Child Rights and International Discrimination Law

Societies and states are at a crossroads in how children are treated and how their rights are respected and protected. Children's new position and their strong rights create tensions and challenge the traditional relationships between family and the state. The United Nations Convention on the Rights of the Child was adopted unanimously by the General Assembly of the United Nations in 1989 and came into force in 1990. Article 2 places states under an obligation to accord primacy to the best interests of the child in all actions concerning children and to ensure and regulate child protection.

This book offers a comparative and critical analysis of the implementation of Article 2 of the United Nations Convention on the Rights of the Child. In order to examine how Article 2 is being implemented, it is essential to have a sound understanding of the obligations it imposes. The opening chapters will explore the precise content of these obligations in terms of the legislative history of the text, its underlying philosophy, its amplification by the United Nations Committee on the Rights of the Child, and subsequent authoritative interpretations of it by courts around the world. The book will then drill down into the conceptual and theoretical challenges posed by the very nature of the obligations and will offer in-depth exploration of the long-running 'rights v welfare' debate that has always presented something of a challenge in giving effect to children's rights. Contributors are leading academics in the children's rights field drawn from a wide range of countries and jurisdictions world-wide, including those with common law, civilian and mixed traditions. Disciplines represented in the book include law, psychology, political science, childhood studies, social work and anthropology.

By drawing together the various facets of Article 2 and analysing it from a range of perspectives, the volume provides a coherent and comprehensive inter-disciplinary analysis on discrimination and the rights of the child.

Marit Skivenes is a Professor at the Department for Administration and Organization Theory at the University of Bergen and the director of Centre for Research on Discretion and Paternalism, University of Bergen, Norway.

Karl Harald Søvig is a Professor of law and the Dean at the Faculty of Law at the University of Bergen, Norway.

Routledge Research in International Law

For a full list of titles in this series, visit https://www.routledge.com/Routledge-Research-in-International-Law/book-series/INTNLLAW

Available:

International Criminal Law and Sexual Violence against Women
The Interpretation of Gender in the Contemporary International Criminal Trial
Daniela Nadj

Unilateral Acts
A History of a Legal Doctrine
Betina Kuzmarov

Regional Developmentalism through Law
Establishing an African Economic Community
Jonathan Bashi Rudahindwa

China's One Belt One Road Initiative and Private International Law
Edited by Poomintr Sooksripaisarnkit and Sai Ramani Garimella

Transnational Terrorist Groups and International Criminal Law
Anna Marie Brennan

Confronting Cyberespionage Under International Law
Oğuz Kaan Pehlivan

Russian Discourses on International Law
Sociological and Philosophical Phenomenon
Edited by P. Sean Morris

Backstage Practices in Transnational Law
Lianne Boer and Sofia Stolk

International 'Criminal' Responsibility
Antimonies
Ottavio Quirico

The Future of International Courts
Regional, Institutional and Procedural Challenges
Edited by Avidan Kent, Nikos Skoutaris and Jamie Trinidad

Child Rights and International Discrimination Law

Implementing Article 2 of the United Nations Convention on the Rights of the Child

Edited by
Marit Skivenes and Karl Harald Søvig

Routledge
Taylor & Francis Group
LONDON AND NEW YORK

First published 2019
by Routledge
2 Park Square, Milton Park, Abingdon, Oxon OX14 4RN

and by Routledge
605 Third Avenue, New York, NY 10017

First issued in paperback 2021

Routledge is an imprint of the Taylor & Francis Group, an informa business

Publisher's Note
The publisher has gone to great lengths to ensure the quality of this reprint but points out that some imperfections in the original copies may be apparent.

British Library Cataloguing in Publication Data
A catalogue record for this book is available from the British Library

Library of Congress Cataloging-in-Publication Data
Names: Skivenes, Marit, editor. | Sovig, Karl Harald, editor.
Title: Child rights and international discrimination law : implementing Article 2 of the UN Convention on the Rights of the Child / Edited by Marit Skivenes and Karl Harald Sovig.
Description: New York, NY : Routledge, 2019. |
Series: Routledge research in international law | Includes bibliographical references and index.
Identifiers: LCCN 2018049170 (print) | LCCN 2018049461 (ebook) | ISBN 9780429020926 (ebk) | ISBN 9780367074630 (hbk)
Subjects: LCSH: Convention on the Rights of the Child (1989 November 20). Article 2. | Children's rights. | Discrimination—Law and legislation. | Children (International law).
Classification: LCC K639.A41989 (ebook) | LCC K639.A41989 C43 2019 (print) | DDC 341.4/8572—dc23
LC record available at https://lccn.loc.gov/2018049170

Typeset in Galliard
by Taylor & Francis Books

ISBN 13: 978-1-03-224145-6 (pbk)
ISBN 13: 978-0-367-07463-0 (hbk)

DOI: 10.4324/9780429020926

This book is dedicated to the memory of Benjamin Labaran Hermansen, who in 2001 at age 15 years old was a victim of a racially motivated murder in Norway. In the wake of this tragedy, the Benjamin Prize – Against Racism and Discrimination, was established in 2002. This prize is awarded to schools that are actively working against racism and all discriminatory attitudes and actions.

Contents

Figures

Acknowledgements

The book has its origin in the fourth annual colloquium for the United Nations Convention on the Right of the Child: Implementation Project (CRC-IP) which took place in April 2017 in Bergen, Norway. Elaine E. Sutherland established the CRC-IP in 2012, with the belief that there is a distinct value of bringing together a smaller group of experts from around the world to discuss the progress that has been made in implementing the Convention and to focus on one article at a time. The first colloquium examined Article 12, the child's rights to be heard, the second addressed Article 6, the child's rights to survival and development. Articles expanding on papers from these colloquia can be found in the *New Zealand Law Review* 2013, 33–504, and the *Stellenbosch Law Review* 2015, 254–442. The third colloquium addressed Article 3, which make the child's best interest a primary consideration. The work from this colloquium is collected in the book *Implementing Article 3 of the United Nations Convention on the Rights of the Child: Best Interest, Welfare and Well-Being* edited by Elaine E. Sutherland and Lesley-Anne Barnes Macfarlane. This volume on Article 2, prohibition of discrimination, is the second book with its origin in the CRC-IP. The book arose out of the debates, presentations, and activities for the colloquium in Bergen, Norway in April 2017. We want to express our appreciation and gratitude to the chapter authors for their collaboration and sharing their expertise and knowledge to make this book possible. A special big thank you to Professor Elaine E. Sutherland for her support and for sharing her valuable insights before and during the process of finalising this volume. We are grateful for the important input and comments to the overall proposal to the book from five anonymous reviewers.

Finally, with no doubt, we could not have made this book without the invaluable help from research assistant Siri Hansen Pedersen, and her marvellous organization and coordination of chapters and correspondence with authors to the final preparation of the manuscript into Routledge style.

The book received funding from Centre for Research on Discretion and Paternalism (http://www.discretion.uib.no/), and from the Norwegian Research Council, project number 262773.

Contributors

David Archard is Emeritus Professor of Philosophy in the School of History, Anthropology, Philosophy and Politics, Queen's University Belfast. David is Honorary Vice-President of the Society for Applied Philosophy and since 2017 he has been the Chair of the Nuffield Council on Bioethics. His work within ethics, moral philosophy and especially on the rights of children and the family is widely known.

Gillian Black graduated LLB (Hons) from the University of Glasgow in 1999 and qualified as a solicitor in Scotland in 2002. She practised in the field of commercial law before taking up a lectureship at the University of Edinburgh in 2005. She completed her PhD in Scots law at the University of Edinburgh in 2009. Gillian has written and taught in the area of Scots private law for 13 years, with specific interests in family law, privacy, personality rights, and contract law.

Trynie Boezaart is Professor in the Department of Private Law at the University of Pretoria. She was the founder of the Centre for Child Law at the University of Pretoria in 1998 and Director until 2008, and still serves on the Board. In 2008 she acted as a Judge in the North Gauteng High Court. She is the editor of and contributed a chapter to Child Law in South Africa (2017) and the co-editor of and contributor to Commentary on the Children's Act (2007), a regularly updated loose-leaf publication (the most recent update being Revision Service 8 in 2018).

Claire Breen is a Professor at Te Piringa Faculty of Law of the University of Waikato, in Aotearoa New Zealand. She teaches public international law, human rights law and the laws of armed conflict, as well as supervising post-graduate and doctoral students. She has published extensively in in the area of children's rights. Her key publications include The Standard of the Best Interests of the Child (Brill, 2002) and Age Discrimination and Children's Rights (Brill, 2006) as well as journal articles in the International Journal of Children's Rights, Human Rights Quarterly and the International Journal of Refugee Law.

Linda D. Elrod is the Richard S. Righter Distinguished Professor of Law and Director of the Washburn University Law School Children and Family Law Center. She served on the Council for the American Bar Association Family Law Section from 1988–2016, was Editor-in-Chief of the Family Law Quarterly from 1992–2016, and was Chair in 2000–2001. She has served on the U.S. Secretary of State Legal Adviser's Advisory Committee on Private International Law since 2009. In 2011 she was a Fulbright Senior Specialist to the Dublin Institute of Technology Law Department. She currently serves as the Reporter for the Uniform Law Commission Joint Editorial Board on Uniform Family Law. She was also the Reporter for the Family Law Arbitration Act (2016) and the Child Abduction Prevention Act (2007).

Comine Howe is currently residing in China. Prior to this she completed her Master's degree in Law and assisted various charities to generate funds for underprivileged girls to gain access to sanitary wear. She has always had a passion for advancing equality and hopes to continue that in the future.

Liu Huawen is Professor and Assistant Director at the Institute of International Law, Chinese Academy of Social Sciences (CASS), China. Professor Liu Huawen is also Executive Director of the Center for Human Rights Studies, CASS. He used to be legal consultant for UNICEF China and the All China Women's Federation (ACWF) for the Project on Revision of Chinese Law on Protection of Minors in 2006, and Chief of the EU Micro-Project on Promotion of the Awareness and Protection of Disadvantaged Children in China from 2007–2008.

Sonia Human is Professor and Emeritus Dean of Law at Stellenbosch University. Her main areas of interest are Family Law and the Law of Persons, with a special focus on Children's Rights. She is a qualified Commercial and Family Law mediator and has co-authored textbooks on Family Law and the Law of Persons. Sonia is an award-winning lecturer and regularly speaks at national and international academic conferences.

Katre Luhamaa is a researcher at the Center for Research on Discretion and Paternalism and holds a PhD in Law. Her field of expertise includes Comparative and International Human Rights Law and Democracy, EU Law and European Studies, and Legal Theory. Her research focuses on the national implementation of international law, EU law and human rights, and in particular children's rights. Katre Luhamaa has previously worked as a Lecturer at The University of Tartu, and as a Counsellor to the Constitutional Review Chamber at the Supreme Court of Estonia.

Lize Mills is a lecturer at the Department of Private Law at Stellenbosch University. Her teaching interests include the Law of Persons, Family Law, Child Law and Consumer Law. Her particular research focuses on how the best interests of the child are given practical consideration in South Africa. She previously served as Chief Examiner of the Film and Publications Board; a Member of a Special Task

Group appointed by the Deputy Minister of Home Affairs, investigating the increase of child abuse images; a research assistant at the Western Cape High Court; and editor and Product Manager of the South African Law Reports.

Tarja Pösö is a Professor in Social Work at the Faculty of Social Sciences, Tampere University, Finland. She has more than 20 years' experience in studying child welfare from various perspectives, and a keen interest in cross-cultural perspectives and exploring methods and ethics for child welfare studies. She is currently working with notions of 'consent' and 'objection' in child protection decision-making.

Marit Skivenes is a professor at the Department of Administration and Organization Theory (University of Bergen), and director of the Centre for Research on Discretion and Paternalism. Skivenes completed her PhD in Political Science at the University of Bergen in 2002, and is a leading international scholar on discretionary decision making, children's rights and child protection systems. Skivenes has an extensive record of scientific publications, as well as being PI for numerous research projects, and she received the prestigious Consolidator Grant from the European Research Council in 2016.

Brian Sloan read for his BA in Law (scholar) and LLM (Wright Rogers scholar) at Robinson College, Cambridge. He then took up a W.M. Tapp doctoral studentship at Gonville and Caius College. After 3 years as Bob Alexander Fellow at King's College, Brian returned to Robinson as a College Lecturer in October 2012, where he teaches Equity, Family Law and Land Law. Brian is a member of the International Advisory Board of FamRz and has been a visiting academic at the Catholic University of Leuven, the University of New South Wales and Utrecht University.

Elaine E. Sutherland is Professor of Child and Family Law at the Law School, University of Stirling, Scotland, and Distinguished Professor of Law Emeritus at Lewis & Clark Law School, Portland, Oregon, USA. She has written extensively on domestic (UK and US), comparative and international child and family law and has taught and presented papers at conferences around the world. In 2012 she founded the United Nations Convention on the Rights of the Child Implementation Project (CRC-IP) which brings together an invited group of internationally-respected child law scholars to address the challenges of implementing the Convention in the domestic and international contexts.

Karl Harald Søvig is Professor and the Dean of the Faculty of Law, University of Bergen. Søvig completed his PhD in Law at the University of Bergen. He is a guest professor at the Faculty of Law at Changchum University of Science and Technology, China. He is also Chair of the European Association of Health Law. His research has focused on different forms of coercive measures within the welfare state, as well as the rights of children. He has authored a report for the government on the implementation of the UN Convention on the Rights of the Child into the Norwegian legal system and chaired an expert committee drafting a new act on adoption.

D. Kelly Weisberg joined UC Hastings College of the Law after obtaining a J.D. at U.C. Berkeley School of Law and a Ph.D. in Sociology at Brandeis University. She has participated in federal studies of juvenile justice, intimate partner violence, and child abuse. She worked as a legal intern at the International Commission of Jurists in Geneva, during the International Year of the Child (1979). At UC Hastings, Professor Weisberg served as Director of the Family Law Concentration. She is editor of Domestic Violence Report, a national newsletter on domestic violence. She has authored several law review articles and books on family law, domestic violence, and children and the law.

1 Discriminating against children

*Katre Luhamaa, Marit Skivenes and Karl Harald Søvig**

Introduction

This book discusses discrimination of children and the effects of discrimination in different areas of life. The textbook definition of discrimination is that a person or a group of individuals are treated differently, in a negative way compared with others. Central to the non-discrimination discourse is a distinction between differential treatment and discrimination. While the former is acceptable and, in some situations, required, the latter amounts to violation. We can talk about discrimination when there is a certain legal criterion whereby the practice or treatment or rule is not justifiable. The prohibition of discrimination does not call for a boundless ban on differential treatment, but once the criteria of discrimination are met, the prohibition applies. As Fredman (2018) points out, central to the divide between differential treatment and discrimination is the discussion of what kind of justifications are acceptable for differential treatment and to what extent the concrete legal system accepts the concept of remedying the effects of discrimination. No one would recommend the same shoe size for all children. Even though this may be regarded as a form of equal treatment, it would obviously be a form of discrimination toward all children not fitting into the given size. This example illuminates how anti-discrimination is a matter of tailor-making, which in turn also explains why discrimination is such a complex issue. Even if the starting points are simple, actual assessments can be a challenging task since so many factors have to be considered. This leaves both the national authorities and supervisory bodies with leeway in terms of discretion, which often results in an assessment of whether a given measure is proportionate to the legitimate aims pursued.

The disadvantages of being treated differently may or may not be directly harmful for the individual or group of individuals to be labelled discrimination, but a clear example of discrimination would be, holding all things equal, boys are given more pay than girls for helping with chores at home. In Chapter 3, David Archard expands on the conceptual dimensions of discrimination. A key point in studying discrimination is that discriminatory actions involve some form of exclusion and may concern both material and non-material matters. The Convention on the Rights of the Child (UNGA 1989) has prohibited discrimination in one of its four main pillars, Article 2:

1 *States Parties shall respect and ensure the rights set forth in the present Convention to each child within their jurisdiction without discrimination of any kind, irrespective of the child's or his or her parent's or legal guardian's race, colour, sex, language, religion, political or other opinion, national, ethnic or social origin, property, disability, birth or other status.*
2 *States Parties shall take all appropriate measures to ensure that the child is protected against all forms of discrimination or punishment on the basis of the status, activities, expressed opinions, or beliefs of the child's parents, legal guardians, or family members.*

Article 2 in the CRC forms a self-standing right of non-discrimination on a wide list of prohibited grounds. Non-discrimination is also a general principle that covers all the rights included in the CRC.[1] Therefore, a wide set of characteristics are listed as a no-zone for discriminatory behaviour, including not only direct discrimination, such as that involving race and gender, but also indirect discrimination owing to, for example, parental beliefs. The topic of discrimination is additionally complicated as it often is expressed as a combination of factors (cf. CRC Committee 2007, para. 8) present in various aspects and times of life.

The facets of discrimination

Discrimination denotes treatment of a person that is less favourable in comparison with others on grounds unrelated to merit, usually because he or she belongs to a particular group or category. The principles of equality and non-discrimination are the foundations of international law and international human rights law as they are principles or rights enshrined in each and every global or regional international human rights instrument (see, e.g. Henrard 2008, paras 6–28 or Makkonen 2012, pp. 113–213).

The general substance of the right to non-discrimination as protected in Article 2 of the CRC has been analysed before: Abramson (2008) and Besson (2011) have commented on the legal meaning of Article 2, and Kutsar and Warming (2014) have edited a textbook on the implementation of Article 2. The theoretical basis of non-discrimination, although debated, is often positioned as dignity and equal respect toward every individual (see e.g. Smith 2011). Both of the concepts are also present in the first paragraph of the preamble of the CRC, which recognises the inherent dignity and equal rights of all members of the human family. Nevertheless, international and regional human rights, as well as national legal systems, are not consistent in their theory and practice toward defining principles and the content of the right to non-discrimination and have developed a wide range of typologies to address this matter. As the current book takes a global although selective approach into the implementation of Article 2 of the CRC, and the approaches of the various authors vary in regard to the substantive meaning of non-discrimination, the relevant theoretical concepts are generally sketched here to assist the reader.

Formal equality requires a consistent procedural practice with foreseeable results. Such an approach fails to respond to the whole range of differences present in society and may lead to unequal results (see e.g. the discussion in Fredman 2018). A wider approach to equality would require *equality of results* seen either as a more equal distribution of benefits, a better result for a specifically identified group of individuals or as requiring a certain outcome. *Equality of opportunity* forms an alternative middle ground for the two former approaches (Fredman 2011, 4–19). All of these approaches are often grounded in the concept of dignity, a principle and a right that also forms part of many current constitutions (see, e.g. McCrudden 2013).

A second and closely connected distinction used is differentiation between *direct* and *indirect discrimination*. Direct discrimination concerns differentiation explicitly on a particular ground, such as gender. While there is no uniform and universally accepted definition of "indirect discrimination", it generally covers measures that are neutral on their face, but that have or are likely to have a disproportionate impact, without objective and reasonable justification, on a group distinguished by that ground (see, e.g. Collins and Khaitan 2018). While direct discrimination can be relatively easily identified in individual cases, indirect discrimination requires a more systematic approach, analyses the effect of the law or policy for a wider group, and is dependent on the legality of the justifications used. New approaches to affirmative action and prevention have blurred the line even further (see e.g. Lippert-Rasmussen 2018).

Structural discrimination has some similarities to the unintended effects of discrimination, and concerns a wide range of institutional social and organisational structures. For example, would the educational system with dominantly white, Caucasian persons being teachers and academic staff represent an institution that is structurally favouring white persons, and thus have an embedded form of discrimination in regard to people of colour? A much too well-known example of structural discrimination involves the Jim Crow laws in the U.S., which commanded the segregation of people of colour and whites in a range of public spaces, including schools, hospitals, and public transportation. There was no differentiation between races, but the result was the massive discrimination of people of colour.

Some of the distinctions mentioned above – direct discrimination and formal equality – are concerned with the concrete individual and their treatment. Others, such as indirect discrimination and equality of results, look at the effects of the treatment of a certain group and whether the cumulative effect for this group disadvantages them. This is a particularly relevant distinction when looking at cultural practices such as female genital mutilation or the effects of a lack of sanitary facilities on girls in school. The topic of discrimination is furthermore complicated by multiple discrimination, which is particularly relevant in regard to children who, by the nature of their existence, constantly face age and other types of discrimination, such as that based in gender, disability or ethnicity.

Remedy and duty bearer

Affirmative action involves measures and policies that aim to compensate for the long histories of discrimination faced by minorities and women. Various mechanisms are involved in affirmative action, and states have different views and approaches on how to best compensate for past discrimination. Often, young minorities and females may receive special consideration when seeking education or employment. Alternatively, some approaches institute a fixed quota system so that a certain percentage of students must be of a specific gender or minority background. Yet another approach, critical to quotas and special considerations, focuses on recruitment strategies and targets certain groups in campaigns and advertising. Recently, the CRC Committee has also stressed the importance of budget-related decisions in combating discrimination (CRC Committee 2016d, paras 41–44), and has recognised and stressed the role of business and the private sector in creating a wider discrimination-free environment and value system (CRC Committee 2013a, paras 13–14).

The core duty bearer of human rights is the state. The obligations rest with all branches of the state, being the legislature, judiciary and administrative organs. A statutory provision can as such be a violation of the right to non-discrimination. However, often, it is not legislation as such that is problematic, but rather how it is enforced – or not – that is the core of the matter. It should also be noted, as with many other human rights issues, that the state can also be held responsible for the conduct of private individuals or entities. The state is responsible for respecting – and securing – the right to non-discrimination. If more boys than girls are born in a country, the state may have an obligation to examine the causes of this situation, even though the driving force is the conduct of individuals (see Chapter 11 by Huawen concerning development in China). Many discriminatory practices are taking place within the family sphere. This leaves the state with a difficult task since it is also under a human rights obligation to respect family life. The right to family life does not prevent the state from intervening to target discriminatory practices, but in such situations, the state – and its supervisory bodies – must balance the interests that are at stake.

CRC Committee's focus on discrimination

As mentioned above, the CRC Committee, in its first years of practice, introduced non-discrimination and Article 2 as one of the first pillars.[2] In General Comment No. 5, it emphasises that the non-discrimination obligation "requires States actively to identify individual children and groups of children the recognition and realisation of whose rights may demand special measures" (2003, para. 12). The Committee highlighted the "need for data collection to be disaggregated to enable discrimination or potential discrimination to be identified". Addressing discrimination may require "changes in legislation, administration and resource allocation, as well as educational measures to change attitudes". The Committee also stressed that "the application of the non-discrimination principle of equal access to rights does not mean identical treatment".

CRC Article 2 is unique in that "disability" is used as a prohibited ground of discrimination (see now also the UN Convention on the Rights of Persons with Disabilities (CRPD) Article 5 regarding quality and non-discrimination). In General Comment No. 9 on the rights of children with disabilities (2007), the Committee held that this explicit mention of disability can be explained by the fact that children with disabilities belong to one of the most vulnerable groups of children (para. 8). The Committee stressed that "discrimination takes place – often de facto – in various aspects of the life and development of children with disabilities", thus emphasising that combating discrimination stretches beyond legislation (see also Chapter 10 by Boezaart). Additionally, the Committee paid attention to girls with disabilities and held that they are often even more vulnerable to discrimination because of gender discrimination. As seen in several contributions to this book, many questions relating to discrimination have a gender dimension (see for example Chapters 7 and 11).

Measures combating discrimination

In General Comment No. 9, the Committee introduced three main measures (para. 12):

1. Legislative tools (e.g. include explicitly disability as a forbidden ground for discrimination)
2. Effective remedies in case of violations; ensure that these remedies are easily accessible to children and their parents and/or others caring for the child
3. Conduct awareness-raising and educational campaigns targeting the public at large and specific groups of professionals with a view to preventing and eliminating de facto discrimination.

Even though these measures are given in the context of children with disabilities, they have the potential to be regarded as general measures of combating discrimination.

Several forms of child discrimination have existed (and have been targeted) for a long period. In recent years, both international and national institutions, as well as public movements, have taken a wider approach to discrimination and expanded the focus of types of discrimination faced by children as well as the different negative results of discrimination. Furthermore, the CRC Committee has shown the importance of proactive measures in budget planning in combating discrimination (CRC Committee 2016d, paras 41–44) and has discussed the effects of discrimination using the example of street children (CRC Committee 2017e, paras 25–27).

Gender and minorities

International and national discussions have seen the mainstreaming of discussions of gender discrimination and have brought the discrimination faced by girls to the forefront. The joint general comment of the CRC Committee and the *Committee on the Elimination of Discrimination against Women* (CEDAW) (2014) took a comprehensive look at the gender-based discrimination faced by girls and targeted four areas of the highest concern: female genital mutilation; child and/or forced marriages; polygamy; and "honor" crimes. These create conflicts in multicultural societies. Children, as the most important component of the formation of a family, are embedded in and an expression of parental identity as well as our cultural practices. Thus, it is no surprise that children are in the midst of many of the discriminatory cultural practices that create most conflicts in multicultural societies. The political scientist Bhikhu Parekh studies cultural diversity in the book *Rethinking Multiculturalism* (2006 p. 265ff) and shows that children, especially female children, are exposed to discrimination on both a cultural and religious basis; examples of this include arranged marriage (which sometimes involves the practice of marrying a family member), children being scarred on the face or other parts of the body, girls not being allowed to take part in gym class or swimming if boys are in the same classes; girls being forced to wear a headscarf or hijab, and children being withheld from school (Roma and Amish) (Ibid). The subsequent attention to gender discrimination by the CRC Committee has been even wider and has focused on discrimination based on ethnicity (CRC Committee 2018c, para. 22), widening the approach to sexuality and specifying that this prohibition of discrimination includes lesbian, gay, bisexual, transgender and intersex children (CRC Committee 2018d, para. 15; CRC Committee 2018b, para. 16), gender-based selective abortion, as well as negative attitudes toward adolescent children (CRC Committee 2016a, para. 21). International activism (the *#METOO* movement) as well as the scholarly community have also extended narrower areas where gender-based discrimination has been commonplace – examples of this include gender discrimination in sports (see e.g. Moses 2015; or Gill 2017) or in access to hygiene (also discussed by Mills and Howe in Chapter 7).

Discrimination relating to children in migration is another area that has recently received focused attention from activists (Amnesty International 2018) and media (Panetta 2018 or Gladstone 2017), as well as from different institutional settings (CRC Committee and Committee on Migrant Workers 2017). The separation of children from their parents in the U.S. and the treatment of unaccompanied asylum seekers in Europe has revealed the reluctance of policymakers to recognise the special status of migrating children. This situation is further complicated by the fact that refugee laws do not specifically target children (see e.g. Arnold 2017).

Disability and health

Children with disabilities comprise a group that faces multiple and intersectional discrimination in its widest sense. The CRC Committee has elaborated on their particular vulnerability:

> As an example, social discrimination and stigmatization leads to their marginalization and exclusion, and may even threaten their survival and development if it goes as far as physical or mental violence against children with disabilities. Discrimination in service provision excludes them from education and denies them access to quality health and social services. The lack of appropriate

> education and vocational training discriminates against them by denying them job opportunities in the future. Social stigma, fears, overprotection, negative attitudes, misbeliefs and prevailing prejudices against children with disabilities remain strong in many communities and lead to the marginalization and alienation of children with disabilities.
>
> (CRC Committee 2007, para. 8)

The practical implementation of the laws and policies relating to the realities of the lives of children with disabilities lies at the heart of concerns of this group (CRC Committee 2017b, para. 52). International emphasis has been placed on such practical steps as physical access to buildings and the lack of specialised but inclusive day care and educational facilities (see e.g. CRC Committee 2017c, para. 38; or CRC Committee 2017a, para. 54). Discrimination in its most subtle form comes from societal attitudes and acceptance toward children with disabilities. Examples of such attitudes can be observed when the numbers of adopted children with disabilities is disproportionally low in comparison with adoptions of other types of children (CRC Committee 2017a, para. 41).

Children's health and discrimination relating to the health sector has been an area for which international scrutiny has widened, including the teenage pregnancy rate, access to contraceptives and safe abortion rights (see, e.g. CRC Committee 2017b, para. 45). Wider health-related topics include early and/or forced marriage (CRC Committee 2016b, para. 18) and the lack of access to medical services for some ethnic (CRC Committee 2016e, para. 38) or social groups of children. Emerging topics include those related to the impact of climate change on the rights of the child (CRC Committee 2016c, para. 48).

What is regarded as discrimination is constantly changing and new questions continue to arise. A returning issue for children has been the status of the relationship between their parents and how this affects their legal ties. The classical issue has been children born out of wedlock, which is still a matter of concern (see below), but new questions have appeared on the agenda. An increasing number of children are born as a result of various forms of artificial insemination, often abroad and in conflict with the domestic legislation. A flagrant example is surrogacy, where domestic legislation may have been constructed to protect the interests of the child. However, when a child is born and raised, he or she must be treated without discrimination based on their birth status; this calls for challenging assessments. On one hand, it is a legitimate aim for a state to avoid surrogacy and enforce domestic legislation for adults who circumvent the rules. On the other hand, children born out of surrogacy should not be put in an unfavourable situation compared with others. Many such questions can be expected to be brought to the table of the CRC Committee in the future.

Individual complaints in the CRC Committee

Further evidence regarding the importance of the non-discrimination principle in the newly developed practice of the CRC Committee in reviewing individual complaints under Optional Protocol 3 (CRC OP3, 39 parties in August 2018) gives everyone (including children) whose rights under the CRC have been violated access to the international individual complaint mechanism of the CRC Committee. CRC OP3 allows communications on behalf of individuals and groups of individuals (Article 5 of the Protocol), and the exhaustion of the domestic remedies clause allows for exceptions when the proceedings are unreasonably prolonged or unlikely to bring effective relief (Article 7(e)).

Non-discrimination and reference to Article 2 is frequent in the complaints procedure of the CRC Committee. As of September 2018, the CRC Committee has concluded discussing the merits of only one case (CRC Committee 2018a) relating to a rejected asylum application and a threat of female genital mutilation of a child in the case of a return to her motherland. Among other provisions, the applicant referred to a violation of Article 2 of the CRC; however, the CRC Committee found this claim to be manifestly ill-founded as it was made in a very general manner (para. 10.3 of the views). Reference to Article 2 seems to be a common feature in the individual complaints submitted to the CRC Committee. As of September 2018, there were 17 further cases pending before the CRC Committee where the applicants had invoked Article 2. Interestingly, the majority of these cases (12) also relate to migration, another sensitive topic in relation to the non-discrimination of children.[3]

Influence of the CRC

It is undisputed that the socialising effect (c.f. Goodman and Jinks 2013) of the CRC has been notable globally – it has directed the international and national practice of child rights, and has been implemented as the child rights standard in both global and regional international law, as well as in national legal settings. For example, the CRC is used by other UN treaty bodies as the standard relating to issues concerning children (see e.g. CRC Committee and CEDAW Committee 2014), it has been referred to as the basis for the cases relating to children by the European Court of Human Rights (ECtHR), European Court of Justice and European Committee on Social Rights (FRA, European Court of Human Rights, and Europarat 2015; Kilkelly 2015), and it has been used in the case law of the Inter-American Court of Human Rights (see, e.g. Inter-American Commission on Human Rights 2017; or Novak 2013); it has also been referred to in the practice of the African Commission on Human and Peoples' Rights (e.g. Sloth-Nielsen 2016). Furthermore, these institutions have included the concepts developed in the children's rights paradigm in the interpretation of human rights.

Attention to non-discrimination has become mainstream and substantively revived in the Human Rights Council (HRC) of the UN, and more specifically, in the Universal Periodic Review (UPR) process.[4] It is a transparent process that is best described as the comprehensive peer review of a state's human rights record, combining self-reporting with scrutiny by other states, input from UN treaty bodies and agencies and civil society. This combination has brought the topic of non-discrimination to the forefront of human rights discussions and has enforced systematic evaluations of discriminatory practices against some groups – most notably the emphasis on ending various types of gender discrimination, the discrimination of persons with disabilities, LGBTI discrimination and the discrimination of indigenous, cultural or religious minorities (e.g. Human Rights Council 2018a; or Human Rights Council 2018b). There is also a continued push to eliminate discrimination against children, e.g. in regard to education, poverty or disabilities (e.g. Human Rights Council 2018d). Also notable is the amount of voluntary commitments undertaken by states to apply recommendations by other states, as well as the possibility of non-governmental organisations to bring forward their concerns. At the same time, the UPR process enables the value-diversity of states to be seen when they make and accept recommendations; most notable is the attitude toward sexual minorities. Nevertheless, the UPR process and the HRC more widely have become an arena for wider discussion of acceptable state actions and best practices, and has brought child rights and the non-discrimination agenda into state diplomatic exchanges that have not traditionally had an excellent human rights record (e.g. Human Rights Council 2018c). It represents a possible arena for states to show their support for certain rights, topics or groups in society.

National implementation of rights

As the CRC has been ratified by almost all countries in the world, which is a unique phenomenon in itself, it provides formal protection of children's rights around the world, including the right to non-discrimination. All children have equal rights; however, the formal implementation of these rights varies as some countries, for example, have made the CRC national legislation and enacted additional legislation to ensure children's rights, whereas others have not. The KidsRights index[5] is a measure of how the CRC signatories uphold the rights of children, and as of 2018, includes 182 countries. The index reports on five areas: Right to Life; Right to Health; Right to Education; Right to Protection; and Enabling Environment for Child Rights. With caution regarding the simplifications that any overarching measurement of complex issues carries with it (cf. Langford and Kirkebø 2018), the index provides information on how well countries fare in respecting children's rights relative to their capabilities. In 2018, the following countries scored highest on all five domains on children's rights, and are therefore considered to perform well according to their implementation capabilities: Norway, Iceland, Portugal, Spain, Switzerland, Netherlands, Finland, Germany, France, and Slovenia. Countries such as New Zealand and U.K. are near the bottom, together with Eritrea, Papua New Guinea, Guinea-Bissau, Central African Republic, Equatorial Guinea, Democratic Republic of the Congo, Chad, Afghanistan, and Sierra Leone. The reason high-income countries such as New Zealand and the U.K. are at the bottom is that the ranking system does not allow for compensations between areas, as all five right domains are considered equally important; therefore, a low score on one domain has a large impact on the overall rankings.

The focus of the KidsRights index is on a country's capability and will to realize children's rights; this has clear parallels to the work United Nations Children's Fund (UNICEF) has done on comparing living conditions for children. The level of living conditions in a society impacts the ability to ensure, as well as to protect and respect, children's rights, and thus, impacts which types of discrimination may be occurring. For example, if basic amenities are missing or not affordable, direct and indirect discrimination of children is the likely result. Children will also be discriminated against because of poverty and structural conditions such as family income. For several years, nation states and their welfare programs have been evaluated from the point of view of the youngest in our societies in response to the question: how does the welfare state fare from the point of view of the child (cf. UNICEF 2009, 2013). In the latest report (2017), the scope of measurement was widened, and states were measured in accordance with sustainable development goals (SDG, United Nations Development Program 2015), which comprise a total of nine areas. The number of countries has also increased; the most recent assessment included 41 high- and middle-income countries from the European Union (EU) and the Organisation for Economic Co-operation and Development (OECD). The SDGs included in the UNICEF measurement cover poverty, hunger and food security, healthy living, education, gender equality, employment, inequality reduction, inclusive cities, sustainable production and peaceful societies. A detailed overview of indicators is presented on p. 6 of the report, and groups countries into high, average and low performance categories. Similar to the KidsRights index, there are some regular countries in the top layer, such as Norway, Iceland, Finland, Switzerland and the Netherlands, while New Zealand, Romania and the U.S. are in the bottom layer. However, the U.K., which was ranked amongst the lowest in the KidsRights index, is in the top layer in UNICEF's SDG measure, which gives us an indication of how different the measurements may turn out. In this book, the chapter on girls that do not have access to affordable sanitary pads because of poverty and a lack of compensatory policies clearly shows discrimination in relation to education and the need for secure health conditions for girls. The types of discrimination involving children are inevitably both correlated with and caused by the welfare level in a society.

The KidsRights index includes an overall measurement on the enabling environment; included in this category is a nation state's respect for the four main pillars of the CRC: Article 2 on non-discrimination, Article 3 on child's best interest, Article 6 on right to life and Article 12 on participation. This gives some indication of how states stand in regard to the non-discrimination of children, but more detailed information on this specific variable is necessary. However, discrimination against children is a major concern. In 2017, the KidsRights Foundation voiced this in the KidsRights Index 2017. The title of the report was: "Violence and Discrimination Against Children Global Concern" (KidsRights Index). In the opening statement, the following was emphasised:

> The highly alarming trend of discrimination against minority groups has continued across the globe in 2017 but is especially distressing in the Middle East and North Africa. Many vulnerable and marginalised groups including refugees and street children are still widely discriminated against. Marc Dullaert, founder and chairman of the KidsRights Foundation, urges all 165 countries listed in the Index to treat non-discrimination as a policy priority in 2017: *"Discrimination*

against vulnerable groups of children and youths should be met head-on by all 165 governments represented in the Index. It is severely hampering the opportunities of future generations to reach their full potential.

Human Rights and children's rights

The understanding that children are holders of human rights represents common ground, at least in mainstream international human rights scholarship (see e.g. Freeman 2010) and practice. Nevertheless, the lack of clarity and added value of children's rights and its relationship to human rights has often been questioned (see e.g. Ferguson 2013). International human rights practice in the UN and regional bodies has connected the two concepts and, when solving a case relating to the rights of children, has stressed the core of applicable human rights together with the added nuances of the rights of the child (see Kilkelly 2001; Skivenes and Søvig 2016). A good illustration would be the utilisation of the principle of the best interest of the child (Article 3 of the CRC; GC No. 14, CRC Committee 2013b; for a wider analysis, see e.g. Eekelaar 2015; Sutherland and Macfarlane 2016). For example, the ECtHR has, when analysing the right to family life of birth parents or the right to property, noted the importance of the best interest principle as a guiding principle.[6] Similarly, the ECtHR has applied Article 12 of the CRC as a guiding principle in cases relating to hearing the child (see e.g. Kilkelly 2015). (More on the ECHR and ECtHR below.) Thus, international child rights form an enforceable part of international human rights law. The concrete substance and nature undoubtably differ, as there are rights that are directly justiciable and others where the focus should be on state obligations. This is, however, no different from other international human rights and their implementation.

Article 2 and European Convention on Human Rights

The influence of the CRC on regional legal systems is well observed in the context of the ECHR and the practice of the ECtHR. The ECHR is ratified by all member states of the Council of Europe (47 states) and is a core instrument within the European legal community. The main body of supervision, and the driving force of developing the convention, is the ECtHR. The ECHR as such does not contain a separate provision concerning minors, but children can normally invoke all the rights and freedoms set forth in the ECHR. The general term used in most provisions is "everyone", which also covers children (it is not necessary to elaborate on the status of the fetus here). Many cases concerning children are within the ambit of Article 8. This provision states that "everyone" has the "right to respect for his private and family life, his home and his correspondence". According to ECHR Article 14, the enjoyment of the rights and freedoms set forth "in this Convention" shall "be secured without discrimination". The prohibited grounds of discrimination are specified as "sex, race, colour, language, religion, political or other opinion, national or social origin, association with a national minority, property, birth or other status", but with the introductory phrase "such as". The ECHR has been developed by the member states in accordance with Protocol 12. Article 1 of Protocol 1 introduces a general prohibition of discrimination without any reference to the enjoyment of the rights and freedoms set forth "in this Convention". So far, Protocol 12 has only been ratified by 18 countries, mainly in Eastern and Southern Europe. Hence, the analysis will therefore concentrate on ECHR Article 14.

Comparing CRC Article 2 and ECHR Article 14, the two provisions are similar as far as they both are "accessory". Respectively, they refer to the "present Convention" and "this Convention", which means that questions concerning discrimination have to relate to a matter covered by other substantial provisions of the treaty. The prohibited grounds of discrimination in ECHR Article 14 are to a large extent exactly the same as those in CRC Article 2, although the latter also includes "disability" (CRC Committee 2007, paras 2–8). The wording concerning national origin is also slightly different ("national … origin" in CRC Article 2 and "association with a national minority" in ECHR Article 14). Still, any differences are of limited interest since both instruments include "other status". This ending phrase provides supervisory bodies with a basis for dynamic interpretations. As pointed out by Abramson (2008, para. 20), the crucial point is not any textual differences between instruments, but how they are developed by the competent enforcement bodies. It is therefore suitable to look into the case law of the ECtHR concerning the discrimination of children, but before that, a short analysis of the relationship between ECHR and CRC is required.

There is no formal connection between the ECHR and the CRC. However, it has become common ground for the ECtHR in cases relating to children to enlist the relevant provisions of the CRC under the heading of "relevant international law", and to refer to the relevant General Comments of the CRC Committee. Thus, the ECtHR acknowledges the CRC and its substantive articles as part of the obligatory child rights standards for member states. Nevertheless, reference to CRC Article 2 of the CRC itself is infrequent.[7] The Court has not discussed directly the added value of Article 2 of the CRC as it prefers reference to its own non-discrimination clause in Article 14. The ECtHR has from the beginning emphasised that the ECHR is a "a living instrument which … must be interpreted in the light of present-day conditions".[8] The CRC Committee has chosen the same approach (CRC Committee 2003, para. 18), but seldom refers to the ECHR, either as such or specifically to ECHR Article 2, even though the approach by the ECtHR may often serve as inspiration.

ECtHR on discrimination

One of the first cases brought before the court was a case "relating to certain aspects of the law on the use of languages in education in Belgium" (Belgian Linguistic case). The applicants were parents of Francophone children living in certain (mostly Dutch-speaking) parts of Belgium. They complained that their children were denied access to an education in French. The ECtHR held that denying certain children access to the French-language schools with a special status in the six communes on the outskirts of Brussels because their parents lived outside those communes was in violation of Article 14 taken in conjunction with

Article 2 (right to education) of Protocol No. 1. However, the Court also held that the Convention did not guarantee a child the right to state or state-subsidised education in the language of her/his parents. Later on, several cases have involved discriminatory practices in the field of education, such as an agnostic child that did not attend religion classes in *Grzelak v. Poland*. The school refused to organize classes in ethics because an insufficient number of children were interested. The ECtHR held that there had been a violation of Article 14 taken in conjunction with Article 9 (freedom of religion), finding in particular that the absence of a mark for "religion/ethics" on his school certificates throughout the entire period of his schooling had amounted to his unwarranted stigmatisation. Interestingly, the complaint by the parents were found inadmissible (incompatible ratione personae), indicating that the ECtHR is increasingly assessing the complaints of the child on an individual basis. *D.H. and Others v. the Czech Republic* concerned the placement of Roma children in "special" schools. The children (18 in total) were placed in schools for children with special needs, including those with a mental or social handicap. The Court noted that, at the relevant time, the majority of children in special schools in the Czech Republic were of Roma origin. Roma children of average/above average intellect were often placed in such schools on the basis of psychological tests, which were not adapted to people of their ethnic origin. The ECtHR held that the domestic legislation at the time had a disproportionately prejudicial effect on Roma children, in violation of Article 14 taken in conjunction with Article 2 of Protocol No. 1. It is noteworthy that in this case, the ECtHR pointed out the discriminatory effect of domestic legislation. The schooling of Roma children was also the crux of the matter in *Oršuš and Others v. Croatia*. The children concerned had been segregated into Roma-only classes. This case differed from *D.H. and Others v. the Czech Republic* (see above) since it had not been a general policy in both schools to automatically place Roma pupils in separate classes. However, the domestic practice was still discriminatory. The segregation was claimed to be justified by a lack of proficiency in Croatian, but the domestic authorities had not monitored the development of the language skills or tried to remedy the pupils' language problems.

Another typical group of cases has concerned children born out of wedlock. A landmark case is *Marckx v. Belgium*. This case was brought before the ECtHR by an unmarried Belgian mother. She complained that she and her daughter had been denied the rights given to married mothers and their children, i.e. that she had to recognise her child. She could only ensure the same rights as a legitimate child by getting married, and then adopting her own daughter (or going through a legitimation process). The ECtHR assessed the various legal situations leading to the different statuses of children born out of wedlock and held that it was both a violation of Article 8 alone, and of Article 8 taken in conjunction with Article 14 regarding both applicants. While the latter case concerned the recognition of children born out of wedlock, several subsequent cases have concerned the limited inheritance rights of such children. In *Camp and Bourimi v. the Netherlands*, the father had died before the son was born and without recognising the offspring or being married to the mother. As a consequence, the father's family was the sole heir. The case was made by the mother on her own behalf and on behalf of her son, and a violation was found only concerning the son. The ECtHR held that excluding a son from his father's inheritance was a disproportionate measure. The ECtHR has followed the same approach in several other cases concerning inheritance rights, and has emphasised the development of the Council of Europe in Member States to establish equal treatment of children regardless of their parent's legal relations.[9] It is noteworthy that such cases concern various member states over several decades, and that discriminatory approaches in this field are still upheld in Europe. It should also be noted that in several of these cases, the ECtHR has not only found a violation of Article 14, taken in conjunction with another substantial provision of the convention, but also remedied the discriminatory outcome by awarding pecuniary compensation to the party being placed in an unfavourable situation.[10] A case of particular interest is *Pla and Puncernau v. Andorra*. This case concerned the interpretation of a domestic court of a clause in a will, stipulating that the heir must be born of a "legitimate and canonical marriage", as referring only to biological children, thereby excluding adopted children. The ECtHR held that the approach by the domestic court was "blatantly inconsistent with the prohibition of discrimination" (ECtHR: Pla and Puncernau v. Andorra, para. 59).

The role of ECtHR and the CRC Committee

The question then is to what extent the case law of the ECtHR can serve as an inspiration for the CRC Committee in their efforts to develop CRC Article 2. As an introductory remark, it should be noted that the complaints brought before the ECtHR are made by parents, either on their own behalf or on behalf of their children. The ECtHR may treat the objections by the children independently, and it seems to an increasing extent to also make a separate assessment of the children's situations, which is a development that may have been influenced by the CRC and the focus on children as subjects of human rights. Still, many cases before the ECtHR are driven primarily by the parents and often pleaded by the same counsels as those appearing for the parents.

The ECtHR and CRC Committee have traditionally had different mandates concerning review, the ECtHR reviews individual complaints and the CRC Committee reviews state reports, but as mentioned above, the CRC Committee has recently been vested with the competence to review individual cases under the optional protocol concerning communication procedures. The crux of the matter in many of the cases decided by the ECtHR has been whether a given measure has been "disproportional". The CRC Committee can seek guidance when it comes to which factors should be taken into consideration and how to balance the conflicting interests. A returning issue for the ECtHR has been the legal protection of children born out of wedlock. In many countries, children are still treated differently based on the legal status between the parents (see also the contributions by Sloan (Chapter 5) and Black (Chapter 13) in this book). The ECtHR has been rather reluctant to accept argumentation by states to accept such differences; this approach could be a source of inspiration for the CRC Committee.

Few cases from the ECtHR have concerned positive obligations and the state's responsibility to introduce measures to combat indirect discrimination, which often are not a result of legislation, but rather discriminatory practices. As mentioned above, the CRC Committee has emphasised the state's obligation area "to take appropriate measures to prevent all forms of discrimination" (CRC Committee 2007, para. 8). The CRC Committee has also paid special attention to children with disabilities and the gender dimension. In these fields, the CRC Committee needs to develop its approach further.

The CRC Committee can be said to have had a rather pragmatic approach where discriminatory practices can be found to be problematic, without referring to a specific provision taken in conjunction with Article 2. A recent example is found in the Concluding Observation to Angola, where the Committee "urges the State party to continue and strengthen its activities to combat discrimination" with reference to specific vulnerable groups, such as children with disabilities, etc. (CRC Committee 2018d, para. 15). When the CRC Committee decides cases concerning individual complaints, it has to be more specific and follow the same approach as the ECtHR, where the specific provision to be read in conjunction with the singling out of Article 2.

Children's experiences of discrimination

Dulin-Keita et al. (2011) note that few studies have examined how race and racial discrimination are experienced by young children. Some of the reasons for this are the complexity of the issue, the difficulties in surveying children, and the ethical aspects of asking children about racial discrimination. The lack of systematic data and overviews of how children experience harmful discrimination are a knowledge gap that clearly needs to be filled. However, there are also studies that evidence the feelings and consequences of discrimination. For example, Dulin-Keita et al. (2011) conducted face-to face interviews with 175 children aged 7–12 years, and their conclusion was that "Hispanic children encountered more racial discrimination, with frequent reports of ethnic slurs. Additionally, after accounting for ethnic identity, perceived racial discrimination remained a salient stressor that contributed to low self-esteem." (p. 662). Another study, to illustrate the scale of discrimination, from the U.S., Pachter et al. (2010) conducted a questionnaire survey on 267 children (aged 8–16 years) asking about situations in which they experienced discrimination. Nine out of 10 had recently experienced at least one incident of racial discrimination the last month, and one in 10 had experienced racism in multiple situations.

Discrimination is widely experienced, as documented by the American Psychology Association, but racial and ethnic minorities face more day-to-day discrimination. The consequences of discrimination are extensive; discrimination has been linked to serve physical and mental problems, and there is no reason to believe that such consequences also are valid for children.

The content of this book

This book focuses on the implementation of Article 2 of the CRC – the right to non-discrimination. The chapter authors provide an important overview of some pressing issues in relation to the discrimination of children across the world. The selection of the included empirical areas was driven by the authors' areas of expertise and countries of origin, but nevertheless, provides general insights that exceed the specific context it departs from. The first three chapters provide insight into the legal and conceptual understandings of discrimination and non-discrimination. In Chapter 2, legal scholar Elaine Sutherland sets the tone by providing a legal understanding of the non-discrimination article in the CRC. The title of her chapter is: "Article 2 of the United Nations Convention on the Rights of the Child: non-discrimination and children's rights". In Chapter 3, philosopher David Archard taps into one of the core discriminatory challenges in relation to children, namely the issue of age. The title of his chapter is: "Respecting age: discrimination against the young and the old". In Chapter 4, legal scholar Claire Breen follows up Archard's discussion with an outline of the core themes in political philosophy in regard to the understanding of children and their autonomy. The title of her chapter is: "The ageing of Article 2(1): the child's right to be free from age-based discrimination".

The present book includes a range of empirical topics, some of which touch upon discriminatory practices that concern an enormous number of children, such as discrimination based on gender or the education system. In Chapter 10, legal scholar Trynie Boezaart discusses educational discrimination. The title of her chapter is: "Hidden discriminatory practices in access to education for children with disabilities: a challenge for children's rights." Furthermore, in Chapter 7, legal scholars Lize Mills and Comine Howe show how disadvantaged girls in low-income families are simply because they are entering puberty and lack basic amenities. Their chapter is titled: "That time of the month: discrimination against girls who cannot afford sanitary health care."

Another way many children are involved is when discrimination is a structural issue, built into a country's system and legislation, as the legal scholar Liu Huawen shows in Chapter 11 on China. His chapter is titled: "Starting from system building: child rights protection and the non-discrimination principle in China." Structural discrimination, which concerns fewer children, is also discussed by legal scholars Brian Sloan (Chapter 5) and Gilling Black (Chapter 13). Sloan brings attention to the ongoing illegitimacy issue in the U.K. and Ireland in his chapter titled: "Illegitimate Consequences of 'Illegitimacy'? Article 2 UNCRC and non-marital children in the British Isles." In addition, Black shows how birth status is still a phenomenon in Scotland in her chapter titled: "Birth and status: the ongoing discrimination against children in Scots law based on parentage."

Children that need protection from the child protection system are a particularly vulnerable group, and the responsibilities of the state regarding how to treat children are explicitly stated. In Chapter 6, Tarja Pösö, a social work scholar, shows how the outsourcing of services has negative effects for children in the care system. The title of her chapter is: "The non-discrimination principle in child protection: A snapshot on a seemingly trivial practice of transitions in care." In Chapter 8, legal scholar D. Kelly Weisberg addresses the deficits in the protection of children in family violence cases in his chapter titled: "Collateral damage: discrimination in failure-to-protect laws for children's wellbeing".

Some current pressing global challenges involve immigration and minority issues, which challenge the cohesion, for example, of the EU and affect national elections. Migration has increased over the last few decades, intensifying multiculturalism and religious diversity in society. In a European context, the "refugee crisis" in 2015 and 2016 multiplied the number of asylum seekers from predominantly Muslim countries, possibly followed by increased support for radical right movements and those with nationalist and anti-immigrant attitudes in many recent national elections. Although the political and social consequences of the influx of refugees remains unclear, it is already evident that children do not have a prominent place in migration discussions or possible solutions. Rather, these children seem to be overlooked without the necessary political will to directly address the children's needs and situations. In Chapter 12, legal scholar Sonia Human brings forward the situation of refugee children in her chapter titled: "The importance of Article 2 of the Convention on the Rights of the Child for refugee children." In Chapter 9, focusing on minorities within a country, legal scholar Linda Elrod discusses the situation of migrant children under the title: "Citizen children and unauthorised immigrant parents: can best interest analysis relieve discrimination based on status?"

Notes

* This project has received funding from the European Research Council (ERC) under the European Union's Horizon 2020 research and innovation programme (grant agreement no. 724460), and from the Research Council of Norway under the Independent Projects – Humanities and Social Science programme (grant no. 262773).

1 For a comparative analysis between the CRC and other UN human rights instruments, see Abramson 2008, 5–12.

2 The practice of the CRC Committee is systematically approached in Chapter 2 by Elaine E. Sutherland.

3 See a list of pending cases at: https://www.ohchr.org/Documents/HRBodies/CRC/TablePendingCases.pdf

4 For a general overview of the UPR process, see de la Vega and Lewis (2012).

5 https://kidsrightsindex.org/Portals/5/The%20KidsRights%20Index%202018.pdf?ver=2018-06-01-112649-877

6 This concept has been in the centre of the Article 8 case law. See e.g. *N.Ts. v. Georgia*, No. 71776/12, judgment 2 February 2016; or *S.L. and J.L. v. Croatia*, No. 13712/11, judgment 7 May 2015.

7 See, e.g. *Abdullahi Elmi and Aweys Abubakar v. Malta*, Appl. Nos 25794/13 and 28151/13, judgment 22 November 2016; or *Ponomaryovi v. Bulgaria*, Appl. No. 5335/05, judgment 21 June 2005.

8 *Tyler v. U.K.*, Appl. No. 5856/72, judgment 25 April 1978, para. 31.

9 See *Mazurek v. France*, Appl. No.34406/97, judgment 1 February 2000; *Merger and Cros v. France*, Appl. No. 68864/01, judgment 22 December 2004; *Brauer v. Germany*, Appl. No. 3545/04, judgment 28 May 2009; *Fabris v. France*, Appl. No. 16574/08, judgment 7 February 2013 (Grand Chamber); *Mitzinger v. Germany*, Appl. No. 29762/10,

judgment 9 February 2017. See also *Genovese v. Malta*, Appl. No. 53124/09, judgment 11 October 2011 (concerning denial of citizenship to a child born out of wedlock).

10 e.g. *Merger and Cros* (see above) awarding the two applicants 612,145 euros and 278,634 euros, respectively, for pecuniary damage.

References

Abramson, B. 2008. *A Commentary on the United Nations Convention on the Rights of the Child: The Right of Non-Discrimination*. Leiden, Netherlands: BRILL. http://ebookcentral.proquest.com/lib/nlibee-ebooks/detail.action?docID=467877.

American Psychological Association. Talking to Kids about Discrimination. Available at: http://www.apa.org/helpcenter/kids-discrimination.aspx (accessed 28. 09. 2018).

Amnesty International. 2018. USA: Policy of Separating Children from Parents Is Nothing Short of Torture. https://www.amnesty.org/en/latest/news/2018/06/usa-family-separation-torture/.

Arnold, S. 2018. *Children's Rights and Refugee Law: Conceptualising Children within the Refugee Convention*. Abingdon: Routledge. doi:10.4324/9781315167633.https://www.taylorfrancis.com/books/9781351683579.

Besson, S. 2011. The Principle of Non-Discrimination in the Convention on the Rights of the Child. In: M. D. A. Freeman and M. Freeman (eds). *Children's Rights: Progress and Perspectives: Essays from the International Journal of Children's Rights*. Leiden, Netherlands: Martinus Nijhoff Publishers.

Collins, H. and Khaitan, T. (eds) 2018. *Foundations of Indirect Discrimination Law*. Oxford: Bloomsbury Publishing.

CRC Committee. 2003. General Comment No. 5: General Measures of Implementation of the Convention on the Rights of the Child (arts. 4, 42 and 44, para. 6). CRC/GC/2003/5.

CRC Committee. 2007. General Comment No. 9: The Rights of Children with Disabilities. CRC/C/GC/9.

CRC Committee. 2013a. General Comment No. 16: State Obligations Regarding the Impact of the Business Sector on Children's Rights. CRC/C/GC/16.

CRC Committee. 2013b. General Comment No. 14 on the Right of the Child to Have His or Her Best Interests Taken as a Primary Consideration (art. 3, para. 1). CRC/C/GC/14.

CRC Committee. 2016a. General Comment No. 20: Implementation of the Rights of the Child during Adolescence. CRC/C/GC/20.

CRC Committee. 2016b. Concluding Observations: Pakistan (Fifth Report). CRC/C/PAK/CO/5.

CRC Committee. 2016c. Concluding Observations: Samoa (Second to Fourth Report). CRC/C/WSM/CO/2–4.

CRC Committee. 2016d. General Comment No. 19: Public Spending and the Rights of the Child. CRC/C/GC/19.

CRC Committee. 2016e. Concluding Observations: Slovakia (Third to Fifth Report). CRC/C/SVK/CO/3–5.

CRC Committee. 2017a. Concluding Observations: Serbia (Second and Third Report). CRC/C/SRB/CO/2–3.

CRC Committee. 2017b. Concluding Observations: Central African Republic (Second Report). CRC/C/CAF/CO/2.

CRC Committee. 2017c. Concluding Observations: Estonia (Second to Fourth Report). CRC/C/EST/CO/2–4.

CRC Committee. 2017d. Concluding Observations: Saint Vincent and the Grenadines (Second and Third Report). CRC/C/VCT/CO/2–3.

CRC Committee. 2017e. General Comment No. 21: Children in Street Situations. CRC/C/GC/21.

CRC Committee. 2018a. I.A.M. v. Denmark. CRC/C/77/D/3/2016.

CRC Committee. 2018b. Concluding Observations: Sri Lanka (Fifth and Sixth Report). CRC/C/LKA/CO/5–6.

CRC Committee. 2018c. Concluding Observations: Montenegro (Second and Third Report). CRC/C/MNE/CO/2–3.

CRC Committee. 2018d. Concluding Observations: Angola (Fifth to Seventh Report). CRC/C/AGO/CO/5–7.

CRC Committee and CEDAW Committee. 2014. Joint General Recommendation/ General Comment No. 31 of the Committee on the Elimination of Discrimination against Women and No. 18 of the Committee on the Rights of the Child on Harmful Practices. CEDAW/C/GC/31-CRC/C/GC/18.

CRC Committee and Committee on Migrant Workers. 2017. Joint General Comment No. 3 and No. 22 on the General Principles Regarding the Human Rights of Children in the Context of International Migration. CMW/C/GC/3-CRC/C/GC/22.

de la Vega, C. and Lewis, T. 2012. Peer Review in the Mix: How the UPR Transforms Human Rights Discourse. In: W. Schabas and C. Bassiouni (eds), *New Challenges in the UN Human Rights Machinery.* Cambridge: Intersentia. https://papers.ssrn.com/abstract=3055828.

Dulin-Keita, A., Hannon, L., Fernandez, J. R. and Cockerham, W. 2011. The defining moment: children's conceptualization of race and experiences with racial discrimination. *Ethnic and Racial Studies*, 34(04), 662–682. doi:10.1080/01419870.2011.535906.

ECHR, European Convention on Human Rights. 1950. *Convention for the Protection of Human Rights and Fundamental Freedoms.* Strasbourg: Council of Europe.

ECtHR. Abdullahi Elmi and Aweys Abubakar v. Malta. Appl. Nos 25794/13 and 28151/13, judgment 22 November 2016. Strasbourg: European Court of Human Rights.

ECtHR. Belgian Linguistic Case. Appl. Nos 1474/62; 1677/62; 1691/62; 1769/63; 1994/63; 2126/64, judgment 23 July 1968. Strasbourg: European Court of Human Rights.

ECtHR. Brauer v. Germany. Appl. No. 3545/04, judgment 28 May 2009. Strasbourg: European Court of Human Rights.

ECtHR. Camp and Bourimi v. the Netherlands. Appl. No. 28369/95, judgment 3 October 2000. Strasbourg: European Court of Human Rights.

ECtHR. D.H. and Others v. the Czech Republic. Appl. No. 57325/00, judgment 13 November 2010 (Grand Chamber). Strasbourg: European Court of Human Rights.

ECtHR. Fabris v. France. Appl. No. 16574/08, judgment 7 February 2013 (Grand Chamber). Strasbourg: European Court of Human Rights.

ECtHR. Genovese v. Malta. Appl. No. 53124/09, judgment 11 October 2011 (concerning denial of citizenship to a child born out of wedlock). Strasbourg: European Court of Human Rights.

ECtHR. Grzelak v. Poland. Appl. No. 7710/02, judgment 15 June 2010. Strasbourg: European Court of Human Rights.

ECtHR. Marckx v. Belgium. Appl. No. 6833/74, judgment 13 June 1979. Strasbourg: European Court of Human Rights.

ECtHR. Mazurek v. France. Appl. No. 34406/97, judgment 1 February 2000. Strasbourg: European Court of Human Rights.

ECtHR. Merger and Cros v. France. Appl. No. 68864/01, judgment 22 December 2004. Strasbourg: European Court of Human Rights.

ECtHR. Mitzinger v. Germany. Appl. No. 29762/10, judgment 9 February 2017. Strasbourg: European Court of Human Rights.

ECtHR. N.Ts. v. Georgia. No. 71776/12, judgment 2 February 2016. Strasbourg: European Court of Human Rights.

ECtHR. Oršuš and Others v. Croatia. Appl. No. 15766/03, judgment 16 March 2010 (Grand Chamber). Strasbourg: European Court of Human Rights.

ECtHR. Pla and Puncernau v. Andorra. Appl. No. 69498/01, judgment 13 July 2004. Strasbourg: European Court of Human Rights.

ECtHR. Ponomaryovi v. Bulgaria. Appl. No. 5335/05, judgment 21 June 2005. Strasbourg: European Court of Human Rights.

ECtHR. S.L. and J.L. v. Croatia. No. 13712/11, judgment 7 May 2015. Strasbourg: European Court of Human Rights.

ECtHR. Tyler v. U.K. Appl. No. 5856/72, judgment 25 April 1978, para. 31. Strasbourg: European Court of Human Rights.

Eekelaar, J. 2015. The Role of the Best Interests Principle in Decisions Affecting Children and Decisions about Children. *The International Journal of Children's Rights*, 23(1) (March 28): 3–26. doi:10.1163/15718182-02301003.

Ferguson, L. 2013. Not Merely Rights for Children but Children's Rights: The Theory Gap and the Assumption of the Importance of Children's Rights. *The International Journal of Children's Rights*, 21(2) (January 1): 177–208. doi:10.1163/15718182-55680015.

FRA, European Court of Human Rights, and Europarat, (eds) 2015. *Handbook on European Law Relating to the Rights of the Child*. Handbook/FRA, European Union Agency for Fundamental Rights. Luxembourg: Publication Office of the European Union.

Fredman, S. 2011. *Discrimination Law*. 2nd ed. Clarendon Law Series. Oxford: Oxford University Press.

Fredman, S. 2018. Direct and Indirect Discrimination: Is There Still a Divide? In: H. Collins and T. Khaitan (eds), *Foundations of Indirect Discrimination Law*. Oxford: Bloomsbury Publishing.

Freeman, M. 2010. The Human Rights of Children. *Current Legal Problems*, 63(1) (January 1): 1–44. doi:10.1093/clp/63.1.1.

Gill, D. L. 2017. Gender and Cultural Diversity in Sport, Exercise, and Performance Psychology. In: *Oxford Research Encyclopedia of Psychology* (April 26). doi:10.1093/acrefore/9780190236557.013.148.http://psychology.oxfordre.com/view/10.1093/acrefore/9780190236557.001.0001/acrefore-9780190236557-e-148.

Gladstone, R. 2017. 300,000 Child Refugees and Migrants Traveled Alone in '15 and '16, U. N. Says. *The New York Times*, December 22, sec. World. https://www.nytimes.com/2017/05/17/world/americas/united-nations-children-refugees-migrants-trafficking.html.

Goodman, R. and Jinks, D. 2013. *Socializing States: Promoting Human Rights through International Law*. Oxford: Oxford University Press. http://www.oxfordscholarship.com/view/10.1093/acprof:oso/9780199300990.001.0001/acprof-9780199300990.

Henrard, K. 2008. Equality of Individuals. *Max Planck Encyclopedia of Public International Law*. Oxford: Oxford University Press. http://opil.ouplaw.com.ezproxy.utlib.ut.ee/view/10.1093/law:epil/9780199231690/law-9780199231690-e788.

Human Rights Council. 2018a. Press Release: HRC Adopts UPR Outcomes of Gabon, Ghana and Peru. https://www.ohchr.org/EN/HRBodies/HRC/Pages/NewsDetail.aspx?NewsID=22836&LangID=E.

Human Rights Council. 2018b. Press Release: HRC Adopts the UPR Outcomes of Guatemala, Switzerland and the Republic of Korea. https://www.ohchr.org/EN/HRBodies/HRC/Pages/NewsDetail.aspx?NewsID=22838&LangID=E.

Human Rights Council. 2018c. Press Release: HRC Adopts Outcomes of UPR of Luxembourg, Barbados, Montenegro and the United Arab Emirates. https://www.ohchr.org/EN/HRBodies/HRC/Pages/NewsDetail.aspx?NewsID=22838&LangID=E.

Human Rights Council. 2018d. Press Release: HRC Adopts UPR Outcomes of Azerbaijan, Tuvalu, Colombia, and Djibouti. https://www.ohchr.org/EN/HRBodies/HRC/Pages/NewsDetail.aspx?NewsID=23600&LangID=E.

Inter-American Commission on Human Rights. 2017. Towards the Effective Fulfillment of Children's Rights: National Protection Systems. OEA/Ser.L/V/II. Doc. 206/17. http://www.oas.org/en/iachr/reports/pdfs/FulfillmentRights-Children.pdf.

KidsRights Index. KidsRights Index 2017: Violence and Discrimination Against Children Global Concern. Available at: https://kidsrightsindex.org/News/ArticleID/18/KidsRights-Index-2017-violence-and-discrimination-against-children-global-concern (accessed: 28. 09. 2018).

Kilkelly, U. 2001. Best of Both Worlds for Children's Rights – Interpreting the European Convention on Human Rights in the Light of the UN Convention on the Rights of the Child. *Human Rights Quarterly* 23: 308–326.

Kilkelly, U. 2015. The CRC in Litigation Under the ECHR. In: T. Leifaar and J. E. Doek (eds), *Litigating the Rights of the Child.* Dordrecht: Springer Netherlands. 193–209. doi:10.1007/978-94-017-9445-9_12.http://link.springer.com/10.1007/978-94-017-9445-9_12.

Kutsar, D. and Warming, D. (eds) 2014. *Children and Non-Discrimination: Interdisciplinary Textbook.* Children's Rights Erasmus Academic Network (CREAN). Tartu: University Press of Estonia.

Langford, M. and Kirkebø, T. L. 2018. The Commitment Curve: Global Regulation of Business and Human Rights. *Business and Human Rights Journal*, 03(03): 157–185. doi:10.1017/bhj.2018.11.

Lippert-Rasmussen, K. 2018. Indirect Discrimination, Affirmative Action and Relational Egalitarianism. In: H. Collins and T. Khaitan (eds), *Foundations of Indirect Discrimination Law* (pp. 173–196). Oxford: Bloomsbury Publishing.

Makkonen, T. 2012. *Equal in Law, Unequal in Fact: Racial and Ethnic Discrimination and the Legal Response Thereto in Europe.* Erik Castrén Institute Monographs on International Law and Human Rights v. 13. Leiden; Boston: Martinus Nijhoff Publishers.

McCrudden, C. (ed.) 2013. *Understanding Human Dignity.* London: British Academy. http://www.britishacademypublications.com/view/10.5871/bacad/9780197265642.001.0001/upso-9780197265642.

Moses, E. 2015. The Importance of Retaining Girls in Sports | HuffPost. *Huffington Post Blog*, August 13. https://www.huffingtonpost.com/edwin-moses/retaining-girls-in-sports_b_7971912.html?guccounter=1.

Novak, F. 2013. The Inter-American Court of Human Rights and Its Contribution to the Protection of Children's Rights. In: N. Boschiero, T. Scovazzi, C. Pitea, and C. Ragni (eds), *International Courts and the Development of International Law, Essays in Honour of Tullio Treves* (pp. 513–533). The Hague, The Netherlands: T.M.C. Asser Press. doi:10.1007/978-90-6704-894-1_38.https://link.springer.com/chapter/10.1007/978-90-6704-894-1_38.

Pachter, L. M., Szalacha, L. A., Bernstein, B. A. & Coll, C. G. 2010. Perceptions of Racism in Children and Youth (PRaCY): Properties of a Self-Report Instrument for Research on Children's Health and Development. *Ethnicity and Health*, 15(01): 33–46. doi:10.1080/13557850903383196.

Panetta, G. 2018. Denmark's Extreme Immigration Policies Include Separating Immigrant Toddlers from Their Parents Every Week to Teach Them "Danish Values". *Business Insider Nordic*, July 2. https://nordic.businessinsider.com/denmark-strict-immigration-policies-ghetto-neighborhoods-2018-7/.

Parekh, B. 2006. *Rethinking Multiculturalism. Cultural Diversity and Political Theory.* 2nd ed. Basingstoke: Palgrave Macmillan.

Skivenes, M. and Søvig, K. H. 2016. Judicial Discretion and the Child's Best Interest – The European Court of Human Rights on Child Protection Adoptions. In: E. Sutherland and L. Macfarlane (eds) *Implementing Article 3 of the United Nations Convention on the Rights of the Child: Best Interests, Welfare and Well-being.* Cambridge: Cambridge University Press.

Sloth-Nielsen, J. 2016. *Children's Rights in Africa: A Legal Perspective.* Abingdon: Routledge.

Smith, N. 2011. *Basic Equality and Discrimination: Reconciling Theory and Law. Applied Legal Philosophy.* Farnham, Surrey; Burlington, VT: Ashgate Publications.

Sutherland, E. E. and Macfarlane, L-A. B. (eds) 2016. *Implementing Article 3 of the United Nations Convention on the Rights of the Child. Best Interest, Welfare and Well-being.* Cambridge: Cambridge University Press.

UNICEF. 2009. *The State of the World's Children: Special Edition. Celebrating 20 Years of the Convention on the Rights of the Child.* New York: United Nations Children's Fund.

UNICEF. 2013. *Child Well-being in Rich Countries: A Comparative Overview. Innocenti Report Card 11.* Florence: UNICEF Office of Research.

United Nations Committee on the Rights of Persons with Disabilities. 2018. General Comment No. 6 on Equality and Non-Discrimination. CRPD/C/GC/6.

United Nations Development Program. 2015. Sustainable Development Goals (SDG). Available at: http://www.undp.org/content/undp/en/home/sustainable-development-goals.html.

United Nations General Assembly (UNGA). 1989. Convention on the Rights of the Child. 20 November 1989. Available at: https://www.ohchr.org/en/professionalinterest/pages/crc.aspx.

United Nations General Assembly (UNGA). 2011. Optional Protocol to the Convention on the Rights of the Child on a Communications Procedure. 19. 12. 2011. A/RES/66/138.

United Nations General Assembly (UNGA). 2015. Transforming Our World: the 2030 Agenda for Sustainable Development, Resolution adopted. 25. 09. 2015. A/RES/70/1.

2 Article 2 of the United Nations Convention on the Rights of the Child

Non-discrimination and children's rights

*Elaine E. Sutherland**

Introduction

The long-standing principle of non-discrimination is enshrined in the UN Charter, where one of the purposes of the organisation is stated as "promoting and encouraging respect for human rights and for fundamental freedoms for all without distinction as to race, sex, language, or religion".[1] That ethos is reflected in the International Bill of Human Rights where the fundamental principle of non-discrimination is repeated and the grounds of prohibited discrimination are expanded to include "political or other opinion, national or social origin, property, birth or other status".[2] Regional human rights instruments take a similar approach.[3]

The landmark United Nations Convention on the Rights of the Child (CRC) continues that tradition, embracing non-discrimination in Article 2. Along with the three other general principles of the CRC,[4] Article 2 underpins the Convention as a whole, applying to all the sectoral rights it guarantees to children and young people.

This chapter sets the scene for those that follow and focusses on two key issues: the grounds of discrimination applicable to children and young people under Article 2 and the nature of the obligation placed on States Parties. The chapter begins by examining the grounds that the drafters of the Convention identified as relevant and, in particular, those that generated most debate in the course of their deliberations. Textual analysis is then employed in probing the duties incumbent on states under the provision. The work of the United Nations Committee on the Rights of the Child (UNCRC) and other bodies, amplifying these obligations, will be used to drill down further, exploring the extent to which the responsibility for ensuring non-discrimination has evolved into an obligation to promote equality, either equality of opportunity or equality of outcomes. Finally, the nature and manifestations of discrimination perpetrated against children and young people around the world today will be surveyed.

Drafting: which children may need protection?

When the drafters of the CRC turned their attentions to the issue of discrimination, they did not come cold to their task since their deliberations took place in the context of the non-discrimination ethos of the United Nations and a developing corpus of human rights jurisprudence.[5] In addition, they had the first Polish draft, modelled on the Declaration of the Rights of the Child of 1959,[6] with which to work. It contained the following two provisions:

Article I,

> Every child, without any exception whatsoever, shall be entitled to the rights set forth in this Convention, without distinction or discrimination on account of race, colour, sex, language, religion, political or other opinion, national or social origin, property, birth or other status, whether of himself or of his family.

Article X,

> The child shall be protected from practices which may foster racial, religious and any other form of discrimination. He shall be brought up in a spirit of understanding, tolerance, friendship among peoples, peace and universal brotherhood, and in full consciousness that his energy and talents should be devoted to the service of his fellow men.[7]

There is a certain irony in the fact that provisions aimed at preventing discrimination should be couched in the masculine, embodying a gender bias that was widespread in international and domestic legal instruments at the time. That shortcoming ran throughout the first Polish draft and, while the issue was raised by New Zealand early in discussions,[8] the text was only rendered gender-neutral rather late in the day, in 1988, at the urging of UNICEF.[9]

What, then, generated debate during the drafting process? As we have seen, prohibiting discrimination on the basis of race, colour, sex, language, religion, political or other opinion, national or social origin, property, birth or other status was already part of an established pattern in human rights instruments by the time the drafters of the CRC set about their task.[10] That normative setting – and their commitment to advancing the rights of children and young people within it – enabled the drafters to accept many of the prohibited grounds without discussion. They were far from passive acceptors of established norms, however, and lively debate surrounded proposals to delete from, and add to, the existing list.

Proposed deletion

The Dominican Republic suggested deleting reference to the child's "political or other opinion" from the text because of a concern that, while the child's incapacity was mentioned in the Preamble to the Convention, these words "could be interpreted as meaning that [the child's] opinions would still have some relevance".[11] To a modern reader, familiar with the importance of respecting the participation rights of children and young people in policy making and the legislative process,[12] as well as the meaningful contribution made by children and young people to the political process,[13] this seems baffling. In the event, the proposal for deletion did not attract support.

Proposed additions

In terms of expanding the enumerate grounds in what became Article 2, the drafters focussed on two issues: non-marital children and what might be described as "immigration status".[14] Commenting on the first Polish draft, the German Democratic Republic called for "an explicit provision ... to preclude discrimination against children of unmarried parents"[15] and a number of other delegations proposed textual amendment designed to have the same effect.[16] These children were already protected by the reference to "birth status"[17] and the support for providing for more explicit protection reflects the widespread discrimination faced by this particular group of children in many countries at the time.

The 1979 revised Polish draft of what was to become Article 2, which adopted the more familiar, bipartite structure, sought to address this issue:

1 The States Parties to the present Convention shall respect and extend all the rights set forth in this Convention to all children in their territories, irrespective of these children's race, colour, sex, religion, political and other opinion, social origin, property, *birth in lawful wedlock or out of wedlock* or any other distinction whatever.
2 The States Parties to the present Convention shall undertake appropriate measures individually and within the framework of international cooperation, particularly in the areas of economy, health and education for the implementation of the rights recognized in this Convention.[18]

Such was the level of concern, however, that a number of delegations, including those from Austria and China, and the NGO Ad Hoc Group, continued to press for a separate article in the Convention guaranteeing to non-marital children the same (or equal) legal rights as those enjoyed by marital children.[19] Opposition came from Australia, Japan, the United Kingdom and the United States on the grounds that such a provision would be inconsistent with their domestic laws on succession.[20]

Disagreement continued throughout the drafting process and, despite efforts by the Federal Republic of Germany to return to the issue,[21] consensus proved elusive and the protection extended to non-marital children remained confined to the original reference to "birth status". In many countries, including some of those most strongly opposed to any separate article, there is the perception that equality for non-marital children is a twentieth-century problem that has now been resolved.[22] The same cannot be said of the other issue that most concerned the drafter: immigration status.

The 1979 revised Polish draft brought another innovation, requiring States Parties to respect and extend Convention rights to "all children in their territories," along with a new Article 5, requiring States Parties to "recognize the right of alien children staying in their territories to enjoy" these rights.[23] This triggered sharp and protracted division between the drafters with numerous different forms of words being proposed.[24] A flavour of the very different views can be gleaned by contrasting the American proposal that a State Party be required to respect and extend Convention rights to "all children lawfully in its territory,"[25] with that from Norway that children should enjoy these rights "irrespective of the legality of their parents' stay".[26] Consensus again proved elusive and something of a compromise was reached when Article 5 was deleted while the obligation on States Parties to respect and extend Convention rights "to each child within their jurisdiction" remained in the text of Article 2(1).

These, then, were the groups of children whose protection from discrimination generated most discussion, but what of those who received little or no attention? While the rights of children with disabilities were acknowledged in a separate article of the first Polish draft,[27] early versions of what was to become Article 2 contained no reference to the child's or the parent's or guardian's disability. That omission was corrected when reference to disability was added to Article 2, without demur, at behest of UNESCO during the 1988 technical review.[28] As the UNCRC pointed out some years later, the CRC was "was the first human rights treaty that contained a specific reference to disability".[29]

In an instrument addressing the rights of children, it is curious that there was no discussion of age discrimination itself: that is, discrimination against children and young people solely on the basis of their youth. As we shall see presently, the Human Rights Committee has made clear that, while different treatment may sometimes be justified, blanket discrimination on the basis of age is not.[30]

To the modern reader, however, the most startling omission from the Convention is express reference to a prohibition on discrimination on the basis of the child's – or the parent's or guardian's – sexual orientation or gender identity. It appears that there was simply no discussion of these grounds, something that is probably no more than a reflection of the temporal context of drafting since these issues had a lower profile in the 1980s than they do today. As the UNCRC has confirmed, discrimination on either ground is covered by "other status".[31]

The final text

Article 2, as adopted by the General Assembly on 20 November 1989, is as follows:

1 States Parties shall respect and ensure the rights set forth in the present Convention to each child within their jurisdiction without discrimination of any kind, irrespective of the child's or his or her parent's or legal guardian's race, colour, sex, language, religion, political or other opinion, national, ethnic or social origin, property, disability, birth or other status.

2 States Parties shall take all appropriate measures to ensure that the child is protected against all forms of discrimination or punishment on the basis of the status, activities, expressed opinions, or beliefs of the child's parents, legal guardians, or family members.

The obligations under Article 2

Just as the drafters of Article 2 were not working in a vacuum, nor is the modern commentator. In the decades since the CRC was adopted, the corpus of human rights law that informed the drafters' deliberations has developed and various UN treaty bodies have provided insights into the obligations embodied in Article 2, with the *General Comments* of the UNCRC being particularly helpful. Strictly speaking, these interpretations are not binding on States Parties, since the CRC, like other human rights treaties, does not give the relevant treaty body express power to adopt binding interpretations of the treaty.[32] However, the views expressed in *General Comments* are widely regarded as "non-binding norms that interpret and add detail to the rights and obligations"[33] contained in the treaty or as a distillation of the particular committee's views[34] and they of immense assistance to those charged with implementing the obligations.

Discrimination

Any exploration of the content of Article 2 begins, necessarily, with establishing what is meant, in the human rights context, by discrimination. While the concept is an ancient one and discrimination is prohibited in all the main human rights instruments, there was an early reluctance to attempt a definition. That approach changed, in 1965, when the International Convention on the Elimination of All Forms of Racial Discrimination provided a definition of "racial discrimination",[35] and the practice was followed in subsequent sectoral treaties.[36] Why this was not done in the CRC is unclear.[37] However, drawing on existing definitions and its own work,[38] the Human Rights Committee has offered the following definition in the context of the CRC: "non-discrimination means that no child should be injured, privileged, punished or deprived of any right" on the basis of any of the grounds enumerated in Article 2(1).[39] It will be remembered, of course, that the prohibition on discrimination applies not only to the child's characteristics, but also to those of the child's parent or guardian.

This is not the place for an in-depth analysis of the nuances and complexities of discrimination to which whole forests have been sacrificed.[40] For our present purpose, it will be helpful to bear two questions in mind. Does the obligation to ensure non-discrimination, under Article 2, create an obligation to promote equality? If it does, is the goal equality of opportunity or equality of outcomes?

Is different treatment ever permissible?

It has long been accepted in human rights law that respecting the principle of non-discrimination does not preclude all forms of different treatment. As long ago as 1989, the Human Rights Committee, commenting on the International Covenant on Civil and Political Rights, noted that "the principle of equality sometimes requires States Parties to take affirmative action in order to diminish or eliminate conditions which cause or help to perpetuate discrimination".[41] Almost a decade later, that Committee offered the following test in the context of the CRC: "not every differentiation of treatment constitutes a discrimination if the criteria for such differentiation are reasonable and objective and if the aim is to achieve a purpose which is legitimate under the Convention".[42]

The UNCRC endorsed that approach, noting, "It should be emphasized that the application of the non-discrimination principle of equal access to rights does not mean identical treatment",[43] and numerous *General Comments* confirm that eliminating discrimination may require targeted and prioritised responses. Thus, for example, when it amplified State Party obligations in respect of the child's right to the highest attainable standard of health, the UNCRC counselled that "children in disadvantaged situations and under-served areas should be a focus of efforts to fulfil children's right to health".[44] Similarly, in addressing the rights of indigenous children, it noted that "the non-discrimination obligation requires States actively to identify individual children and groups of children the recognition and realization of whose rights may demand special measures".[45]

The endorsement of different treatment, designed to eliminate discrimination, should not, however, be regarded as signalling approval of generalised age discrimination.[46] To suggest that youth, in itself, justifies different or lesser treatment risks perpetuating what Pierce and Allen identified, long before the CRC was conceived, as "childism": that is, "the automatic presumption of superiority of any adult over any child".[47] Similarly, to assume that non-age necessarily implies disability is wholly inconsistent with the concept of the child's evolving capacity, articulated in Article 5, and the child's participation rights, guaranteed by Article 12. Rather, any age-based difference of treatment requires justification, applying the Human Rights Committee's test, that the difference is reasonable, objective and designed to achieve a purpose which is legitimate under the Convention.

The content of the State's obligation under Article 2

Textual analysis of Article 2 gives an indication of the nature of the obligation it places on States Parties. As we have seen, after considerable debate, the provision applies to "each child within their jurisdiction": that is, the child's presence is the controlling factor and how the child came to be there – whether by legal or illegal means – is irrelevant. By requiring that States "shall respect and ensure"[48] Convention rights to all such children, Article 2(1) creates positive and negative, non-optional duties. The requirement to "respect" creates "an affirmative and immediate obligations to take all necessary measures to enjoy and exercise the relevant rights," while the obligation to "ensure" requires the State "to abstain from adopting measures that may preclude the exercise of such rights or may violate them."[49] Similarly, an element of proactivity is reflected Article 2(2), by the requirement that States "take appropriate measures to ensure that the child is protected" from the various kinds of discrimination enumerated there. Finally, it is worth noting that these prohibited grounds of discrimination, which apply not only to the child, but also to the child's parent or legal guardian, are not an exhaustive list, something indicated by the use of the words "of any kind" and "or other status".[50]

So much for the text, but what does Article 2 actually require of states? Again, the UNCRC has elaborated in respect of sectoral rights in numerous *General Comments*. In terms of implementation, more broadly, *General Comment 5* and its younger sibling, *General Comment 19*, are particularly helpful.[51] *General Comment 5* sets out, in unambiguous terms, the two-step process required of a State Party. First, it must "identify individual children and groups of children the recognition and realization of whose rights may demand special measures."[52] To this end, the UNCRC has stressed the need to collect disaggregated data in order that discrimination or potential discrimination can be identified. Thereafter, the State should address the discrimination, using mechanisms including "legislation, administration and resource allocation, as well as educational measures to change attitudes."[53] In all of this, it will be remembered that targeted responses, prioritising the needs of particular children or groups of children, are unobjectionable provided that they are founded on reasonable and objective criteria and designed to achieve one of the Convention's purposes.

This emphasis on identifying the children and young people who are experiencing discrimination and taking steps to eliminate it, whether by affirmative action or otherwise, is arguably designed not simply to secure equality of opportunity, but also to achieve equality of outcomes. Further support for that position is found in *General Comment No. 19*, addressing public budgeting – the allocation of resources by the state – in order to realise children's rights. It will be remembered that Article 4 of the CRC requires States Parties to realise civil and political convention rights immediately and to implement economic, social and cultural rights "to the maximum extent of their available resources", anticipating that full realisation of the latter group of rights may be a progressive process.

In *General Comment No. 19*, the UNCRC acknowledged that significant progress has been made by States Parties in implementing children's rights through legislation, policies and programmes, but reminded States of its concern that the allocation of insufficient resources would impede their full realisation and advised on how resource allocation could be undertaken most effectively to address that problem.[54] One facet of that is for States to take proactive measures in allocating and spending sufficient funds, with the UNCRC advising, "in order to achieve substantive equality, States Parties should identify groups of children that qualify for special measures and use public budgets to implement such measures."[55] Equality of outcomes, it seems, is regarded by the UNCRC as a "given".

That the goal of Article 2 is equality is entirely consistent with the modern human rights climate. The 2030 Agenda for Sustainable Development, which launched the Sustainable Development Goals,[56] makes express reference to "equality and non-discrimination".[57] While the 17 Goals span a wide range of concerns, a number focus on equality-related issues, like the elimination of poverty, and specific mention is made of reducing inequalities, generally, and of gender inequality. Both the World Health Organisation[58] and UNICEF[59] emphasise equality of outcomes. Many of the publications emanating from the UNICEF Office of Research-Innocenti, which undertakes research on critical issues facing children and young people around the world, focus on equality, sometimes equating it with equity or fairness.[60]

Continuing discrimination: grounds and manifestations

The crucial question, of course, is whether children and young people continue to experience discrimination, on which there is no shortage of information. Again, the *General Comments* of the UNCRC provide valuable insights, but a particularly rich resource is its *Concluding Observations* on the reports that States Parties are required to submit 2 years after ratifying the CRC and every 5 years thereafter.[61] In the paragraphs below, selective examples, taken from 100 recent *Concluding Observations*, are used to give a flavour of how discrimination continues to manifest itself.

While there have been improvements in many countries, *de jure* and *de facto* discrimination continues, with a lack of adequate legislation prohibiting discrimination in some countries,[62] a dilution of statutory protection in others[63] and a lack of awareness or enforcement of existing laws and policies in yet others.[64]

Two observations are worth offering at the outset. First, childhood, itself, may be a source of discrimination, with negative public attitudes towards the young leading to stereotyping, stigmatisation and social exclusion.[65] Adolescents often fare particularly badly,[66] facing the paradoxical situation of being viewed as "dangerous or hostile", on the one hand, and "incompetent and incapable", on the other.[67]

Secondly, discrimination does not always stem from only one ground and some groups of children face intersectional discrimination: that is, they may be discriminated against on multiple grounds. So, for example, a poor, female child with disabilities from an ethnic minority may experience discrimination deriving from all of her characteristics.[68] Where discrimination targets teenage, single mothers, it is likely to have an adverse impact on the young women and their children simultaneously.[69]

Race, colour or national, ethnic or social origin

Discrimination on the basis of race, colour or national, ethnic or social origin features frequently in the *Concluding Observations.* Children from racial or ethnic minorities are particularly at risk[70] and there are local variations: in Costa Rica[71] and Panama,[72] it is children of African descent; in Kuwait, it is Bidoon children[73]; in Turkey, it is Kurdish children[74]; in Cyprus and Greece, it is Turkish children[75]; in India, it is children from scheduled castes and scheduled tribes.[76] Across Europe, Roma children face prejudice.[77] In countries where immigrants, often from Europe, quickly outnumbered the indigenous population, indigenous children experience discrimination.[78] A harbinger of the horrors to come is seen in the discrimination against Rohingya children in Myanmar, noted by the UNCRC in 2012.[79]

The drafters of the CRC showed a chilling prescience in their lengthy discussion of immigration status, since unaccompanied minors and migrant, asylum-seeking and refugee children often face discrimination[80] and the UNCRC has given particular attention to the problem, publishing a *General Comment* of its own, in 2005,[81] and two jointly with the Committee on Migrant Workers more recently.[82]

How these particular forms of discrimination manifest themselves varies between countries, but examples include specific groups of children being denied access to services like health care,[83] social security,[84] education[85] and, in at least one case, clean drinking water.[86] Another manifestation is stigmatisation and marginalisation by other children,[87] with children in the Russian Federation joining nationalist movements that are involved in hate crimes against minority groups.[88]

Sex

Sex discrimination persists in many parts of the world and is highlighted, depressingly often, in *Concluding Observations.* [89] In a relatively small number of countries, discrimination against girls and young women is expressly embodied in the law on such matters as education,[90] marriage,[91] inheritance rights,[92] family name,[93] and land ownership rights.[94] A more pervasive problem, however, stems from social and cultural norms[95] and persistent patriarchal attitudes,[96] sometimes advancing a view that females are inferior to males.[97] This can result in physical and psychological abuse of girls and young women,[98] including female genital mutilation[99] and child marriages,[100] in some countries, and in sex-selective abortions, female infanticide and abandonment of girls, in others.[101]

Gender stereotyping may impact the position of females in a given society, more generally, confining women and girls to certain tasks and roles within society[102] and can have a particularly negative impact on access to services, including health care and education.[103] Specific examples, highlighted by the UNCRC, in the context of education, include gender stereotypes in Catholic school textbooks that undermine girls' education and life opportunities[104] and the *Chbap Srey* (code of conduct for women), used in Cambodian schools, which legitimises the perceived inferiority of girls and women in the society.[105]

Disability

It will be remembered that the CRC was the first human rights treaty to include disability in the list of the grounds on which discrimination is prohibited. The UNCRC has published a *General Comment* expanding on States Parties' obligations to children with disabilities,[106] and a more recent *General Comment* on equality and non-discrimination from the Committee on the Rights of Persons with Disabilities includes guidance in respect of children as well as adults.[107]

Children with disabilities continue to face discrimination around the world.[108] This often takes the form of prejudice, harassment and stigmatisation,[109] leading to the children being marginalised, and numerous *Concluding Observations* make reference to children with disabilities being denied access to services, including health care and education.[110]

Birth status

The need to protect children born outside of marriage was of particular concern to the drafters of the Convention. While discrimination on the basis of parental marital status has diminished or been eliminated in many countries,[111] it continues in others.[112] The very fact that children may be classified as "illegitimate" opens the door to discrimination[113] and the problem is exacerbated where identity documents disclose that status.[114] In addition to societal discrimination, numerous *General Comments* note *de jure* discrimination experienced by these children, particularly in respect of family name and inheritance rights.[115]

Religion, language and property

Discrimination on the basis of religion was mentioned in only a small number of the *Concluding Observations* reviewed and the target group varies by country: in China, it is Tibetan, Uighur, Falun Gong practitioner children[116]; in Greece, it is children belonging to the Muslim community of Thrace[117]; and, in Hungary, it is Jewish children.[118] Language-related discrimination was noted only in respect of Turkmenistan, where Kazakh and Uzbek children "have limited access to language classes in their mother tongue".[119]

While discrimination on the basis of property was not mentioned explicitly in the *Concluding Observations* reviewed, there are frequent references to the adverse impact on children of living in poverty[120] and, more obliquely, in "marginalised and disadvantaged" situations.[121] The latter term may refer to children living in geographically remote communities,[122] but includes those living in rural and urban settings[123] and in street situations.[124] In each case, the lack of property is at the heart of the prejudice and stigmatisation these children experience and their difficulties in gaining access to resources, including health care and education. What is presented here is a vicious circle of children facing discrimination because they are poor and that, in turn, keeping them in poverty.

Other status

By prohibiting discrimination on the basis of "other status", the CRC seeks to ensure that the treaty is capable of addressing issues, unanticipated at the time of drafting, that come to the fore in the future. One such issue is children living with HIV/AIDS, either because they are infected or they have a parent who is. In *General Comment No. 3*, the UNCRC made clear that "other status" includes the "HIV/AIDS status of the child or his/her parent(s)" and has offered further guidance on States Parties' obligations to these children.[125] They experience discrimination in many countries, sometimes impeding their access to medical treatment.[126]

While the drafters of the CRC simply did not discuss discrimination on the basis of sexual orientation or gender identity, the UNCRC made clear, in *General Comment No. 4*, [127] that such discrimination comes within the ambit of "other status" and has elaborated on the nature and unacceptability of it more recently in *General Comment No. 20*. [128]

LGBTI+ young people face discrimination in many parts of the world, as do children of same sex parents. In some countries, discrimination is enshrined in the criminal law. For example, in the Russian Federation, "propaganda of unconventional sexual relationships" is a criminal offence[129] while, in Gambia, anyone convicted of "aggravated homosexuality" is liable to a term of life imprisonment.[130] In other countries, the problem stems from the absence of laws protecting LGBTI+ youth[131] or the failure of the legal system to recognise same sex families.[132]

Discrimination may take the form of stigmatisation and stereotyping, and the UNCRC has expressed concern about past statements from the Holy See which contributed to both stigmatisation of, and violence directed at, LGBTI+ young people and the children of same sex couples.[133] In numerous countries, both groups are subject to hate speech, intimidation and physical violence.[134] Other consequences include an adverse impact on access to services, including education[135] and health care,[136] and the UNCRC has condemned "the imposition of so-called 'treatments' to try to change sexual orientation and forced surgeries or treatments on intersex adolescents".[137]

Conclusions

The drafters of the United Nations Convention on the Rights of the Child took a wise course in using the established ground of prohibited discrimination found in other instruments as the basis for their work, expanding them to embrace discrimination on the ground of disability. Their foresight in ensuring that protection from discrimination extends to all children in a State Party's territory, regardless of how they came to be there, has proved to be another prudent measure.

By requiring States Parties to respect and ensure Convention rights to every child "without discrimination of any kind" and including "other status" in the list of grounds on which discrimination is prohibited, the drafters secured the Convention's capacity to accommodate specific concerns, unanticipated at the time of drafting, that came to prominence later. As a result, the United Nations Committee on the Rights of the Child has been able to take a proactive approach in its *General Comments* and *Concluding Observations* in addressing the needs of children living with HIV/AIDS, LGBTI+ youth and the children of same sex parents. Effectively, the Convention was "future-proofed" and will be able to meet new challenges that emerge in the years to come.

Yet there is no denying that many children around the world continue to face discrimination and, often, on the well-established grounds with which we are thoroughly familiar. That is not a failing of Article 2. The Convention provides the tools for addressing discrimination and the Committee on the Rights of the Child has taken the process further, elaborating on the obligations on States Parties, generally, and identifying instances of discrimination in particular countries and how they can be tackled.

The Committee's work and other contributions from the United Nations human rights system make clear that Article 2 is not confined to eliminating discrimination on the enumerated grounds, but extends to the more challenging goal of achieving equality for children. It falls to governments, non-governmental organisations – and to each of us – to play our part in turning that goal into reality. The children of the world deserve no less.

Notes

* My thanks go to Samantha MacBeth, now a Lewis and Clark Law School alumna, for her diligent and resourceful research assistance.

1 Charter of the United Nations 1 U.N.T.S. XVI (1945), Art. 1(3).

2 Universal Declaration of Human Rights, GA Res. 217 A (III) (1948), Art. 2; International Covenant on Economic, Cultural and Social Rights, 993 U.N.T.S. 3 (1966), Art. 2(2); International Covenant on Civil and Political Rights, 993 U.N.T. S. 17 (1966), Art. 2(1).

3 See, the European Convention on Human Rights, E.T.S. No 5 (1950), Art. 14; the American Convention on Human Rights, 1144 U.N.T.S. 144 (1969), Art. 1(1); the African Charter on Human and Peoples' Rights, OAU Doc CAB/LEG/67/3 rev. 5 (1981), Art. 2; and the Arab Charter on Human Rights (2004), Art. 3.

4 The others require States Parties to prioritise the child's best interests and to ensure their care and protection (Art. 3); recognise the child's right to life and ensure the child's survival and development (Art. 6); and assure to the child what have come to be known as participation rights (Art. 12). See, United Nations Committee on the Rights of the Child (2003b) para. 12, referring to the "general principles".

5 The Convention on the Elimination of all Forms of Discrimination Against Women, 1249 U.N.T.S. 17, had only recently been adopted, on 18 December 1979.

6 General Assembly Resolution 1386(XIV) (1959).

7 Save the Children Sweden and the Office of the United Nations High Commissioner for Human Rights, *Legislative History of the Convention on the Rights of the Child*, (2007) (hereinafter, *Legislative History*): Vol 1, 314. The *Legislative History* was published in two volumes and can be found at: www.ohchr.org/Documents/Publications/Legisla tiveHistorycrc1en.pdf and www.ohchr.org/Documents/Publications/LegislativeHistor ycrc2en.pdf For earlier discussions of the travaux préparatoires to the Convention, see, Sharon Detrick (ed) with Jaap Doek and Nigel Cantwell, *The United Nations Convention on the Rights of the Child: A Guide to the "Travaux Préparatoires"*.

8 E/CN.4/1324/Add.5 (1980); *Legislative History*: Vol 1, 318.

9 *Legislative History* (n 7): Vol 1, 330.

10 See n 2.

11 E/CN.4/1324 (1978); *Legislative History*: Vol 1, 314.

12 United Nations Committee on the Rights of the Child (2009b), *General Comment No. 12: The Right of the Child to be Heard*, CRC/C/GC/12, paras. 127–129. It must be acknowledged that there are considerable national variations in this respect. See further, van Bueren (2011) and "Children's Voices in Public Decision-Making" in Parkes (2013).

13 Their role in bringing about the end of apartheid in South Africa is a particularly striking example but, around the world, the emergence of Youth Parliaments and the practice of consulting children and young people as part of the political process illustrate their valuable contribution.

14 The Federal Republic of Germany raised the issue of specific protection for adopted children and foster children. While their status is not mentioned expressly in Article 2, their rights are addressed in Articles 20 and 21.

15 E/CN.4/1324 (1978): *Legislative History* (n 7): Vol 1, 315.

16 For example, Spain proposed the insertion of the words "in or out of wedlock" between the word "birth" and the words "other status": E/CN.4/1324 (1978): *Legislative History* (n 7): Vol 1, 316.

17 It is arguable that such discrimination was also covered by the "other status" of the child and the parents.

18 E/CN.4/1324 (1979), reissued for technical reasons; *Legislative History* (n 7): Vol 1, 319, emphasis added.

19 E/CN.4/1986/39 (1986); *Legislative History* (n 7): Vol 1, 325.

20 E/CN.4/1986/39 (1986); *Legislative History* (n 7): Vol 1, 326.
21 E/CN.4/1988/WG.1/WP.3 (1988); *Legislative History* (n 7): Vol 1, 327.
22 That is not to suggest that discrimination based on birth status has been eliminated. See endnotes 111–115 and accompanying text.
23 E/CN.4/1349; *Legislative History* (n 7): Vol 1, 319.
24 *Legislative History* (n 7): Vol 1, 320–325.
25 HR/(XXXVII)/WG.1/WP.7; *Legislative History* (n 7): Vol 1, 320.
26 HR/(XXXVII)/WG.1/WP.10; *Legislative History* (n 7): Vol 1, 320.
27 E/CN.4/1292; *Legislative History* (n 7): Vol 2, 564. This formed the basis of what became Article 23 of the Convention.
28 E/CN.4/1989/WG.1/CRP.1; Legislative History (n 7): Vol 1, 329.
29 United Nations Committee on the Rights of the Child (2006), para. 2.
30 See endnotes 46–47 and accompanying text.
31 See endnotes 127–137 and accompanying text.
32 International Law Association: Committee on International Human Rights Law and Practice (2014), paras. 16 and 18.
33 Keller and Grover (2012: 131).
34 Alston (2001: 775).
35 660 U.N.T.S. 195 (1966), Art. 1.
36 See, the Convention on the Elimination of All Forms of Discrimination against Women, 1249 U.N.T.S. 13 (1980), Art. 1, defining "discrimination against women".
37 While the International Convention on the Protection of the Rights of All Migrant Workers and Members of Their Families, 2220 U.N.T.S. 3 (1990), adopted the year after the CRC, does not define discrimination, the Convention on the Rights of Persons with Disabilities 2515 U.N.T.S. 3 (2006), Art. 2, defines "discrimination on the basis of disability".
38 Human Rights Committee (1989) para. 7, defining "discrimination" in the context of the International Covenant on Civil and Political Rights.
39 Office of the United Nations High Commissioner for Human Rights (1997: 418).
40 For an accessible overview, see Moeckli (2017), ch. 8.
41 Human Rights Committee (1989), para. 10.
42 Office of the United Nations High Commissioner for Human Rights (1997: 418).
43 United Nations Committee on the Rights of the Child (2003b) (arts. 4, 42 and 44, para. 6, para. 12).
44 United Nations Committee on the Rights of the Child, *General Comment No. 15 (2013) on the right of the child to the enjoyment of the highest attainable standard of health (art. 24)*, CRC/C/GC/15, para. 11.
45 United Nations Committee on the Rights of the Child (2009a), para. 24.
46 See further, Breen (2006) and Webb (2011).
47 Pierce and Allen (1975: 266). They continued, by noting that this "results in the adult's needs, desires, hopes, and fears taking unquestioned precedence over those of the child" and "goes beyond the biologic necessity that requires adults to sustain the species by means of authoritative, unilateral decisions": The term returned to prominence with the work of Elisabeth Young-Bruehl. See, Young-Bruehl (2012), taking forward her earlier work in Young-Bruehl (2009).
48 The second Polish draft used the phrase "shall respect and *extend*" and its amendment resulted from the input of UNICEF during the 1988 Technical Review. UNICEF argued that "extend" was not found in the principal human rights instruments in place at the time, where the word "ensure" was used, denoting a higher level of obligation: *Legislative History* (n 7): Vol 1, 229–330.
49 Office of the United Nations High Commissioner for Human Rights (1997: 417).
50 *Id.*
51 United Nations Committee on the Rights of the Child (2016a), which the UNCRC notes, at para. 6, "builds on general comment No. 5".

52 United Nations Committee on the Rights of the Child (2003b) para.12.
53 *Id.*
54 United Nations Committee on the Rights of the Child (2016a), para. 11.
55 United Nations Committee on the Rights of the Child (2016a), para. 42.
56 The Sustainable Development Goals are the successor to the Millennium Development Goals. For a helpful overview, see, Sachs (2012).
57 Transforming our world: the 2030 Agenda for Sustainable Development, GA A/RES/70/1, adopted 25 September 2015, para. 8.
58 World Health Organisation (2016), *Growing up Unequal: Gender and Socioeconomic Differences in Young People's Health and Well-being.*
59 UNICEF (2015), *For Every Child, a Fair Chance: The Promise of Equity.*
60 See, for example, Stewart (2013); *Innocenti Report Card – No 13 (2016) – Fairness for Children: A League Table of Inequality in Child Well-being in Rich Countries*; Toczydlowska and Bruckauf (2017).
61 Article 44. In the future, another valuable resource will be the individual cases under the communications procedure created by the third Optional Protocol to the CRC: Optional Protocol to the Convention on the Rights of the Child on a communications procedure, GA/RES/66/138 (2011).
62 See, for example: Congo, CRC/C/COG/CO/2–4, 2014, para. 28; the Russian Federation, CRC/C/RUS/CO/4–5, 2014, para. 22.
63 Sweden, CRC/C/SWE/CO/5, 2015, para. 15(b) (the term "race" has been deleted in the new Anti-Discrimination Act and there is no explicit legal provisions declaring illegal and prohibiting organisations promoting and inciting racial hatred); Italy, CRC/C/ITA/CO/3–4, 2011, para. 24(b) (amendments to the Criminal Code reduced sentences for propaganda advocating racial or ethnic superiority).
64 See, for example: Dominican Republic: CRC/C/DOM/CO/3–5, 2015, para. 17(a); Lithuania, CRC/C/LTU/CO/3–4, 2013, para. 16.
65 See, for example: Fiji, CRC/C/FJI/CO/2–4, 2014, para. 22; Uruguay, CRC/C/URY/CO/3–5, 2015, para. 23.
66 United Kingdom of Great Britain and Northern Ireland: CRC/C/GBR/CO/5, 2016, para. 23.
67 United Nations Committee on the Rights of the Child (2016b), para. 20.
68 Seychelles, CRC/C/SYC/CO/2–4, 2012, para. 34.
69 See, for example: Republic of Korea, CRC/C/KOR/CO/3–4, 2012, para. 28; Tanzania, CRC/C/TZA/CO/3–5, 2015, para. 25.
70 See, for example: Ireland, CRC/C/IRL/CO/2, 2006, para. 20; Netherlands, CRC/C/NLD/CO/3, 2009, para. 26; Viet Nam, CRC/C/VNM/CO/3–4, 2012, para. 29(b).
71 Costa Rica, CRC/C/CRI/CO/4, 2011, para. 29.
72 Panama: CRC/C/PAN/CO/3–4, 2011, para. 34.
73 Kuwait, CRC/C/KWT/CO/2, 2013, para. 27.
74 Turkey, CRC/C/TUR/CO/2–3, 2012, para. 28.
75 Cyprus, CRC/C/CYP/CO/3–4, 2012, para. 21; Greece, CRC/C/GRC/CO/2–3, 2012, para. 26.
76 India, CRC/C/IND/CO/3–4, 2014, para. 31.
77 See, for example: Finland: CRC/C/FIN/CO/4, 2011, para. 25; Italy: CRC/C/ITA/CO/3–4, 2011, para. 24; Portugal, CRC/C/PRT/CO/3–4, 2014, para. 25; Bosnia and Herzegovina: CRC/C/BIH/CO/2–4, 2012, para. 29.
78 See, for example: Australia, CRC/C/AUS/CO/4, 2012, para. 29(a); Canada: CRC/C/CAN/CO/3–4, 2012, para. 32(a); New Zealand, CRC/C/NZL/CO/5, 2016, para. 15.
79 Myanmar, CRC/C/MMR/CO/3–4, 2012, para. 35.
80 See, for example: Canada, CRC/C/CAN/CO/3–4, 2012, para. 32(a); Switzerland, CRC/C/CHE/CO/2–4, 2015, para. 24; Namibia, CRC/C/NAM/CO/2–3,

2012, para. 30(a); United Kingdom of Great Britain and Northern Ireland, CRC/C/GBR/CO/5, 2016, para. 21(c); South Africa. CRC/C/ZAF/2, 2016, para 23.

81 Committee on the Rights of the Child (2005).

82 United Nations Committee on Migrant Workers and the United Nations Committee on the Rights of the Child (2017a, b).

83 See, for example: China, CRC/C/CHN/CO/3–4, 2013, para. 25; Colombia, CRC/C/COL/CO/4–5, 2015, para. 19; Indonesia, CRC/C/IDN/CO/3–4, 2014, para. 19; Panama, CRC/C/PAN/CO/3–4, 2011, para. 33.

84 Italy, CRC/C/ITA/CO/3–4, 2011, para. 24.

85 See, for example: Turkey, CRC/C/TUR/CO/2–3, 2012, para. 28; Portugal, CRC/C/PRT/CO/3–4, 2014, para. 25; Germany, CRC/C/DEU/CO/3–4, 2014, para. 24.

86 Slovenia, CRC/C/SVN/CO/3–4, 2013, para. 24(b).

87 Sweden, CRC/C/SWE/CO/5, 2015, para. 15(c).

88 Russian Federation, CRC/C/RUS/CO/4–5, 2014, para. 22.

89 See, for example: Albania, CRC/C/ALB/CO/2–4, 2012, para. 27; Bahrain, CRC/C/BHR/CO/2–3, 2011, para. 30; Hungary, CRC/C/HUN/CO/3–5, 2014, para. 19; Madagascar, CRC/C/MDG/CO/3–4, 2012, para. 23; Russian Federation, CRC/C/RUS/CO/4–5, 2014, para. 22; Thailand, CRC/C/THA/CO/3–4, 2012, para. 33; Uruguay, CRC/C/URY/CO/3–5, 2015, para. 23.

90 Kuwait, CRC/C/KWT/CO/2, 2013, para. 29.

91 Jordan, CRC/C/JOR/CO/4–5, 2014, para. 17.

92 Algeria, CRC/C/DZA/CO/3–4, 2012, para. 29; Kuwait, CRC/C/KWT/CO/2, 2013, para. 29; Syrian Arab Republic, CRC/C/SYR/CO/3–4, 2012, para. 32.

93 Morocco, CRC/C/MAR/CO/3–4, 2014, para. 24.

94 Namibia, CRC/C/NAM/CO/2–3, 2012, para. 31(c).

95 Guinea, CRC/C/GIN/CO/2, 2013, para. 35; Jordan, CRC/C/JOR/CO/4–5, 2014, para. 17.

96 Andorra, CRC/C/AND/CO/2, 2012, para. 24; China, CRC/C/CHN/CO/3–4, 2013, para. 27; Cuba, CRC/C/CUB/CO/2, 2011, para. 24; Fiji, CRC/C/FJI/CO/2–4, 2014, para. 22; India, CRC/C/IND/CO/3–4, 2014, para. 33; Venezuela, CRC/C/VEN/CO/3–5, 2014, para. 27.

97 Cambodia, CRC/C/KHM/CO/2–3, 2011, para. 28; Yemen, CRC/C/YEM/CO/4, 2014, para. 29.

98 Colombia, CRC/C/COL/CO/4–5, 2015, para. 19(b); Iraq, CRC/C/IRQ/CO/2–4, 2015, para. 17; Jordan, CRC/C/JOR/CO/4–5, 2014, para. 17.

99 Guinea-Bissau, CRC/C/GNB/CO/2–4, 2013, para. 24.

100 Iraq, CRC/C/IRQ/CO/2–4, 2015, para. 17.

101 India, CRC/C/IND/CO/3–4, 2014, para. 33; Armenia, CRC/C/ARM/CO/3–4, 2013, para. 18; Viet Nam, CRC/C/VNM/CO/3–4, 2012, para. 29(a).

102 Guinea, CRC/C/GIN/CO/2, 2013, para. 35; Cambodia, CRC/C/KHM/CO/2–3, 2011, para. 28.

103 Liberia, CRC/C/LBR/CO/2–4, 2012, para. 33; Namibia, CRC/C/NAM/CO/2–3, 2012, para. 31(a); Turkey, CRC/C/TUR/CO/2–3, 2012, para. 28.

104 Holy Sea, CRC/C/VAT/CO/2, 2014, para. 28.

105 Cambodia, CRC/C/KHM/CO/2–3, 2011, para. 28.

106 United Nations Committee on the Rights of the Child (2006).

107 United Nations Committee on the Rights of Persons with Disabilities (2018).

108 See, for example: Armenia, CRC/C/ARM/CO/3–4, 2013, para. 18; Azerbaijan, CRC/C/AZE/CO/3–4, 2012, para. 30; Bahrain, CRC/C/BHR/CO/2–3, 2011, para. 30; Canada, CRC/C/CAN/CO/3–4, 2012, para. 32(b); Finland, CRC/C/FIN/CO/4, 2011, para. 25; India, CRC/C/IND/CO/3–4, 2014, para. 31; Lithuania, CRC/C/LTU/CO/3–4, 2013, para. 16; Morocco, CRC/C/MAR/CO/3–4, 2014, para. 24(d); Republic of Korea, CRC/C/KOR/CO/3–4, 2012, para. 28; Switzerland, CRC/C/CHE/CO/2–4, 2015, para. 24; Togo,

CRC/C/TGO/CO/3–4, 2012, para. 31; Uruguay, CRC/C/URY/CO/3–5, 2015, para. 23; Yemen: CRC/C/YEM/CO/4, 2014, para. 29.

109 See, for example: Andorra, CRC/C/AND/CO/2, 2012, para. 24; Liberia, CRC/C/LBR/CO/2–4, 2012, para. 33; Togo, CRC/C/TGO/CO/3–4, 2012, para. 32 (b); Viet Nam, CRC/C/VNM/CO/3–4, 2012, para. 29(a).

110 See, for example: Colombia, CRC/C/COL/CO/4–5, 2015, para. 19; Germany, CRC/C/DEU/CO/3–4, 2014, para. 24; China, CRC/C/CHN/CO/3–4, 2013, para. 25; Indonesia, CRC/C/IDN/CO/3–4, 2014, para. 19(b); Namibia, CRC/C/NAM/CO/2–3, 2012, para. 31(a); Panama, CRC/C/PAN/CO/3–4, 2011, para. 33; Turkey, CRC/C/TUR/CO/2–3, 2012, para. 28; Viet Nam, CRC/C/VNM/CO/3–4, 2012, para. 29(a).

111 Even where discrimination has been largely eliminated, it may continue in respect of a particular group of children. See Chapter 13.

112 See, for example: Algeria: CRC/C/DZA/CO/3–4, 2012, para. 29; Gambia: CRC/C/GMB/CO/2–3, 2015, para. 29(b); Guinea: CRC/C/GIN/CO/2, 2013, para. 35; Italy: CRC/C/ITA/CO/3–4, 2011, para. 24; Jordan: CRC/C/JOR/CO/4–5, 2014, para. 15; Yemen: CRC/C/YEM/CO/4, 2014, para. 29; Syrian Arab Republic: CRC/C/SYR/CO/3–4, 2012, para. 33; Tuvalu: CRC/C/TUV/CO/1, 2013, para. 23.

113 Concluding Observations on Holy See, CRC/C/VAT/CO/2, 2014, para. 25.

114 See, for example: Gambia, CRC/C/GMB/CO/2–3, 2015, para. 29; Hungary, CRC/C/HUN/CO/3–5, 2014, para. 20; Jordan, CRC/C/JOR/CO/4–5, 2014, para. 16; Morocco, CRC/C/MAR/CO/3–4, 2014, para. 25.

115 See, for example: Morocco, CRC/C/MAR/CO/3–4, 2014, para. 24; Tuvalu, CRC/C/TUV/CO/1, 2013, para. 23; Luxembourg, CRC/C/LUX/CO/3–4, 2013, para. 22; Togo, CRC/C/TGO/CO/3–4, 2012, para. 31.

116 China, CRC/C/CHN/CO/3–4, 2013, para. 25.

117 Greece, CRC/C/GRC/CO/2–3, 2012, para. 26.

118 Hungary, CRC/C/HUN/CO/3–5, 2014, para. 20.

119 Turkmenistan, CRC/C/TKM/CO/2–4, 2015, para. 18.

120 See, for example: Armenia, CRC/C/ARM/CO/3–4, 2013, para. 18; Azerbaijan, CRC/C/AZE/CO/3–4, 2012, para. 30; Jordan, CRC/C/JOR/CO/4–5, 2014, para. 15; Seychelles, CRC/C/SYC/CO/2–4, 2012, para. 34; Myanmar, CRC/C/MMR/CO/3–4, 2012, para. 35.

121 See, for example, the Concluding Observations on: Canada, CRC/C/CAN/CO/3–4, 2012, para. 32(c); Gambia, CRC/C/GMB/CO/2–3, 2015, para. 29(d); Hungary, CRC/C/HUN/CO/3–5, 2014, para. 19; Lithuania, CRC/C/LTU/CO/3–4, 2013, para. 16; Mauritius, CRC/C/MUS/CO/3–5, 2015, para. 27; Sweden, CRC/C/SWE/CO/5, 2015, para. 5(a); Switzerland, CRC/C/CHE/CO/2–4, 2015, para. 24.

122 See, for example, the Concluding Observations on: Cook Islands, CRC/C/COK/CO/1, 2012, para. 25; Congo, CRC/C/COG/CO/2–4, 2014, para. 28(b); Guinea, CRC/C/GIN/CO/2, 2013, para. 35; Morocco, CRC/C/MAR/CO/3–4, 2014, para. 25(c); Uruguay, CRC/C/URY/CO/3–5, 2015, para. 23.

123 See, for example, the Concluding Observations on: Colombia: CRC/C/COL/CO/4–5, 2015, para. 19(a); Dominican Republic: CRC/C/DOM/CO/3–5, 2015, para. 17(d); Panama: CRC/C/PAN/CO/3–4, 2011, para. 33.

124 See, for example, the Concluding Observations on: Algeria, CRC/C/DZA/CO/3–4, 2012, para. 29; Colombia: CRC/C/COL/CO/4–5, 2015, para. 19(a); Greece: CRC/C/GRC/CO/2–3, 2012, para. 26; Syrian Arab Republic, CRC/C/SYR/CO/3–4, 2012, para. 33; South Africa, CRC/C/ZAF/2, 2016, para. 23; Thailand: CRC/C/THA/CO/3–4, 2012, para. 33. See also, United Nations Committee on the Rights of the Child (2017).

125 United Nations Committee on the Rights of the Child, *General Comment No 3: HIV/AIDS and the rights of the child* (2003), CRC/GC/2003/3, para. 9.

126 See, for example: Armenia: CRC/C/ARM/CO/3–4, 2013, para. 18; China: CRC/C/CHN/CO/3–4, 2013, para. 25; Fiji, CRC/C/FJI/CO/2–4, 2014, para. 22; India, CRC/C/IND/CO/3–4, 2014, para. 31; Madagascar, CRC/C/MDG/CO/3–4, 2012, para. 23; Venezuela, CRC/C/VEN/CO/3–5, 2014, para. 27.
127 United Nations Committee on the Rights of the Child (2003a), para. 6.
128 United Nations Committee on the Rights of the Child (2016b), para. 34.
129 Russian Federation, CRC/C/RUS/CO/4–5, 2014, para. 24.
130 Gambia, CRC/C/GMB/CO/2–3, 2015, para. 29(e).
131 Australia, CRC/C/AUS/CO/4, 2012, para. 29(e); Switzerland, CRC/C/CHE/CO/2–4, 2015, para. 24.
132 Slovenia, CRC/C/SVN/CO/3–4, 2013, para. 26
133 Holy See, CRC/C/VAT/CO/2, 2014, para. 25, also noting, as encouraging, the more progressive statements made by the Pope in 2013.
134 See, for example: Dominican Republic, CRC/C/DOM/CO/3–5, 2015, para. 17 (d); Sweden, CRC/C/SWE/CO/5, 2015, para. 15(d); Venezuela, CRC/C/VEN/CO/3–5, 2014, para. 27.
135 Slovenia, CRC/C/SVN/CO/3–4, 2013, para. 26.
136 Colombia, CRC/C/COL/CO/4–5, 2015, para. 19.
137 United Nations Committee on the Rights of the Child (2016b), para. 34.

References

Abramson, B. 2008. A *Commentary on the United Nations Convention on the Rights of the Child, Article 2: The Right of Non-Discrimination.* Leiden: Brill/Nijhoff.

Alston, P. 2001. The Historical Origins of the Concept of "General Comments" in Human Rights Law. In Boisson de Chazournes, L. and Gowlland-Debbas, V. (eds), *The International Legal System in Quest of Equity and Universality: Liber Amicorum Georges Abi-Saab.* The Hague: Matinus Nijhoff.

Breen, C. 2006. Age *Discrimination and Children's Rights: Ensuring Equality and Acknowledging Difference.* Leiden: Brill.

Detrick, S., Doek, J. and Cantwell, N. 1992. *The United Nations Convention on the Rights of the Child: A Guide to the "Travaux Préparatoires".* Dortrecht: Martinus Nijhoff.

Human Rights Committee. 1989. General Comment No. 18: Non-Discrimination, HRI/GEN/1/Rev.6.

International Law Association: Committee on International Human Rights Law and Practice, 2014. Final Report on the Impact of Finding of the United Nations Human Rights Treaty Bodies. London: International Law Association.

Keller, H. and Grover, L. 2012. General Comments of the Human Rights Committee and their Legitimacy. In Keller, H., Ulfstein, G. and Grover, L. (eds), *UN Human Rights Treaty Bodies: Law and Legitimacy.* Cambridge: Cambridge University Press.

Moeckli D. 2017. Equality and Non-Discrimination. In Moeckli, D., Shah, S. and Sivakumaran, S. (eds), *International Human Rights Law.* 3rd ed. Oxford: Oxford University Press.

Office of the High Commissioner for Human Rights. 1997. Manual on Human Rights Reporting Under Six Major International Human Rights Instruments. Geneva: OHCHR. HR/PUB/91/1 (Rev.1).

Office of the High Commissioner for Human Rights. 2007. Legislative History of the Convention on the Rights of the Child, 2 Vols. New York and Geneva: OHCHR.

Parkes, A. 2013. *Children and International Human Rights Law: The Right of the Child to be Heard.* Abingdon: Routledge.

Pierce, C.M. and Allen, G.B. 1975. Childism. *Psychiatric Annals*, *5*(*7*), 266–270.

Sachs, J.D. 2012. From Millennium Development Goals to Sustainable Development Goals. The Lancet, *739*(*9832*), 2206–2211.

Stewart, F., 2013. *Approaches Towards Inequality and Inequity: Concepts, Measures and Policies*. Florence: UNICEF Office of Research-Innocenti.

Toczydlowska, E. and Bruckauf, Z. 2017. *Growing Inequality and Unequal Opportunities in Rich Countries*. Florence: UNICEF Office of Research-Innocenti.

UNICEF Office of Research-Innocenti. 2016. Innocenti Report Card – No 13 (2016) – Fairness for Children: A League Table of Inequality in Child Well-being in Rich Countries. Florence: UNICEF Office of Research-Innocenti.

United Nations Committee on the Elimination of Discrimination against Women and United Nations Committee on the Rights of the Child. 2014. Joint General Recommendation No. 31 of the Committee on the Elimination of Discrimination against Women/General Comment No. 18 of the Committee on the Rights of the Child on harmful practices. CEDAW/C/GC/31/CRC/C/GC/18.

United Nations Committee on Migrant Workers and the United Nations Committee on the Rights of the Child. 2017a. Joint General Comment No. 3 of the Committee on the Protection of the Rights of All Migrant Workers and Members of Their Families and No. 22 of the Committee on the Rights of the Child on the General Principles Regarding the Human Rights of Children in the Context of International Migration. CMW/C/GC/3-CRC/C/GC/22.

United Nations Committee on Migrant Workers and the United Nations Committee on the Rights of the Child. 2017b. Joint General Comment No. 4 of the CMW and No. 23 of the CRC in the Context of International Migration: States Parties' Obligations in Particular with Respect to Countries of Transit and Destination. CMW/C/GC/4-CRC/C/GC/23.

United Nations Committee on the Rights of the Child. 2003a. General Comment No. 4: Adolescent Health and Development in the Context of the Convention on the Rights of the Child. CRC/C/GC/2003/4.

United Nations Committee on the Rights of the Child. 2003b. General Comment No 5: General Measures of Implementation of the Convention on the Rights of the Child. CRC/GC/2003/5.

United Nations Committee on the Rights of the Child. 2005. General Comment No. 6: Treatment of Unaccompanied and Separated Children Outside their Country of Origin. CRC/GC/2005/6.

United Nations Committee on the Rights of the Child. 2006. General Comment No. 9: The Rights of Children with Disabilities. CRC/C/GC/9.

United Nations Committee on the Rights of the Child. 2009a. General Comments No. 11: Indigenous Children and their Rights under the Convention. CRC/C/GC/11.

United Nations Committee on the Rights of the Child. 2009b. General Comment No. 12: The Right of the Child to be Heard. CRC/C/GC/12.

United Nations Committee on the Rights of the Child. 2016a. General Comment No. 19 on Public Budgeting for the Realization of Children's Rights (art. 4). CRC/C/GC/19.

United Nations Committee on the Rights of the Child. 2016b. General Comment No. 20 on the Implementation of the Rights of the Child During Adolescence. CRC/C/GC/20.

United Nations Committee on the Rights of the Child. 2017. General Comment No. 21 on Children in Street Situations. CRC/C/GC/21.

United Nations Committee on the Rights of Persons with Disabilities. 2018. General Comment No. 6 on Equality and Non-Discrimination. CRPD/C/GC/6.

van Bueren, G. 2011. Multigenerational Citizenship: The Importance of Recognizing Children as National and International Citizens. *The Annals of the American Academy of Political and Social Science, 633(1)*, 30–51.

Webb, E. 2011. An Exploration of the Discrimination-Rights Dynamic in Relation to Children. In Invernizzi, A. and Williams, J. (eds), *The Human Rights of Children*. Farnham: Ashgate.

Young-Bruehl, E. 2009. Childism – Prejudice against Children. *Contemporary Psychoanalysis, 45(2)*, 251–265.

Young-Bruehl, E. 2012. *Childism: Confronting Prejudice Against Children*. New Haven, CT: Yale University Press.

3 Respecting age

Discrimination against the young and the old

David Archard

Introduction

Article 2 enjoins State Parties to ensure that the rights listed elsewhere in the Convention are enjoyed 'without discrimination of any kind'. It does not, in one sense, give children any new right. Rather it stipulates that children should not be discriminated in their possession and exercise of those rights that are listed in the other Articles. It is, one might say, a higher order right about the enjoyment of first order rights, a right to the equal enjoyment of those latter rights. Article 2 thus properly belongs at the outset of the Convention and it does so coming after Article 1 that provides a certain specification of scope. Article 1 defines who it is that enjoys the rights subsequently listed, namely any child. Article 2 defines the manner in which children – all children – shall enjoy those rights, namely without discrimination.

Now non-discrimination might seem to be nothing more or other than equal treatment. Indeed for many, especially those writing about human rights law, equality and non-discrimination do mean the same thing. Anne Bayefsky writes for instance that 'It is my view that equality and non-discrimination are positive and negative statements of the same principle' (Bayefsky 1990 p. 1 fn. 1). She supplies extensive citations from legal documents and other writers to support her view. To treat equally, on that view, just is not to discriminate; and to discriminate just is not to treat equally. Others are less sure that equality and non-discrimination are simply two sides of the same normative principle (Besson 2013; Holmes 2005).

Non-discrimination

It is thus worth spelling out what might be meant by non-discrimination. At its most basic, to discriminate is to treat differently. Such differential treatment is either as such morally wrongful or it is a further matter as to whether treating differently is to be condemned (Altman 2018). Those who think it is an open question as to whether discrimination is wrong can point to those forms of it that are 'positive', such as compensatory discrimination in favour of groups who have previously suffered inequitable treatment. For those who think discrimination is wrongful there is the matter of what makes it wrong. There are three elements of discrimination that might be judged wrongful (Lippert-Rasmussen 2006). First, there is treatment of someone in some area in ways that are different from how others are treated. Second, such differential treatment is disadvantageous for that person. Third, the differential treatment of a person is to be explained by that person's membership of a well-defined and prominent social group. This tripartite definition fits well then with those understandings of discrimination to be found in human rights documents that view it as unfavourable treatment based on a 'prohibited ground'. In simple terms what appears to be wrong with discrimination is that someone suffers worse treatment than others and for a bad reason, namely their status or salient social character, something that should not explain such a poorer outcome.

Bad reasons

It is perhaps worth saying something more about what might count as a bad reason. Richard Arneson defines as wrongful discrimination 'when an agent treats a person identified as being of a certain type differently than she otherwise would have done from unwarranted animus or prejudice against persons of that type' (Arneson 2006, p. 787). Now one way to understand a prejudice or animus is as a hostile negative attitude. Some forms of discrimination are indeed animated by such attitudes. Think only of the standard examples of racist or sexist behavior. Yet discrimination might be animated by an entirely favorable attitude, albeit one that depends upon a wholly false belief or set of beliefs. Thus, some who supported the exclusion of women from the suffrage, including many women at the time, did so because of a belief that the sensitivities of the 'gentle sex' were ill-suited to the brutal world of politics. That belief is not best described as an animus against women. As a result it would be better to say that wrongful discrimination is based upon a false belief as to the nature or character of the group discriminated against. It is in this epistemic rather than straightforward moral sense that the reason for treating differently is 'bad'.

Equal and differential treatment

It should be noted that to discriminate is not in any straightforward way not to treat equally. For to treat equally in circumstances where it would be appropriate to treat differently is as much an instance of discrimination as treating unequally in circumstances that call for equal treatment. To explain what this means by way of a straightforward example: non-discriminatory or equal provision of medical care would require that such care is sensitive to the particular needs of those seeking treatment. Thus it would be wrong to provide everyone, irrespective of their diagnosed condition, with the same treatment; just as it would be wrong to treat those with the same condition in different ways, for reasons such as the social status of the patient. In general it is important to distinguish between discrimination understood simply as differential treatment and discrimination as differential treatment that is not justified by its relevance to or proportionate to the differences between those treated.

The idea of prohibited grounds also merits discussion in this context. Article 2 construes 'discrimination of any kind' by reference to those respects in which it is wrong to treat a child differently, namely 'the child's or her or his parent's or legal guardian's race, colour, sex, language, religion, political or other opinion, national, ethnic or social origin, property, disability, birth or other status.' However, it would be a mistake to think that treating a child differently because of his or her status in any of these regards would be wrong. Clearly a child's religion, for instance, could be a proper ground for providing that child with resources or goods not afforded to other children. A child might legitimately be entitled to a certain kind of education or access to opportunities to practice her faith because of her religion. Or again, a child with a disability would surely be entitled to assistance that would not be appropriate for able-bodied children.

What is crucial is not that there should be equal treatment understood as the same treatment, but rather that no-one should be disadvantaged in relation to others on account of their status. A ground may be prohibited as an explanation of disadvantageous treatment; but the same ground need not be ruled out for advantageous treatment, understood as compensating for or taking account of disadvantages that would otherwise be suffered in the absence of positive discrimination.

Age

But is not age a prohibited ground? And, if it is, are children discriminated against on account of their age? And, if so, is this not in violation of Article 2? Grounds for differential treatment are not 'prohibited', in the sense indicated, in all circumstances. As already pointed out, someone's religion, for example, might well be the appropriate ground for receipt of special treatment. As might the other grounds listed in Article 2. How is it with age? There are certainly forms of discrimination on the basis of age that merit the description 'ageism'. This term is deliberately employed to echo the charges of 'racism' and 'sexism' that might be made of wrongful discrimination. These are forms of prejudiced displays of the disadvantageous treatment of another on the grounds of their race or sex. Ageism similarly is an unjustified display of preferential treatment for someone of a certain age and to the disadvantage of those of a different age. Thus it is ageist not to employ older people for certain jobs on the simple grounds of their greater age. I will return later to the differences in ageism in respect of the young and the old.

Is it then ageist to discriminate against children? It may well be. However, in the first place, the treatment of children in ways that are different from that of adults need not be explained solely in terms of a difference of age. It might rather be that age is associated with features or characteristics of persons that do justify differential treatment. Thus it is worth noting the crucial paragraph within the Convention's Preamble, bearing in mind that, as indicated in the Declaration of the Rights of the Child, 'the child, by reason of his physical and mental immaturity, needs special safeguards and care, including appropriate legal protection'. In other words the critical feature of a child is not his or her age as such but rather the 'physical and mental immaturity' which is associated with that age.

Yet it might still be ageist if, either there is no such association of age and immaturity that might justify the special treatment, or if such an association does not justify the forms of special treatment it is argued to do. The first response is made by those characterized as 'child liberationists' (Holt 1974; Farson 1974; Firestone 1970; Cohen 1980) who explicitly denied that children lacked those capacities that entitled adults to the enjoyment of rights denied to children. The term liberationist in this context consciously echoed its use in others – those of women and race – where a charge of injustice and oppression was also made.

It is probably fair to comment that child liberationism both was a creature of its particular time and is an ideologically overstated if understandable reaction to a perception that children were maintained in a socially constructed space of 'childish' vulnerability and dependence. I will briefly return to this criticism later.

The second response is different. It does not deny that children do differ from adults and in more than simply age. It argues, however, that such differences as there are do not warrant the differences in treatment of children and adults. Here it is worth pausing to be clear about the forms of discrimination that Article 2 is directed at and which it repudiates.

Discrimination against one person or group is necessarily to be understood as differential treatment by reference to another group. It is to treat that individual or group worse than another. So children as a group can be discriminated against in relation to adults. However, that is not the discrimination that Article 2 concerns. This is about the discriminatory treatment of some children by comparison with other children. It affirms the entitlement of all children, whatever their differences in respect of religion, sex, language, etc., to the full possession and enjoyment of all the rights listed in the Convention.

Now it would be easy, if mistaken, to think that in some sense the interdiction on discrimination within the group of children extends, or should be extended, to a denial that adult-children discrimination is ever warranted. Moreover, it will perhaps also be said that the grant to children of rights is itself sufficient to show that adults and children do not differ in moral, legal or political status. If children, just like adults, have rights – as the existence of the Convention shows – then it would be wrong to discriminate between them.

Different types of rights

The mistake in such reasoning lies in failing to see that what is critical is not the possession and enjoyment of rights as such, but rather the nature of those rights that are given, respectively, to adults and children. Joel Feinberg's famous and influential defence of a child's right to an open future opens with a distinction between the various rights that might be given, and denied, to children (Feinberg 1980). A-rights are those rights that adults alone have. A-C-rights are those rights that both adults and children have. C-rights are those rights that children alone have. Examples of the first might be the right to vote or to marry. Examples of the second from the Convention include a right to life (Article 6) and a right to freedom of expression (Article 13). Examples of the third might be Feinberg's own 'right to an open future.' One could add to this last list the right to be loved that is defended by Matthew Liao (Liao 2015).

The existence of A-rights testifies to the fact that children do not have the same moral and legal status as adults, even if, by way of A-C rights, they have some of the rights that adults do. C-rights are accorded to children in virtue of their difference from adults. Indeed, C-rights can acknowledge the respects in which children lack capacities that adults have. Thus, the Convention has a number of protection rights that an adult would not claim. Article 32, for instance, accords to the child a right to be 'protected from economic exploitation and from performing any work that is likely to be hazardous or to interfere with the child's education, or to be harmful to the child's health or physical, mental, spiritual, moral or social development.' No such right is likely to be claimed by an adult who would insist on the right to choose such work as he or she sees appropriate and whatever its risks to the employee.

Indeed, central to an adult individual's moral and legal status is the right to make autonomous choices, to be free to live his or her life as she wishes. By contrast a child has no such right. In the first place, as Article 3 states, the child's best interests are a primary consideration in all decision-making respecting a child. A judgment of what is in a child's best interests need not accord with what the child might wish for. Even though Article 12 affords every child 'the right to express those views freely in all matters affecting the child', such a right is to be exercised only by a child 'who is capable of forming his or her own views'. And, crucially, those views are to be 'given due weight in accordance with the age and maturity of the child'. That amounts to the following: only some children can express views as to what they wish for in their own case; and such views are not determinative of what should happen. A child, unlike an adult, cannot choose what will happen and does not have complete autonomy. A child's views as to what will happen can make some difference to whether it does or does not, but only such difference as is proportionate to his or her maturity.

Article 2 insists that all of the rights listed in the Convention should be possessed and enjoyed by all children equally, that is without discrimination in respect of any other features such as sex or language or religion that might distinguish them. Ironically then, Article 2's statement of non-discrimination reinforces the distinction in moral and legal status that the other Articles of the Convention gives effect to. Indeed, Article 2 is explicit that it is only 'the rights set forth in the present Convention' that should be enjoyed 'without discrimination of any kind'. The obligation on State Parties not to discriminate between children does not extend beyond the Convention. Nor is it one not to discriminate between adults and children.

Ageism?

So can we ask once again, is it ageist to discriminate against children? It is true that children are treated differently from adults. Are children disadvantaged as a result? And is the differential treatment attributable to a prejudicial or false belief about the difference between adults and children? The answer to the second question that would be given by child liberationists is evidently 'yes'. If the belief in question is that age alone warrants differential treatment, then their answer would have credibility. However, as we have seen, it is not age alone that marks the difference, but rather the correlation of age with important differences – in maturity, vulnerability and dependence. These are the marks of childhood that, as its Preamble makes clear, justify the Convention's attribution to children of certain kinds of rights. The real burden of the child liberationist argument is that the belief in a child's 'childishness' – and hence its lack of those competences that would make the possession of adult rights appropriate – is the essential feature of a modern conception of childhood that can be exposed as an ideological social construction.

This view cannot be fully assessed here (Archard 2015: Chapter 5). However, it derives support from two contestable claims. First, that any conception of childhood as distinct from adulthood is exclusively modern. Such work thus made much use of the work of social historians, most obviously Philippe Ariès (1960), who maintained that the view of childhood as essentially distinct from adulthood is a modern one. That claim is open to criticism from both historians and others (Archard 2015, Part One).

The second contestable claim is that any particular understanding of childhood – for instance, as one of vulnerability, dependence, ignorance and incapacity – is only a social construction without roots in well-established facts of human development. The proper response to this claim is as follows: that we understand childhood in particular ways as a result of our social context is entirely distinct from a view that such an understanding is entirely constructed and has no basis in evidences that are independent of our particular society. We may indeed understand childhood in particular ways within our society; it does not follow that any view of childhood as different from adulthood has no basis in reality. Nevertheless, the basic claim that a certain view of children is socially constructed has a value in correcting the exaggerated view of children as lacking any ability to possess and enjoy rights.

More interesting is the first question. In effect this broaches the issue of whether granting children the rights within the Convention, which Article 2 stipulates that all children, without discrimination, should enjoy, does ensure that they are not, as an age group, disadvantaged. The Convention accords to children those rights that they ought, as children, to have, and because, as children, they are possessed of certain features that properly distinguish them from adults. I want to say something about this by talking about the goods of childhood, and by comparing children, as an age group with another – the old.

However, in order is a final couple of thoughts about the purported disadvantage or discrimination children suffer by being denied adult rights. These are thoughts to be found in the seminal critique of children's rights by Onora O'Neill (1988). O'Neill is concerned to argue there that children have *no* rights. She does so as someone who is skeptical about the value and function of rights in general, and who wants to insist on the moral and political priority of duties. However, her critical points about the discrimination allegedly suffered by children carry weight even if children have some rights, albeit not all those that some think they should have. First, the purported disadvantaging of children is universal. Thus, only some suffer disadvantage on the basis of gender or ethnicity. But everybody has been young. Second, being of a certain age is not a permanent condition: we pass from childhood into adulthood. By contrast it is normally – and if at all possible only at considerable cost and in highly contested ways – not possible to change one's gender and ethnicity. For O'Neill the discrimination that children allegedly suffer is of a very different order to that suffered by some adults in relation to others.

Goods of childhood

What then of the goods of childhood? The question arises because as we saw at the outset non-discrimination could be understood simply, and minimally, as equal treatment. Yet, as we also saw, discrimination is as much about treating equals unequally in relevant circumstances as failing – by treating equally – to recognise appropriate differences between the members of distinct groups. Should non-discrimination in respect of children then require that they receive goods, benefits, resources, and entitlements that are not given to adults? One interesting way in which the question of non-discrimination *within* the class of children (Article 2) broadens out into the distinct question of non-discrimination against the class of children arises as follows. Some of the Convention rights acknowledge that some children are owed forms of treatment not owed to others. For instance, Article 23 accords to a mentally or physically disabled child the right to a 'full and decent life' and thus particular consideration and treatment inasmuch as he or she is disabled. It thus further stipulates that a disabled child should be accorded a right to '*special* care' and the recognition of his or her '*special* needs' (emphasis added). The general principle that underlines such a right is that some important and salient differences between individuals – and not just children – justify forms of treatment not appropriate to others. Equal treatment of those who are unequal in some regards is – to repeat – discriminatory.

So what might be owed to children and not to others? It is conventional to regard the Convention as according three P-types of rights: protection, participation, and provision. We have already noted a protection right in the Article 32 protection of the child against economic exploitation and hazardous employment. There are others. Participation rights include the rights to free speech (Article 13), freedom of association and assembly (Article 15), and, most centrally, Article 12's right of a child to express views on matters affecting his or her interests. Provision rights include the right of the child to 'the enjoyment of the highest attainable standard of health' (Article 24), to a standard of living adequate for the child's physical, mental, spiritual, moral and social development (Article 27) and to education (Article 28).

The question that arises in consideration of provision rights is whether, and if so why, children might be owed some things that are not provided, as a matter of entitlement, to others. This question has received attention in recent years through work on the question of the possible 'goods of childhood' (Gheaus 2015; Macleod 2010; Brennan 2014). This work represents a subtle but important shift away from a framing of the question of discrimination against children in terms of rights. The source of the idea of 'goods' in this context is John Rawls' liberal theory of justice (Rawls 1999). A theory of justice is a theory of the fair distribution within a society of those things that can be socially distributed and which matter to individuals within society. Social goods are contrasted with natural goods – such as intelligence and physical prowess – that are not a matter of social distribution. For Rawls what is distributed are primary social goods, those goods that 'every rational man is presumed to want' and that are under the control of whatever social arrangements are decided upon (Rawls 1999, p. 54). Rawls listed these as rights, liberties and opportunities, income and wealth. Famously, Rawls' two principles of justice prescribe an equal distribution of the good of liberty and an unequal distribution of the other goods so long as this is to the advantage of the worst-off in society.

Much subsequent criticism of Rawls' theory of justice has concerned the putative fairness of his two principles. But there has also been criticism of what is distributed by those two principles, the so-called distribuenda of the theory of justice. From this follows an interest in primary social goods and the extent to which some goods might be valuable to some groups within society but not to others. The focus on the goods of childhood has also been stimulated by important work on the idea that the existence of the family might be justified within a liberal theory of justice by an appeal to the distinct, perhaps incommensurable, and enormously valuable goods of parenting that are realized within and by families (Brighouse and Swift 2014). Famously, Rawls thought that the existence of the family posed an obstacle to the full realization of justice, since it permitted parents to pass on advantages to their children denied to others, and, conversely, meant some children suffer disadvantages as a result of their family not afflicting others more fortunate. He even asked, rhetorically, it might seem, 'Is the family to be abolished then?' (Rawls 1999, p. 448).

The work of Brighouse and Swift is an answer to that question. For them a liberal theory of justice can and should accommodate the existence of the family by recognizing that it makes it possible for adults, as parents, to enjoy the good of parenting, one that is of great significance and, crucially, cannot be compared to and thus enjoyed in any other way than by parenting. Brighouse and Swift are also clear that children can only enjoy certain goods, that of being exclusively cared for and reared by some adults, within the family.

That is the background context as to the source of the idea. Yet the notion of the goods of childhood can be considered in its own right and it is of evident relevance to the question of what not discriminating against children might mean. Discrimination against children should encompass the denial to children of childhood goods, those that, by definition, are not goods for adults. Are there then childhood goods? What is meant by this are goods that are good for and only for children, and whose value may or may not derive from the value of childhood as such. Two features of such goods should be emphasized. First, there may be goods that are valuable only for children, as opposed to, for instance, goods that have a value for all ages but a special or additional, value for children. Thus play, leisure and recreation – recognized as an entitlement in Article 31 – may be valuable for someone of any age but arguably be of especial importance to the young. By contrast, sexual innocence might be argued to be valuable for the young but not for adults. Indeed it is surely arguable that such innocence is not valuable for adults.

Second, some things might be good for children only inasmuch as they are children, whereas those same things or others might derive their value from their contribution to the welfare or flourishing of the future adults. Thus one might think that education has value for a child as a critical part of what makes a childhood a healthy one of encouraged curiosity about and informed sensitivity to oneself and one's world; or by contrast that it has value in developing the future adult who can play his or her proper and full part in society. Indeed Article 29 directs the education of a child both to 'the development of the child's personality, talents and mental and physical abilities to their fullest potential' and 'the preparation of the child for responsible life in a free society'. In other words one should educate the child as a child *and* as a future adult.

Take as further examples the two C-rights that were mentioned earlier. Joel Feinberg was very clear that the right to an open future was a right in trust, that is a right whose exercise was directed at children but whose beneficiary is the adult that child will grow into. Thus, the education of the child and the provision of opportunities to make informed choices as the child grows to maturity are intended to allow the adult to have and to enjoy a maximally autonomous existence as a member of a liberal society.

Take, again, the right to be loved that Matthew Liao defends. The value and importance of this right is principally defended by Liao on the grounds that being loved as a child ensures the sound psychological development of the child. Only a child that is genuinely loved by those who rear it can and will develop into a flourishing and healthy adult individual. But he could equally see, and would not be averse to seeing, a loved child as enjoying, as a child, a much better life. It would be a better life for the child, independently of its developmental benefits to the later adult.

Young age and old age

We can gain an interesting and a better sense of how we should understand the goods of childhood by offering a brief contrast of them with another set of possible age-specific goods, namely the goods of old age. It is, in the first instance, notable that the charge of 'ageism' that we have considered in relation to children is most often made in contemporary debates in regard to the old. Indeed, those who write on ageism both acknowledge that ageism can be true of both young and old whilst deliberately choosing to focus on the case of the old as somehow most clearly and dramatically exemplifying ageism (Iversen et al. 2009).

Yet a comparison of childhood with old age shows that whilst there may be goods that have a particular significance and value for the old there are no goods of old age in the sense that there are claimed to be goods of childhood. Thus the good of having and sustaining relationships with others matters greatly to the old for whom loneliness and social isolation are especially problematic. Yet this good is not one that is exclusive to the old. Again, the good of individual autonomous choice may be of great value to those who must make momentous choices. That of when and how to end one's life is such a choice, and it is one that particularly matters to old people. Yet the good of choice is of value to any adult.

The difference between childhood and old age in respect of distinctive goods is also revealed by attending to the place of the former in a human life. Anca Gheaus contrasts the instrinsic and instrumental good of childhood, as a stage of life, by characterizing its instrumental value as being 'in preparation for adulthood' (Gheaus 2015, p. 35). It is a familiar theme in childhood studies, and especially within the sociology of childhood, that we should distinguish between the child as 'being' and as 'becoming'. In the present context this signifies a basic contrast between the child as a child and the child as developing into and as 'not yet' an adult. The latter understanding is normally, within much philosophical writing on childhood, informed by a pejorative view of childhood as a state that must be overcome if one is to achieve the full status of a human being. To remain a child is a 'misfortune of the utmost gravity' (Lomasky 1987, p. 202); childhood is a 'predicament' characterized by an absence of full agency (Schapiro 1999, p. 716).

The 'becoming' understanding of childhood has then two features. First, it is prospective, in that it is a looking forward to and anticipating of adulthood; second, it is negatively defined in terms of what is to come, adulthood, whose positive features it lacks. To be a child is to fail to be an adult. Yet consider how it is with old age. This is not a preparation for any succeeding stage of life; indeed it is the last before death. It may be negatively defined as lacking what preceding stages of life possessed. Consider Shakespeare's famous characterization in Jacques' speech from *As You Like It* of the last 'scene' of life as the 'second childishness'. This does not necessarily hold for all instances of old age. Old age need not as such be a second childhood nor be 'sans everything' (Shakespeare [1623] 2005 Act II, Scene vii).

But then – if we subtract the negative features of old age that mirror those of childhood – can we make any sense of what would be its intrinsic good or value? It cannot be as it is with childhood by means of a contrast with a prospective anticipation of what is to come. For in old age only 'oblivion' is to come. Its putative value may consist in its being a retrospective completion of any life. That *would* make it a mirror of childhood. This is the preparation for what is to come whilst old age is the completion of what has already taken place. Yet such a view of old age is deeply contentious. Either it rests on a 'narrative' view of life (MacIntyre 1981, p. 219) in which old age is the final chapter, and the last chance to provide one's personal life narrative with the sought after unity. Such a narrative view is philosophically contentious and subject to various criticisms (Lamarque 2007; Strawson 2004). Or old age is the time to complete one's life defining projects. Yet the simple and probably fatal problem with this view is that it may just be far too late in old age to complete one's life projects, since life has already assumed a certain, determinate shape as a result of earlier activity (Velleman 1991).

Old age has a distinctive character and place in our life. We can be guilty of ageism in our treatment of the old. Yet the brief comparison of childhood with old age suggests that discrimination against the old cannot consist in the failure to provide the old with age-specific goods. By contrast there are goods of childhood and we do discriminate against them in failing to provide such goods. We need however to be clear whether such goods derive their value from what matters to a child as and inasmuch as he or she is a child; or from what matters to the adult into whom the child will grow up. We should also be sensitive in speaking of the intrinsic goods of childhood – such as innocence – that we do not thereby support and sustain a particular pejorative view of a child, one that sees the child only in terms of what he or she is not, namely a competent independent adult.

Concluding remarks

In conclusion, discrimination against children as a group, as opposed to discrimination *between* children, is wrongful only if any differences in treatment disadvantage children as a group and rest on false or prejudicial views of what the differences between children and adults are. Yet children do differ from adults in relevant respects and those differences are acknowledged in the Convention's own Preamble. Children are given rights by the Convention but these are not – or do not amount to all of – those rights that adults have and enjoy. Thus the Convention's according to children of rights that are appropriate to their age is not a concession of a moral and legal status to children that is equivalent to that accorded to adults. On the contrary it marks the difference between them. However such differential treatment is not disadvantageous to children precisely because the distinctive set of rights given to children protects them as children.

Yet that is not the whole story that might be told about discrimination in respect of children. For we cannot determine what it might mean to be ageist and to discriminate against someone on the basis of their age without agreeing whether we owe to age groups goods that are specific to their age. It has been suggested that there are goods of childhood but not of old age. This is in part but not only because of the unique place and meaning of childhood as a stage of life.

The Curious Case of Benjamin Button is a 2008 film that derives from a short story by F. Scott Fitzgerald. It imagines someone who lives their life in reverse to that of other human beings. He starts as an old man and progressively gets younger. In such a life the significance of being a child and that of being old are starkly opposed to that which they have for us. Inasmuch as we humans do age, mature, and develop from birth into senescence and eventual death each stage of our life, each 'age', has its meaning and value. To make sense of what each age is, and what its value for us is, we need to understand that inevitable, ordered, linear and unidirectional progress.

In this manner a consideration of Article 2's apparently simple and straightforward injunction not to discriminate between children has led into a discussion of what it means to discriminate as such. Further it has meant thinking, more particularly, what it might mean to discriminate against children. That in turn has prompted consideration of whether the fair provision of certain goods is owed to children but not to adults, and in answering that question the much broader and more complex issues of what the different stages or ages of a human life mean and how they should be valued have been broached.

References

Altman, A. 2018. Discrimination. *Stanford Encyclopedia of Philosophy.* Available at: https://plato.stanford.edu/entries/discrimination [Accessed 1. 6. 2018].

Archard, D. 2015. *Children, Rights and Childhood.* 3rd edition. London: Routledge.

Ariès, P. 1960. *L'Enfant et la vie famiale sous l'ancien regime.* Paris: Librarie Plon. Translated from the French by Robert Baldick as *Centuries of Childhood.* London: Jonathan Cape, 1962.

Arneson, R. 2006. What is Wrongful Discrimination? *San Diego Law Review*, 43: 775–808.

Bayefsky, A. 1990. The Principle of Equality and Non-discrimination in International Law. *Human Rights Law Journal* 11(1–2): 1–34.

Besson, S. 2013. The Egalitarian Dimension of Human Rights. *Archv für Sozial- und Rechtsphilosophie*, 136: 19–52.

Brennan, S. 2014. The Goods of Childhood and Children's Rights. In F. Baylis and C. McLeod (eds) *Family-Making: Contemporary Ethical Challenges* (pp. 29–48). Oxford: Oxford University Press:.

Brighouse, H. and Swift, A. 2014. *Family Values: The Ethics of Parent-Child Relationships.* Princeton, NJ: Princeton University Press.

Cohen, H. 1980. *Equal Rights for Children.* Totowa, NJ: Littlefield, Adams and Co.

Daniels, N. 1996. The Prudential Life-span Account of Justice Across Generations. In Daniels, N. *Justice and Justification* (pp. 257–283). Cambridge: Cambridge University Press.

Farson, R. 1974. *Birthrights.* London: Macmillan.

Feinberg, J. 1980. The Child's Right to an Open Future. In W. Aiken and H. LaFollette (eds) *Whose Child? Parental Rights, Parental Authority and State Power* (pp. 124–153). Totowa NJ: Rowman and Littlefield.

Firestone, S. 1970. *The Dialectic of Sex: The Case for Feminist Revolution.* New York: Farrar, Straus and Giroux.

Fries, J. 1980. Aging, Natural Death and the Compression of Morbidity. *New England Journal of Medicine,* 303(3): 130–135.

Gheaus, A. 2015. The 'Intrinsic Goods of Childhood' and the Just Society. In A. Bagattini and C. Macleod (eds) *The Nature of Children's Well-Being: Theory and Practice* (pp. 35–54). Dordrecht: Springer.

Holmes, E. 2005. Anti-Discrimination Rights without Equality. *The Modern Law Review,* 68(2): 175–194.

Holt, J. 1974. *Escape from Childhood.* Boston: E. P. Dutton.

Iversen, T., Larsen, L. and Solem, P.E. 2009. A Conceptual Analysis of Ageism. *Nordic Psychology,* 61(3): 4–22.

Lamarque, P. 2007. On the Distance between Literary Narratives and Real-Life Narratives. *Royal Institute of Philosophy Supplements,* 60: 117–132.

Liao, M. 2015. *The Right To Be Loved.* New York: Oxford University Press.

Lippert-Rasmussen, K. 2006. The Badness of Discrimination. *Ethical Theory and Moral Practice,* 9(2): 167–185.

Lomasky, L. 1987. *Persons, Rights and the Moral Community.* Oxford: Oxford University Press.

MacIntyre, A. 1981. *After Virtue: A Study in Moral Theory.* Notre Dame, IN: University of Notre Dame Press.

Macleod, C. 2010. Primary Goods, Capabilities and Children. In H. Brighouse and I. Robeyns (eds) *Measuring Justice: Primary Goods and Capabilities* (pp. 174–192). Cambridge: Cambridge University Press.

O'Neill, O. 1988. Children's Rights and Children's Lives. *Ethics*, 98: 445–463.

Rawls, J. 1999. *A Theory of Justice. Revised Edition*. Oxford: Oxford University Press.

Schapiro, T. 1999. What is a Child? *Ethics*, 109: 715–738.

Shakespeare, W. [1623] 2005. As You Like It. In *William Shakespeare: The Complete Works*. Edited by S. Wells, G. Taylor, J. Jowett and W. Montgomery. Oxford: Oxford University Press.

Strawson, G. 2004. Against Narrativity. *Ratio*, 17(4): 428–452.

Velleman, D. 1991. Well-Being and Time. *Pacific Philosophical Quarterly*, 72: 48–77.

4 The ageing of Article 2(1)

The child's right to be free from age-based discrimination

Claire Breen

Introduction

In international and domestic law, age-based distinctions are not uncommon and may often serve a practical purpose; indeed, Article 1 of the CRC defines a child as everyone under the age of 18 years, and, in so doing, uses age to delineate the particular group whose rights are protected by that treaty. However, when such distinctions directly or indirectly nullify or impair a right, age-based distinctions become age-based discrimination, unless such limitations are justified (Breen 2006). Article 2(1) of the CRC makes no explicit reference to this type of discrimination and its absence is a further indicator of the inequality experienced by children, particularly in relation to adults but also in relation to other children at different ages and stages, in spite of the almost universal adoption of the CRC. It is against this background that this chapter will explore some of the reasons for which children have been treated differently in terms of the protection and promotion of their rights.

The chapter will open with a consideration of the historical conceptions of both rights and children that echo through the centuries and influence our conceptions of inequality as it relates to children today. The chapter will also canvass some of the attempts to overcome such approaches that served to limit – or negate – the manner in which we conceive of children as rights-holders that are entitled to be treated equally. Alternative conceptions of what it means to be a rights-holder also bring with them the invitation to reconsider the meaning of equality and non-discrimination. To that end, this chapter explores the manner in which the inequality faced by children can be overcome by understanding equality as a product of historical, entrenched and hierarchical power imbalances. The chapter then proceeds to consider the comparatively recent recognition of age as a prohibited ground of discrimination in the UN human rights treaty framework more generally, and its emerging recognition by the Committee on the Rights of the Child (CRC Committee). These developments represent a maturation of the rights to equality and non-discrimination, which allow for closer scrutiny of age-based distinctions to reveal whether they are legitimate grounds for differential treatment or whether they comprise age-based discrimination and inequality that children continue to experience simply because they are children.

Autonomy, rationality and rights: the legacy of liberalism for the child's right to non-discrimination

The child's right to non-discrimination on the basis of age presents a rather unique challenge, even against the broader background of age-based discrimination. The challenge stems from the need to consider the discrimination that the individual child experiences, a discrimination that is temporary as it will be overcome when the child reaches adulthood, and the permanent discrimination faced by children as a societal group. Fredman explains this distinction:

> We have all been young, and we will all, if we are fortunate, become old. Thus, the basic opposition between "self" and "other" which marks much of racism and sexism is not present in the same way.
>
> (Fredman 2003, 21)

For O'Neill, this distinction between permanent and transient discrimination is a key distinction in the debate about whether children should have rights. In arguing that children's rights are not analogous to movements to recognise the rights of traditionally oppressed groups, such as women, African Americans or persons with disabilities, O'Neill argues that children's dependent, subordinate status is justified in a sense because children need to be cared for; their stage of dependence is temporary and will generally not be prolonged unlike other (genuine) oppressors who have a vested interest in maintaining the relationship of dependence (O'Neill 1988). This view is the exemplar challenge to the child's right to non-discrimination on the basis of age and it suggests only permanent characteristics, such as race and gender, can be the bases of prohibited grounds of discrimination. But if this view was followed through to its logical conclusion, we could simply argue that those who experience discrimination on the basis of their religion or political opinion could avoid such discrimination by changing their beliefs; but we do not.

O'Neill's views reflect classical liberal theory, which was not aimed at constructing a framework of rights for children. From the late seventeenth century onward, nations and scholars sought to conceptualise new ways of ordering political organisation and political participation in opposition to authoritarian and arbitrary governments that had previously been the norm. The concept of the "social contract" re-emerged as a hypothetical device to explain why and how individuals came together to form a political community.

Thomas Hobbes and John Locke both emphasised the individual's rational nature as the basis for giving consent to be ruled. The emphasis on rationality had the effect of Hobbes excluding children from the category of people that could enter his version of the social contract as, along with "fools and madmen", they had no use of reason (Hobbes 1651). Locke identified natural rights as a means to protect the individual from the exercise of authoritarian and arbitrary state power. He also linked freedom with rational thinking, a characteristic that he believed came with age, which led him to conclude that children were not actually free

(Locke 1690). Jean Jacques Rousseau was also concerned with striking a balance between the freedom of the individual and the need to co-exist in a political state. Rousseau is noteworthy for his particular thoughts on children, education and child development, and the social contract. In *Emile*, he advanced the idea that children, in their natural states, were the prototypes of human freedom and goodness. Society as a whole would benefit if children were secluded from the corrupting influences of the adult world. But this period of seclusion also served an important purpose whereby education – as Rousseau perceived it – could be used to strengthen children's innate goodness and so produce a more autonomous adult that would be ready to participate more fully and equally in his version of the social contract (Rousseau 1762). Immanuel Kant believed that children had certain moral rights that originated in their innate right to freedom. However, the fullness of the political freedom and its related rights that Kant articulated did not extend to children because they were dependent on their parents (Kant 1785).

The relationship between rights and the ability to make rational decisions remained a dominant theme in twentieth-century political theory. Writing as a mid-twentieth-century legal positivist, H.L.A. Hart argued that submitting to legal rules, undertaking the duties that they entail and imposing obligations upon others requires a type of power which originated in the ability to exercise this power and this ability is something that only rational adults possessed (Hart 1961). John Rawls' version of the social contract – the Original Position – is premised on notions of equality and autonomy but there are a number of signals in Rawls' work that suggest that children do not play a central role in his political theory. He refers to representative men and heads of families which compromises his proposed veil of ignorance somewhat. Not only that, Rawls was of the view that equal justice for children could be achieved through paternalistic decision-making, which he conceptualised as a sort of substituted judgement procedure. His reference to moral development suggests that he too regards children as lacking in the cognitive development that precludes them from being participants in the Original Position (Rawls 1989). Each of these efforts, which are only a small account of the multitude of theories of rights, highlights the uneasy place of children's rights within liberal rights theory.

The exclusion of children from the category of the liberal right-holder also stems from their location within the family unit. The idea of the social contract did not extend to the family unit, which fell outside the sphere of state influence and to the extent that the State was concerned with the family, it dealt with the father as the centre of power within the family. This view meant that there was no need for the State to regulate its relationship with the child. Rather, familial relationships were premised on notions of responsibility and duty. The outcome for children in the Hobbesian world view was potentially extreme:

> Children therefore, whether they be brought up and preserved by the father, or by the mother, or by whomsoever, are in most absolute subjection to him or her, that so bringeth them up, or preserveth them. And they may alienate them, that is, assign his or her dominion, by selling, or giving them, in

> adoption or servitude to others; or may pawn them for hostages, kill them for rebellion, or sacrifice them for peace, by the law of nature, when he or she, in his or her conscience, think it to be necessary.
>
> (Hobbes, 1640, 23.8)

Locke took a somewhat more sympathetic approach and identified some rights for children, which were based on the right to self-preservation so that children had the right to be maintained and nourished by their parents (Locke 1960). More recently, as noted above, Rawls also drew a distinction between families and participants in his version of the social contract; he identifies representative men and heads of families as the individuals in the Original Position (Rawls 1989). These assumptions of parental – or paternal – autonomy and the family's right of privacy further excluded the granting of rights to children.

Distinctions such as these have served to further exclude children from the basic concepts that underpin political and social life. The effect of such exclusion has been law and policy measures that perpetuate children's inequality and non-discrimination.

Towards a more nuanced understanding of autonomy

Context and the (cap)ability to choose

Liberal thinking emphasised autonomy as a means to govern relationships between the individual and the State, and amongst individuals themselves. Thus, autonomy, even if understood in the narrowest of senses, is still influenced by some external factors. This view of autonomy was explained by Joseph Raz whereby choices, of which we must have an adequate range of options to choose from to secure autonomy, were influenced by the general character of our environment and culture (Raz 1986). Amartya Sen argued that the capability for autonomy depends not just on the choices, but on the very capability to make choices, where that capability is a combination of the kinds of functioning (beings and doings) that people can achieve and which range from basic elements such as nutrition and adequate health, to other more complex functionings such as self-respect (Sen 1985). Together, Raz and Sen highlight that autonomy can be understood in terms of the kind of connections and relations that people have either with each other and/or with social and political institutions.

Context and the connection with others

To the extent that the dominant conception of rights presumes both autonomy and a direct relationship between the individual and the State, rights for children are even more problematic than rights for adults because children's dependence – or lack of autonomy – stems from the reality of their lives where they are dependent upon others, as well as the construction of legal rules that often govern that reality with its tendency to favour paternalism rather than liberty (Minow 1986).

The feminist critique of liberalism insists that individuals are a product of their social context and some of our most essential characteristics, such as our capacity for language and the conceptual framework through which we see the world, are not made by us, but are developed by us, or in us, through our interactions with others. Much of this argument has a strong resonance with recent feminist writings on relational autonomy. According to Jennifer Nedelsky, to be autonomous a person must feel a sense of her own power. This sense of power does not mean power over others; rather, it means having a presence or the ability to have an impact – any impact – on our relationships. That feeling of power, as Nedelsky describes it, is only possible within a structure of relationships conducive to autonomy; thus, social relationships enable the development of autonomy (Nedelsky 1989).

Context and the connection with others also opens us up to the need to ensure that the voices of different others are heard. A key part of that process is to ensure that those affected by the process of determining rights and their content are included in the decision-making process not only because it is ultimately more useful to know what is important to whom but also because, as Iris Marion Young contended in the context of her theory of deliberative decision-making, such inclusion serves to legitimate the process itself (Young 2000). In difference-centred theories, freedom is understood in terms of the right to participate differently in the social institutions and culture of society. Lack of freedom is defined in terms of a lack of recognition of the participation and contribution of people of "difference" as a result of their difference from normative assumptions of participation and participants (Moosa-Mitha 2005). This difference-based approach allows us to examine the specific, socio-historical realities that children live in, especially to the extent that such experiences are oppressive. It allows us to recognise the difference between the autonomy of children and the autonomy of adults. It allows us to move away from conceiving autonomy as solely based on rational decision-making that is independent of any relationships and to move towards a reconceptualisation of autonomy as one that includes children's ability to influence the multiple relationships in which they participate.

Context as choice, capability and connection

Choices made in the here and now are a consequence of the development of the individual's preferences over time, a development that needs to be understood. From this view, the rational decision-maker does not just materialise to make this choice or that one, neither are choices unfettered by political, social or economic circumstance; rather, choices are made in response to contexts and surroundings. Understandably, this view has many potential pitfalls because context can serve to explain and justify the status quo. In an attempt to moderate the potential polarisation of views, it should be remembered that the human rights enterprise is concerned with empowering the disempowered and regulating the exercise of power over *all* persons in vulnerable positions.

The child's autonomy: a contest of choices

The question of autonomy continued to underpin attempts to formulate specific theories of children's rights in the latter part of the twentieth century. According to Michael Freeman, children have the right to autonomy, not only present autonomy but also the capacity for future autonomy. Freeman draws from Rawls' version of the social contract and he supports limiting children's autonomy where the aim is to protect the child and develop her/his future capacity for self-determination. In this way, Freeman's concept of "liberal paternalism" – or what he now describes as limited paternalism – seeks to confine paternalism for children without totally eliminating it (Freeman 1987). John Eekelaar's concept of "dynamic self-determinism" is another way of balancing paternalism and autonomy. Not only is the child provided with scope to determine what her or his best interests are, her or his scope of decision-making is enhanced by the provision of an extended range of possible outcomes that enhances her or his capability of choosing between these possible outcomes. The aim of Eekelaar's formulation is to allow children to make an increasing number of decisions as they grow up, but it does not allow them to make a decision which would unduly restrict their life choices when reaching adulthood (Eekelaar 1994). David Archard also strives to find a middle way between the liberationist and paternalistic approaches to children's rights; his "care-taker" approach to children's rights holds that rights should reflect children's developing competence, offering them protection as long as they need it. This protection is combined with empowerment that can take effect as soon as children are ready for it; any restrictions on children's freedom and autonomy are only those that can be justified in terms of maximising their future choices (Archard 2015).

These views reflect the understanding that the autonomy of children and young persons is an evolving process and that the balancing act that is the decision-making around children also takes into account the child's relationship with others. These views also resonate with what we now know about how children think. More generally, moral development, as an aspect of psychology, allows us to consider how children, in particular, think (Buss 2009) and how they accommodate cultural norms and proscriptions of society, whether those codes are based on an ethic, or autonomy, or on a basis of community. Freeman has called for childhood to be viewed as a social practice rather than as a period or stage of development (Freeman 1998). In this way, sociology of childhood also recognises children's experiential knowledge as being a vital aspect of recognising children's rights (Mayall 2000) and it supports the image of children as competent, rational and able to deal with complexity.

These theories, although mentioned briefly, are consonant with attempts to describe the development of children's judgements and social reasoning about phenomena, such as rights, and are also consonant with more nuanced approaches to autonomy.

The child's rights to equality and non-discrimination

Equality, to varying degrees, underpins the above-mentioned political theories that strive to describe our relationships with the State and with each other. Efforts to advance a more nuanced understanding of autonomy that facilitates a more nuanced approach to the equality that comes with such freedom reveal some of the fundamental historical and societal structures that perpetuate the inequality experienced by children.

The types of barriers to children's equality – when measured in terms of participation – are structural (socio-historical) and institutional barriers. The identity that adults give children – an identity that most children will internalise – is one of being lesser and, as other chapters in this edited collection indicate, this identity as lesser can then be compounded by other, often negatively construed identities such as disability, gender, race, ethnicity and/or sexual orientation. Adults can sideline children's social relationships – both within and outside of the family – which means that although children are active agents and do participate in society, adults may choose not to respond to the expression of such agency. The failure to respond is a barrier to participation which serves to exclude children, and requires positive steps (as articulated within the framework of substantive equality) to be taken.

The child's right to equality

The 1970's Child Liberation movement may have argued for children and adults to be treated the same, and such arguments might have been readily refuted, but their challenge to the validity of the incapacity argument on ethical grounds is what is important; they regarded the incapacity argument as a form of inequality (Farson 1974; Holt 1974).

However, treating two individuals, who are in different situations, alike may only reinforce inequality especially when the origins of the equal treatment will favour one individual over the other; past inequalities continue to resonate through to the present. Children are different from adults and to treat them the same as adults (as advocated by child liberationists), where the adult is the comparator or the standard of equality to be achieved, simply perpetuates the unequal treatment of children. An insistence on formal equality reinforces children's difference from the norm that is assumed and reflected in social institutional practices and beliefs. This means that children are regarded as less than equal, and, on a tangible level, it means that children often end up feeling that their personal concerns or interests are not important because they fall outside of mainstream/adult values and norms. What counts for inequality and discrimination and the resulting injustice, harm or oppression needs to include children's experiences of exclusion (Moosa-Mitha 2005).

Moreover, and as importantly, this approach does little to challenge the existing power relationships and hierarchies. Thus, formal equality does not account for or value difference:

> the problem is not the diversity of characteristics, but the detrimental treatment attached to it. Thus the aim should not be to eliminate difference, but to prohibit the detriment attached to such difference, preferably by adjusting existing norms to accommodate difference so that equality can also stem from differential but legitimate treatment.
>
> (Fredman 2011, 13)

Rather, focusing on difference might help set us free from pre-conceived notions of how we will know when equality is achieved.

Fredman calls for substantive equality which goes beyond formal equality's requirement that individuals in similar situations should be treated alike. According to Fredman, substantive equality can be understood as equality of opportunity, which requires the removal of barriers to the advancement of vulnerable or disadvantaged groups. This approach suggests those that are excluded presumably are best placed to identify the barriers that must be removed. Substantive equality can also be described in terms of equality of results which requires measures to be taken to ensure that persons from all sections of society have a genuinely equal chance of satisfying the criteria for access to a particular social good such as education, employment, health-care and political representation. Having a genuinely equal chance of accessing a social good should mean that pre-existing and/or prevailing thinking around the measures designed to ensure accessibility will need to be revisited (Fredman 2011).

In the context of children then, equality would be measured with reference to children, where (children's) difference is not a negative or a "less-than". Stepping away from difference as a negative would be one way of removing barriers as called for by substantive equality. It would be one way of overcoming structural inequalities wherein patriarchy or age-based hierarchies predominate to the detriment of children by perpetually excluding them from participating in any societal or political discourse that could serve to include them more fully. Instead, children are viewed as active participants in society through the multiple relationships that they, and we all, have.

In a similar vein, difference-centred theorists define citizenship through an examination of the specific, socio-historical reality within which citizens' lived experiences of oppression are situated. Difference-based theories offer alternative interpretations of equality where difference is the basis, rather than the site of exclusion, for membership in society. Instead of the liberal definition of equality as the right of citizens to be equal and different, equality should be re-interpreted to mean that all citizens are "differently equal". By emphasising difference first, it is suggested that it is through difference that equality is defined, rather than difference being transcended through a claim to equality (Yuval-Davies 1999). In short, difference is no longer regarded as a negative characteristic to be overcome to achieve equality.

The child's right to non-discrimination

In terms of human rights law, the right to non-discrimination can be regarded as a tool for achieving equality whereby the grounds of discrimination – like equality – were initially set out in neutral and abstract terms. Law or policy that is directly aimed at treating one individual negatively because of a particular characteristic, such as ethnicity or gender, is discriminatory. However, in as much as formal equality does not take into account structural and systematic inequality resulting from historic and socially based differences, it has been argued that, "conventional discrimination analysis mirrors the power relations that form hierarchies that define inequalities rather than challenging and equalizing them" (MacKinnon 2013, 1023.)

Conduct that treats a child negatively because of a particular characteristic, such as ethnicity or gender, may be regarded as direct discrimination and a violation of the child's right to non-discrimination. However, conduct that is aimed at treating an individual negatively because they are a child is often less clearly prohibited as is evidenced by the fact that domestic legal provisions that prohibit age-based discrimination may contain age-related exemptions that explicitly exclude children. For example, in Aotearoa New Zealand, section 21(1)(i) of the Human Rights Act 1993 prohibits age-based discrimination but the prohibition only applies to individuals aged 16 years or over. Exemptions such as these are a manifestation of the types of existing power relationships and aged-based hierarchies that serve to minimise or exclude societal participation by children. They serve to perpetuate historic and socially-based differences or biases against children. They are a reflection of liberal theory's conception of the adult as the norm that also regards children as not yet adults and whose rights to autonomy and equality are rights in the making and, consequently, not fully realisable. The result is structural and systematic discrimination against children because they are children.

Recognising that discrimination may be indirect allows situations of structural bias, where the equal treatment of individuals results in unequal outcomes, to be challenged. Indirect discrimination also allows an individual to challenge intentional discrimination or conduct which is not designed to produce a discriminatory effect but which, nonetheless, imposes a specific disadvantage on members of certain groups. The recognition of indirect discrimination also allows situations of unintentional discrimination to be challenged, meaning that a failure to take into account the impact of such conduct on the specific situation of members of certain groups, which resulted in negative consequences, can also be challenged (Fredman 2011). The main advantage of this approach for the child's right to non-discrimination on the basis of age is that it can challenge situations of structural bias and conduct that was not designed to be discriminatory, or simply not assessed for its potential discrimination against children. Nonetheless, the contribution of this view of discrimination is contingent on children being regarded as a group who must not be discriminated against.

Article 2(1) and the child's right to non-discrimination based on age

The prohibition of age-based discrimination in human rights mechanisms is a relatively recent development. Age is not enumerated as a prohibited ground of discrimination in the majority of the core UN human rights treaties, with the exception of the Convention on the Protection of Migrant Workers and their Families 1990 and the Convention on the Rights of Persons with Disabilities 2006.

Nonetheless, the jurisprudence of the UN treaty monitoring bodies reveals a slow, but steadily increasing, evolution in the recognition of age-based discrimination on the grounds of other status. For example, in 1996, the Committee on Economic, Social and Cultural Rights (CESCR Committee) stated that it was not possible to conclude that discrimination on the grounds of age was comprehensively prohibited by the International Covenant on Economic, Social and Cultural Rights 1966 and went on to note that the range of matters in relation to which such discrimination could be accepted would be very limited (CESCR 1996). However, in 2009, the CECSR Committee affirmed that age is a prohibited ground of discrimination in several contexts (CESCR 2009). Similarly, the Committee on the Elimination of Racial Discrimination identified age as being a factor that can contribute to the circumstances of multiple or double discrimination against children or women of a specific group (CERD 2005). These jurisprudential developments support a broader interpretation to include age-based discrimination.

Article 2(1) of the CRC does not make express reference to age as a prohibited ground of discrimination. States Parties are required to extend the rights contained in the CRC to all children within their jurisdiction without discrimination of any kind and Article 2(1) enumerates the grounds of prohibited discrimination that are the child's, or his or her parent's or legal guardian's, race, colour, sex, language, religion, political or other opinion, national, ethnic or social origin, property, disability, birth or other status. Article 2(2) supplements the prohibition on discrimination contained in Article 2(1) as it requires States Parties to ensure that children are not discriminated against or punished because of the status, activities, expressed opinions, or beliefs of their parents, legal guardians, or family members (Detrick 1989). In sum, Article 2's right to discrimination means that the child is to be protected from discrimination based on her or his own status, as well as that of her or his parents.

The wording of Article 2 accommodates the prohibition of age-based discrimination because (i) it prohibits discrimination "of any kind" and (ii) the phrase "or other status" now includes age-based discrimination stemming from the age of the child and/or stemming from the age of her or his parents or legal guardians. Although the CRC is premised on the categorisation of children as a group distinct from adults and Article 2 frames age-based discrimination in terms of differences between children and adults, it must be remembered that children are not a homogeneous group and that age-based distinctions may also arise as between children themselves.

The jurisprudence of the CRC Committee indicates an evolving recognition that children may be subject to age-based discrimination. In general terms, the Committee has identified discrimination against children as a barrier to the implementation of Article 12's provision regarding the child's right to have his or her voice heard (CRC 2009). This recognition is key because Article 12 seeks to address the particular legal and social status of children, who, according to the CRC Committee, are the subjects of rights. Given that narrow conceptions of autonomy can lead to structural inequality for children, especially where such inequality stems from children's difference being regarded as "less than", it is perhaps somewhat unfortunate that children's special status is described in terms of what children lack, which is the full autonomy of adults. Having said that, the adoption of this view is mitigated by the CRC Committee's requirement that States Parties presume that a child has the capacity to form his or her own views and the Committee's discouragement of the introduction of any age limits by States Parties which would restrict the child's right to be heard (CRC 2009). In its

General Comment on the best interests of the child, the CRC has emphasised that the term "children" refers to all persons under the age of 18 years without discrimination of any kind, in line with Articles 1 and 2 of the Convention (CRC 2013), a view that can now be understood to incorporate the prohibition of age-based discrimination. In relation to the child's right to health, the Committee has stated that attention should be given to any other forms of discrimination that might undermine children's health, and the implications of multiple forms of discrimination should also be addressed (CRC 2013).

In 2014, the CRC Committee explicitly identified age as a basis for discrimination when the Committee on the Elimination of All Forms of Discrimination against Women (CEDAW) and the CRC Committee in their Joint General Comment on harmful practices noted that harmful practices are deeply rooted in social attitudes and are grounded in discrimination based on age, among other things (CEDAW and CRC 2014). Both the CRC Committee and the Committee on Migrant Workers have stated that all children involved in or affected by international migration are entitled to the enjoyment of their rights, regardless of, inter alia, their age. It is also worth noting that, in the Committees' view, de facto equality will not necessarily be ensured if States Parties only address de jure discrimination. The Committees called upon States Parties to fulfil the rights under both Conventions by adopting positive measures to prevent, diminish and eliminate the conditions and attitudes that cause or perpetuate de facto discrimination against children (CMW and CRC 2017). This call for States to take a more proactive stance reflects the need to tackle substantive inequality and discrimination.

The CRC Committee's Concluding Observations also reveal direct and indirect expressions of concern that age is a factor that compromises the effective realisation of the rights identified in the CRC. For example, the Committee expressed concern regarding the lack of consistent age limits across New Zealand statutes (CRC 2016) having previously expressed similar concerns in relation to Norway (CRC 2010). In relation to Aotearoa New Zealand, it has recommended that Aotearoa New Zealand ensures full protection against discrimination on any ground (CRC 2016). At a more general level, the concerns raised about the extent to which the substantive rights of children are being violated raise the question of whether the situation of children is a manifestation of inequality and discrimination against a societal group whose common feature is their age range (CRC 2016).

The Committee has expressly referred to age-based discrimination. For example, in its Concluding Observations to Norway, the Committee expressed concern about age-based discrimination and called for measures to combat such discrimination. Significantly, the Committee noted the ongoing debate as to whether age discrimination of children should be included in the law and whether children should be given the right to file complaints if they are discriminated against due to their age. It recommended that Norway carefully examine the possibility of expanding legislation to provide protection to children against discrimination on the grounds of their age (CRC 2010). The Committee welcomed the inclusion of protection against age discrimination in Sweden's Discrimination Act (CRC 2015). Similarly, the Committee expressed concern that a number of provisions under the United Kingdom's Equality Act (2010) exempt children from protection against age discrimination and, in Northern Ireland, the proposed legislation on age discrimination excludes children under 16 years of age. The Committee recommended that the United Kingdom consider the possibility of expanding legislation to provide protection to all children under 18 years of age against discrimination on the grounds of their age (CRC 2016).

The CRC Committee's move towards addressing age-based discrimination is a welcome development. Equally welcome is the Committee's recognition that the discrimination experienced by children may be more deeply rooted in negative attitudes towards children. In this way, the Committee's comments are beginning to reflect the fact that the discrimination that is experienced by children is historical, structural and hierarchical. Its calls upon States Parties to address such discrimination reflect Abramson's view that Article 2(1) of the CRC should be read in light of Article 1 so that where the State is exercising its powers and if the exercise of such powers results in unjustifiably detrimental impacts upon a certain group – the shared characteristic being that they are under the age of 18 years – for the purposes of the CRC, then children are being discriminated against because they are children (Abramson 2008).

There is one final point to be made in relation to age-based discrimination as it relates to children. As the previous paragraphs and sections indicate, the question of age-based discrimination tends to turn on the comparison of children with adults. However, within the category of children itself, care must be taken to ensure that children at different stages and different ages do not experience discrimination. That children are not a homogeneous group has been recognised by the CRC Committee in relation to the right of the child to have his or her voice heard (CRC 2009). The CRC Committee's recognition of the specific needs of children in early childhood (CRC 2005), as well as its statement that adolescence can be a source of discrimination (CRC 2016), is further evidence that the CRC Committee recognises the specific needs of children at different stages of development and thus the basis for any potential discrimination amongst children themselves on the part of States.

Conclusion

Children and adults are different and it is vital to recognise this difference in order to secure the child's rights to equality and non-discrimination; but we must approach our understanding of this difference with care. Categorising such difference in terms of children as lacking in autonomy and rationality and regarding them "as adults in the making" simply perpetuates the conceptualisation of children in terms of adult characteristics. Such views echo 300 years of liberal thinking, with its emphasis on rationality, reason, decision-making and the distinction that it drew between the private and public spheres. The concepts of autonomy and rationality still have strong connotations with action that is strongly individualistic and adult-orientated. However, as this chapter shows, there are other ways of thinking about autonomy and rationality that take account of differences between adults and children. If accounting for difference – and, more importantly, ensuring that difference does not equate to detriment – lies at the core of the rights to equality and non-discrimination, the next step in the evolution of children's rights is to ensure that autonomy and rationality are understood more broadly.

The wording of Article 2(1) indicates that law certainly recognises diversity but its initial failure to identify age as a ground of prohibited discrimination reaffirms adult and political conceptions of diversity. The failure to identify childhood/age as a site of discrimination can mean that the law and those working within the parameters of the law, such as the CRC Committee, cannot easily access, explore, and embrace the differences between children and adults, or indeed as between children themselves. Recent efforts on the part of the CRC Committee to identify and elaborate the consequences of age-based discrimination is a welcome step away from simply repeating liberal rights theory's view of children's difference as being less than adults. Continued efforts by the Committee in this vein will serve as a conduit to equality and non-discrimination for children.

References

Abramson, B. 2008. *A Commentary on the United Nations Convention on the Rights of the Child, Article 2: The Right of Non-Discrimination*. Leiden: Brill.

Archard, D. 2015. *Children, Rights and Childhood*. 3rd ed. London: Routledge.

Breen, C., 2006. *Age Discrimination and Children's Rights: Ensuring Equality and Acknowledging Difference*. Leiden: Martinus Nijhoff Publishers.

Burns, J.H. and Hart, H.L.A. 1970. *Jeremy Bentham, An Introduction to the Principles of Morals and Legislation*. London: Methuen.

Buss, E. 2009. What the Law Should (and Should Not) Learn from Child Development Research. *Hofstra Law Review*, 38(1): 13–68.

CEDAW and CRC. 2014. Joint General Recommendation No 31 of the Committee on the Elimination of Discrimination against Women/General Comment No 18 of the Committee on the Rights of the Child on Harmful Practices. CEDAW/C/GC/31/CRC/C/GC/18.

CERD. 2005. General Recommendation XXXI on the Prevention of Racial Discrimination in the Administration and Functioning of the Criminal Justice System. CERD/C/GC/31/Rev.4.

CESCR. 1996. General Comment No 6: The Economic, Social and Cultural Rights of Older Persons. E/1996/22.

CESCR. 2009. General Comment No 20: Non-discrimination in Economic, Social and Cultural Rights (Art 2, Para 2 of the International Covenant on Economic, Social and Cultural Rights). E/C.12/GC/20.

CMW and CRC. 2017. Joint General Comment No 3 (2017) of the Committee on the Protection of the Rights of All Migrant Workers and Members of Their Families and No. 22 (2017) of the Committee on the Rights of the Child on the General Principles Regarding the Human Rights of Children in the Context of International Migration. CRC/C/GC/22.

CRC Committee. 2003. CRC General Comment No 4: Adolescent Health and Development in the Context of the Convention on the Rights of the Child. CRC/GC/2003/4.

CRC Committee. 2005. General Comment No 7: Implementing Child Rights in Early Childhood. CRC/C/GC/7/Rev.1.

CRC Committee. 2009. General Comment No 12: The Right of the Child to be Heard. CRC/C/GC/12.

CRC Committee. 2010. Consideration of reports submitted by States Parties under Article 44 of the Convention, Concluding Observations: Norway. CRC/C/NOR/CO/4.

CRC Committee. 2013. General Comment No 15 on the Rights of the Child to the Enjoyment of the Highest Attainable Standard of Health (Art 24). CRC/C/GC/15.

CRC Committee. 2015. Concluding Observations on the Fifth Periodic Report of Sweden. CRC/C/SWE/CO/5.

CRC Committee. 2016. General Comment No 20 on the Implementation of the Rights of the Child during Adolescence. CRC/C/GC/20.

CRC Committee. 2016a. Concluding Observations on the Fifth Periodic Report of the United Kingdom of Great Britain and Northern Ireland. CRC/C/GBR/CO/5.

CRC Committee. 2016b. Concluding Observations on the Fifth Periodic Report of New Zealand. CRC/C/NZL/CO/5.

Detrick, S. 1989. *A Commentary on the United Nations Convention on the Rights of the Child.* The Hague, Boston, London: Martinus Nijhoff Publishers.

Eekelaar, J. 1994. The Interests of the Child and the Child's Wishes: The Role of Dynamic Self-Determinism. *International Journal of Law and the Family*, 8: 42–63.

Farson, R. 1974. *Birthrights.* New York: Macmillan Publishing.

Fredman, S. 2003. The Age of Equality. In: S. Fredman and S. Spencer (eds). *Age As an Equality Issue.* Portland: Hart Publishing.

Fredman, S. and Spencer, S. 2003. *Age as an Equality Issue: Legal and Policy Perspectives.* Oxford: Hart Publishing.

Fredman, S. 2011. *Discrimination Law.* 2nd ed. Oxford: Oxford University Press.

Freeman, M. 1987. Taking Children's Rights Seriously. *Children and Society*, 1(4): 299–319.

Freeman, M. 1998. The Sociology of Childhood and Children's Rights. *The International Journal of Children's Rights*, 6(4): 433–444.

Hart, H.L.A. 1961. *The Concept of Law.* Oxford: Oxford University Press.

Hobbes, T. 1651/1968. *Leviathan*; edited with an Introduction by C.B. Macpherson. London: Penguin.

Hobbes, T. 1640/1999. *The Elements of Law, Natural and Politic: Part I, Human Nature, Part II, De Corpore Politico; with Three Lives.* Gaskin, J.C. ed. Oxford: Oxford University Press.

Holt, J.C. 1974. *Escape from Childhood; The Needs and Rights of Children.* Boston, MA: EP Dutton.

Kant, I. 1785 (1965). *The Metaphysics of Morals*; John Ladd trans. Indianapolis, IA: The Bobbs-Merrill Co.

Locke, J. 1689/1960. *Two Treatises of Government: A Critical Edition with an Introduction and Apparatus Criticus by Peter Laslett.* Cambridge: Cambridge University Press.

Locke, J. 1690/1996. *An Essay Concerning Human Understanding*, Winkler, K.P. ed. Indianpolis, IA: Hackett Classics.

MacKinnon, C. 2013. Intersectionality as Method: A Note, Signs. *Journal of Women in Culture and Society*, 38(4): 1019–1030.

Mayall, B. 2000. The Sociology of Childhood in Relation to Children's Rights. *The International Journal of Children's Rights*, 8(3): 243–259.

Minow, M. 1986. Rights for the Next Generation: A Feminist Approach to Children's Rights. *Harvard Women's Law Journal*, 9: 1–24.

Moosa-Mitha M. 2005. A Difference-Centred Alternative to Theorization of Children's Citizenship Rights. *Citizenship Studies*, 9(4): 369–388.

Nedelsky, J. 1989. Reconceiving Autonomy: Sources, Thoughts and Possibilities. *Yale Journal of Law and Feminism*, 1(1): 7–36.

O'Neill, O. 1988. Children's Rights and Children's Lives. *Ethics*, 98, 445–463.

Rawls, J. 1989. *A Theory of Justice Revised Edition*. Oxford: Oxford University Press.

Raz, R. 1986. *The Morality of Freedom*. Oxford: Clarendon Press.

Rousseau, J.J. 1762/1979. *Emile, or On Education*, Allan Bloom, trans. New York: Basic Books.

Sen, A. 1985. *Commodities and Capabilities.* Oxford: Oxford University Press.

Young, I. 2000. *Inclusion and Democracy.* Oxford and New York: Oxford University Press.

Young, I.A. 2011. *Responsibility for Justice*. Oxford: Oxford University Press.

Yuval-Davis, N. 1999. Ethnicity, Gender Relations and Multiculturalism. In: Rodolfo D. Torres, Louis F. Miron, Jonathan Xavier Inda (eds). *Race, Identity and Citizenship: A Reader*. Oxford: Blackwell.

5 Illegitimate consequences of 'illegitimacy'?

Article 2 UNCRC and non-marital children in the British Isles

Brian Sloan

Introduction

Against the background of Article 2 UNCRC's protection against discrimination on the basis of parental status, this paper considers the legal position of children whose parents are unmarried in the British Isles. While all three target jurisdictions (England and Wales, the Republic of Ireland and Scotland)[1] have purported to remove the historically stigma-affected status of 'illegitimacy',[2] this has not entirely removed the differential treatment of children based upon the marital status of their parents. This paper focuses on one issue affecting children who would previously have been 'illegitimate': the differing approach to conferral of 'parental responsibility' depending on the child's parents' marital status, specifically the fact that legal fathers not married to the mothers of their children (hereafter 'unmarried fathers')[3] are not (unlike married ones) automatically granted 'parental responsibility' in any of the jurisdictions, and can acquire it only revocably even where their *parenthood* is not terminated by adoption.[4] For the sake of clarity, the paper will hereafter use the abbreviation 'PR' to refer to the generic concept of parental responsibility and the full terms 'parental responsibility', 'guardianship' and 'parental rights and (parental) responsibilities' to refer to those concepts specifically used in England and Wales, Ireland and Scotland respectively. All concern involvement in major decisions on a child's upbringing.

The paper's first substantive section considers the approach of the UNCRC and the UN Committee on the Rights of the Child to PR. It then considers the understanding of PR present in each jurisdiction, before analysing their approach to the allocation of PR against the requirements of the UNCRC. It will be argued that the allocation of PR is a children's rights issue, and that while the recognition of children's relationships with their unmarried fathers has improved in each jurisdiction,[5] it is still unclear that the law in any of them is necessarily compatible with Article 2.

The UNCRC, non-marital children and PR

While the European Convention on Human Rights has been given effect in the UK (Human Rights Act 1998) and Ireland (European Convention on Human Rights Act 2003) in a manner that provides domestic remedies to individuals, the

UNCRC has not been fully incorporated into UK or Irish domestic law but is becoming increasingly influential in UK judicial decisions.[6]

It is tolerably clear that 'status' for the purposes of Article 2 UNCRC includes marital status, and that the article covers situations where a child is treated differently based on the marital status of her parents. On its own, therefore, the text of Article 2 might be said to support equality of treatment between married and unmarried fathers in relation to other relevant Convention rights (discussed further below). This might mean that all parents should be presumptively granted PR. (This is arguably necessary to ensure parity of treatment between mothers on the one hand and fathers – married or unmarried – on the other, if motherhood and fatherhood are themselves relevant 'statuses'.) Alternatively, Article 2 might simply mean that, whatever the situation regarding mothers, fathers should be granted and stripped of PR on the same basis irrespective of their marital status per se (even if it is thought that their relationship with the child's mother has some relevance to PR allocation).

There are, however, possible objections to the invocation of Article 2 as regards the allocation of PR. It might be countered that PR, although couched in terms of responsibility, is essentially a matter of parents' rather than children's rights, and therefore that PR does not come within the scope of Article 2 because its allocation does not risk discrimination against children themselves. Erlings (2016, p. 625) has gone so far as claiming that 'the principle of parental responsibility as currently applied under English law erodes children's rights'. A related objection is that the Convention's overriding objective in Article 3 is to promote a child's best interests, that PR is less important than that objective, and/or that treating married and unmarried fathers equally on this question potentially undermines that objective, and is not therefore an 'appropriate' measure for the purposes of Article 2(2) even if it can be understood as purporting to eliminate discrimination.

As Unicef's *Implementation Handbook* emphasises (Hodgkin & Newell, 2007: 33), '[t]he Convention is indivisible and its articles interdependent', suggesting that Article 2 must be read in conjunction with the other articles. This fact, however, variously supports and undermines the arguments canvassed above, and the *Handbook* asserts that Article 2 'has been identified as a general principle by the Committee on the Rights of the Child, and needs to be applied to all other articles' rather than the other way around. There are several ways in which the UNCRC recognises the role of parents in making decisions about their children, and the importance of the relationships between parents and children. Article 5 instructs states to 'respect the responsibilities, rights and duties of parents ... to provide, in a manner consistent with the evolving capacities of the child, appropriate direction and guidance in the exercise by the child of the [Convention] rights'. Moreover, under Article 3(2), states 'undertake to ensure the child such protection and care as is necessary for ... her well-being, taking into account the rights and duties of ... her parents'. Article 18 obliges states to 'render appropriate assistance to parents and legal guardians', who 'have the primary responsibility for the upbringing and development of the child', 'in the performance of their child-rearing responsibilities'. Article 7 states that a child has 'as far as possible, the right to know *and be cared for* by ... her parents' (emphasis added), and holding PR is arguably an important method through which a father could 'care for' a child with whom he is not living. Article 8 obliges states to respect a child's right to her identity and 'family relations'. None of these are expressly limited to marital parents, and they appear to support a wide granting of PR.

In response to welfare-related concerns about the invocation of Article 2 to support equal granting of PR to all fathers, it is true that Article 3 requires a child's best interests to be a primary consideration, and that the UNCRC explicitly seeks not to 'affect any provisions which are more conducive to the realization of the rights of the child' in national or international law (Article 41), but as I have argued elsewhere (Sloan, 2013), the relational rights outlined above should be used to provide clues to the nebulous meaning of 'best interests'. Admittedly, on particular facts the exercise of PR by a parent could jeopardise not only the general 'best interests' provision in Article 3 but also a number of specific rights, PR as a concept can damage children's rights, and in General Comment No 14 the UN Committee on the Rights of the Child (2013, [67]) has specifically said that it is 'contrary to [best] interests if the law automatically gives parental responsibilities to either or both parents'. Nevertheless, these very facts can still support the argument that PR should be open to the same *limitation* whether the child's father is married to her mother or not.

Objectors might draw an analogy with the European Court of Human Rights' approach to this question. A general difference between married and unmarried fathers on the allocation of PR is apparently justifiable under Article 8 ECHR because of the range of potential relationships that 'varies from ignorance and indifference to a close stable relationship indistinguishable from the conventional family-based unit'.[7] Somewhat consistently, Wallbank (2009, p. 281) has expressed concern about 'mothers bearing the brunt' of proposals to extend the situations where unmarried fathers are given PR. But there is also a range of potential marital relationships (even if it is a narrower one) and the European Court's justification facilitates the determination of the question of (non-judicial) conferral of PR with reference to assumptions based upon a father's relationship with the mother (arguably a third party)[8] rather than the father's actual or potential relationship with the child.

For its part, the UN Committee on the Rights of the Child has at times taken a relatively formalistic approach to 'legitimacy'. In Concluding Observations on a report of the Philippines, for example, it stated (Committee on the Rights of the Child, 2005, para. 21):

> As regards children born out of wedlock, the Committee requests the State Party to review its domestic legislation in order to secure their right to equal treatment … and abolish the discriminatory classification of those children as 'illegitimate'.

It could be argued that England, Ireland and Scotland have acted consistently by essentially abolishing illegitimacy and formally treating marital and non-marital children equally notwithstanding the differences on PR. There is, however, some evidence of a more substantive approach on the question of non-marital families in

Convention-related documentation. Hodgkin & Newell, (2007, p. 296) opine that '[s]tates should reconsider … laws that do not permit fathers of children born outside marriage to have any potential rights in adoption procedures', and the Committee on the Rights of the Child (2004, [42]) has referred to the need for 'both legal parents' to consent to adoption. The UN Guidelines on the Alternative Care of Children (UN General Assembly, 2010, [10]), moreover, provide that '[s]pecial efforts should be made to tackle discrimination on the basis of any status of the child or parents', including *inter alia* 'birth out of wedlock'.

As regards the jurisdictions considered in this paper, when addressing discrimination in its Concluding Observations on the United Kingdom's fifth periodic report, the UN Committee on the Rights of the Child (2016, para. 20) mentioned only concerns surrounding exempting children from protection against age discrimination and the potential discrimination against children belonging to minorities other than those of unmarried parents. The UK Government (2014, para. 13–16) did not expressly mention non-marital children in the report itself. In the first UK Concluding Observations, the Committee (1995, para. 12) was worried 'about the possible adverse effects on children of the restrictions applied to unmarried fathers in transmitting citizenship to their children, in contradiction of the provisions of articles 7 and 8 of the Convention'.

Discrimination against children from other minorities was the primary discrimination-related concern of the Committee in its Concluding Observations on the Irish Government's second (2006, para. 20) and third and fourth reports (2016a, para. 27). The Children's Rights Alliance, by contrast, in its *appendix* to the Irish Government's Report (2013), regarded '[r]eform[ing] the law on guardianship to address discrimination against children of non-marital families' as a key priority, albeit writing before the Children and Family Relationships Act 2015 ('CFRA') discussed below. In its Concluding Observations on Ireland's initial report, moreover, the Committee (1998, para. 17) was concerned 'about the disadvantaged situation of children born of unmarried parents due to the lack of appropriate procedures to name the father in the birth registration of the child', which 'also has an adverse impact on the implementation of other rights in relation to adoption which, under current regulations, can take place without the consent of the father' (an issue discussed further below).

The mere fact that the references to PR in the relevant jurisdictions are non-existent, sparing or ambiguous in the Committee's reports should not, in any case, be taken to mean that the current law is definitively compliant with Article 2.

Conclusion

Whatever the uncertainties, it is arguable that the UNCRC requires the relationship of father and child to be recognised through the conferral of PR facilitating involvement in major decisions affecting the child unless that would be contrary to the child's best interests; and, conversely, requires PR to be suspended or removed where necessary (taking into account the range of rights protected by the Convention) to protect the child's rights or interests. In neither case should the child's best interests be determined via crude assumptions arising from the relationship between the father and the child's mother. The next section examines the nature of PR in England and Wales, Ireland and Scotland before the final substantive section analyses whether the law on conferral of PR matches up to the UNCRC's possible ideal.

The nature of PR in England and Wales, Ireland and Scotland

England and Wales

'Parental responsibility' is distinct from legal parenthood (which generally governs matters such as inheritance (Administration of Estates Act 1925, s 46) and financial support (Child Support Act 1991)), and is defined as 'all the rights, duties, powers, responsibilities and authority which by law a parent of a child has in relation to the child and his property' (Children Act 1989 ('CA'), s 3(1)). George (2012, p. 131) has attempted a more substantive list. While the language is that of 'responsibility', there is a strong argument that parental responsibility 'appears primarily concerned with parents and their powers over children' (Erlings 2016, p. 631).

While both legal parenthood and parental responsibility are often held by the same people, not all fathers necessarily have parental responsibility. Moreover, it can be held by more than two people and the acquisition of parental responsibility by one person does not itself cause it to be terminated in respect of anyone else (CA, s 2(6)). The CA section 2(7) expressly provides that '[w]here more than one person has parental responsibility for a child, each of them may act alone and without the…others…in meeting that responsibility' unless legislation provides otherwise on a particular issue. Section 2(8) prohibits acts inconsistent with a court order (likely to be triggered by a dispute between holders of parental responsibility), though the judiciary have generated a duty of *consultation* between all holders of parental responsibility on certain important matters such as education or medical treatment (Herring, 2017, pp. 450–451). In practice, however, the person(s) with whom a child is living will have greater day-to-day control over the child's upbringing than a holder of parental responsibility with whom she is not living, and parental responsibility does not in itself carry a right to or expectation of contact with the child.

Ireland

In Ireland, guardianship 'of the person', according to a non-exhaustive and outdated statutory definition in the Guardianship of Infants Act 1964 ('GOIA'), s 10 (2)(a) confers an entitlement *as against non-guardians* to 'the custody of the child and … to take proceedings for the restoration of his custody of the child against any person who wrongfully takes away or detains the child and for the recovery, for the benefit of the child, of damages for any injury to or trespass against the person of the child'.[9] Guardianship is broadly equivalent to 'parental responsibility',[10] and the Supreme Court has recently said that it in fact includes 'duties to maintain and properly care for a child, and rights to make decisions about that child's … education, health requirements, and general welfare'.[11] Again, it is distinct from parenthood and does not in itself carry a right to 'access'.

At one time, the Department of Justice and Equality (2014) proposed to repeal the GOIA entirely and overhaul the concept of 'guardianship'. The final CFRA adopts a rather more cautious approach by making relatively modest amendments to the 1964 Act (not apparently affecting s 10, Part 4), albeit that a greater range of people are able to apply for guardianship while both parents remain alive was previously the case (GOIA, s 6C).

Scotland

The Children (Scotland) Act 1995 ('C(S)A') *prima facie* separates parental responsibilities (in s 1) from parental rights (in s 2), which is a distinctive approach as compared to the other two jurisdictions. That said, rights are expressly conferred 'in order to enable [the holder] to fulfil his parental responsibilities in relation to [the relevant] child', and each right effectively correlates to one or more responsibilities. Again, parental responsibilities and rights are distinct from legal parenthood.

Under section 1, parental responsibilities are defined as those to 'safeguard and promote the child's health, development and welfare', to provide guidance and direction 'in a manner appropriate to the stage of development of the child' (there being a right to control, direct and guide), to 'maintain personal relations and direct contact with the child on a regular basis' where the child is not living with the holder (there being a correlative right to maintain such relations in such circumstances under section 2, but also a general right 'to have the child living with him or otherwise to regulate the child's residence'), and to act as the child's legal representative (the subject of a correlative s 2 duty). The obligation to exercise parental responsibilities is limited to circumstances where the exercise of the responsibility is 'practicable and in the interests of the child'.

Understandably, holding parental rights and responsibilities does not (by virtue of s 3) 'entitle that person to act in any way which would be incompatible with any court order relating to the child'.

It seems that parental responsibilities and parental rights constitute less of a status than do parental responsibility in England and Wales or guardianship in Ireland. Courts in Scotland can adopt a nuanced approach by conferring only some rights and responsibilities and not others.[12] This means that there will be no right to contact (for example) unless that particular parental right has been granted.

The allocation of PR

Non-judicial conferral

Under section 2 of the CA, parental responsibility is conferred automatically on all mothers in England and Wales, as well as on fathers married to the mother regardless of when the marriage occurred. Fathers who are not married to the mother do not automatically have parental responsibility (there are equivalent provisions for second female parents). They can acquire it under section 4. One method is by agreement with the mother. The 'parental responsibility agreement' must be made and recorded in a prescribed manner.[13] The more straightforward acquisition of parental responsibility by registration on the child's birth certificate (available since December 2003) is also contractual in nature, since the mother's co-operation with the registration is currently in substance vital.[14] While only 5.2 per cent of births were registered by the mother alone in 2016 (Office for National Statistics, 2017, p. 8), suggesting that the vast majority of fathers are given parental responsibility with no difficulty, if PR is a rights issue then it is necessary to focus on the children whose fathers to not receive it via this method in England and Wales.

Schedule 6 to the Welfare Reform Act 2009 (passed under the last Labour Government) would have obliged mothers not married to the fathers of their children to register those fathers as such, except in limited circumstances (including where the identity or whereabouts of the father is unknown or where the mother has reason to fear for her or the child's safety if the father is contacted), thereby *prima facie* giving them parental responsibility (Department for Children, Schools & Families, 2009). It seems, however, that schedule 6 is not due to be brought fully into force (Clifton, 2014). It was vociferously opposed by Wallbank (2009, p. 281), for example, on the basis that, presumably where the mother objects:

> there is little if anything to be gained from children being able to name the man who was biologically responsible for their birth. Indeed, there may be more damage to the developing child who starkly realises that the named man has never had and perhaps never will have any relationship whatsoever with the child.

This unconvincingly implies that there should be a presumption against conferring parental responsibility on unmarried fathers coupled with a power to facilitate it, rather a presumption in favour with a power to withhold it or remove it for good reason. The reform proposal was described by Bainham (2008, p. 459) as 'consistent both with the fundamental rights of the child, especially those enshrined in the … UNCRC…, and also with the historical function of birth registration'. The system as proposed would arguably have been consistent with my interpretation of UNCRC requirements, but for the moment mothers remain in control unless and until the father applies to a court.

Irish child law has undergone major reform following a Government commitment to 'ensure that children's rights are strengthened' (Coalition Government of Ireland, 2011, p. 18). By virtue of a 2015 amendment, the Irish Constitution now asserts in Article 42A.1 that '[t]he State recognises and affirms the natural and imprescriptible rights of all children and shall, as far as practicable, by its laws protect and vindicate those rights'[15] (Children's Rights Alliance, 2012; Collins, 2013). One purpose of the changes is said to be to ensure that there is 'no discrimination between children based upon the marital status of their parents' in various contexts (Department of Children and Youth Affairs, 2012).

It is particularly significant that, until the implementation of the CFRA, only married parents were automatically joint 'guardians' of the child (GOIA, s 6(4)). The rights of even an unmarried mother in relation to the child were said to 'derive from the fact of motherhood and from nature itself'.[16] Her marital status did not prevent her from being the child's 'guardian' automatically. Fathers who are not married to the mothers of their children are not always so fortunate, albeit that their situation was improved under the 2015 Act. Previously, this state of affairs was bolstered by the view that the relationship between children born out of wedlock and their fathers was not protected by the Constitution, such that a father not married to that mother had 'no constitutional right to the guardianship or custody of or access to a child of which he is the natural father'.[17]

Unmarried fathers do not all automatically acquire 'guardianship' for their children. Under the pre-CFRA GOIA, an unmarried father could obtain it non-judicially only through a statutorily declared agreement with the child's mother (GOIA, s 2(4)) or a deed/will (s 7) of the mother. This approach undermined the status of an unmarried father's relationship with his child, particularly in cases where a child's parents no longer have (or never substantially had) an amicable relationship, and notwithstanding the fact that at least access is almost always granted between a father and child.[18]

Citing principles of the primacy of child welfare and equality, the Law Reform Commission (2010) almost reiterated the recommendation, originally made in Law Reform Commission (1982), that all unmarried fathers be given automatic guardianship. The 2010 Report sought to achieve generally automatic guardianship through a linkage between guardianship and compulsory joint registration of a child's birth. The Commission (2010, para. 2–23) proposed, however, that registration would not be compulsory where 'the mother does not know who the father of the child is or where there is a risk to the safety and welfare of the mother or the child'.

The original General Scheme of the Children and Family Relationships Bill 2014 would have given an unmarried father automatic guardianship if the father and mother 'cohabited for at least 12 consecutive months before the child's birth, which cohabitation ended (if applicable) not less than 10 months before the child's birth' (Head 31(3)(b)), but this was changed in the September 2014 version so that a father would be a guardian if he 'cohabited for at least 12 consecutive months including at least three months after the birth of the child' (Head 34(3)(b)), albeit that there may have remained a lack of clarity on the meaning of 'cohabited' for these purposes (Shannon 2014). The final CFRA's formulation is that an unmarried father will be a guardian if he 'and the mother of the child concerned have been cohabitants for not less than 12 consecutive months occurring after the date on which [the relevant] subsection comes into operation, which shall include a period, occurring at any time after the birth of the child, of not less than three consecutive months during which both the mother and the [father] have lived with the child' (GOIA, s 2(4A)), and it is expressly provided that '"cohabitant" shall be construed in accordance with' the Civil Partnership and Certain Rights and Obligations of Cohabitants Act 2010 (CFRA, s 2).[19] The new provision is clearly an improvement on the previous law, though it still places much control for the automatic granting of guardianship in the hands of the mother (Treoir, 2014, para. 2.1.1). Shannon (2014, para. 7.9–7.12) criticised the originally proposed time requirements for their arbitrariness, but also sought to justify them in the particular context of guardianship on the basis that they ensure a 'significant degree of stability to the relationship' before automatic guardianship can be conferred. This reinforces the notion that a relationship between a father and his child should to a significant extent be determined by his relationship with that child's mother, even where there is no real suggestion that the father's involvement could harm the child. That said, Ireland appears to be the only jurisdiction considered in this paper where an unmarried father can *obtain* PR without either the active co-operation of the child's mother or a court order.

The Constitution as previously formulated must take a share of the blame for the discriminatory treatment of unmarried fathers, which continues in spite of the purported equality statutorily granted to children born outside marriage. It should be re-emphasised, however, that was improved when the relevant parts of the CFRA were commenced in January 2016,[20] and that (as discussed earlier) reforms similar to the Law Reform Commission's proposals have not yet been fully implemented in England and Wales even in the absence of constitutional constraints.

By virtue of section 3 of the Scottish C(S)A, 'a child's mother has parental responsibilities and parental rights in relation to him whether or not she is or has been married to his father'. For fathers, however, the position is different. While the father will have parental rights and responsibilities where he is 'married to the mother at the time of the child's conception or subsequently', if he is unmarried he will have such rights and responsibilities if he has been registered as the father on the child's birth certificate (from May 2006, under s 3) (including re-registration, unlike in England and Wales), by registered agreement with the mother (s 4) or by court order (s 11). Importantly, as Norrie (2013, para. 6.09) describes and as reflects the current situation in England and Wales, '[t]he father must have the co-operation of the mother to be registered [on the birth certificate], and so, in the absence of any court decree, the mother is the "gatekeeper" to the father's entitlement to parental responsibilities and parental rights', albeit that (again broadly consistently with England and Wales), only 4.3 per cent of birth registrations in 2016 were sole ones (National Records of Scotland, 2017). Tellingly, the provisions detailing the circumstances in which parental rights and responsibilities are held have to be set out in section 3 '[n]otwithstanding Section 1(1) of the Law Reform (Parent and Child) (Scotland) Act 1986 (provision for disregarding whether a person's parents are not, or have not been, married to one another in establishing the legal relationship between him and any other person)'. As Norrie (2013, para. 6.09) puts it, 'it cannot yet be said that the question … whether … the parents are married to each other is completely irrelevant to the acquisition of parental responsibilities and parental rights' (cf Scottish Government, 2018, part 7). This may be problematic for the purposes of Article 2.

Judicial conferral

Parents not married to the child's mother in England and Wales can also acquire parental responsibility via a court order (CA, ss 4(1)(c)-4ZA(1)(c)). The threshold is low notwithstanding the paramountcy of child welfare (s 1), and according to the Ministry of Justice (2012, Table 2.4) (2011 being the last year for which specific figures are available) parental responsibility orders were actively refused in only 0.7 per cent of private law cases in which they were sought. The courts will consider:

> (1) the degree of commitment which the father has shown towards the child; (2) the degree of attachment which exists between the father and the child, and (3) the reasons of the father for applying for the order.[21]

A fact-specific approach is taken.[22]

In Ireland, the principle that 'in the resolution of all proceedings' *inter alia* 'concerning the adoption, guardianship or custody of, or access to, any child' 'the best interests of the child shall be the paramount consideration' is now enshrined in the Constitution (article 42A.4.1; see also GOIA, s 3). When summarising the courts' approach to applications for a guardianship order under GOIA, s 6A in the pre-CFRA Supreme Court case of *J McB v LE*,[23] Fennelly J emphasised the importance of child welfare and said that the court would consider 'all the circumstances of the relationship which exists between the father and the child',[24] including the rights of the mother and the child. He accepted that the biological link between father and child was 'an important element', but said that the strength of the relationship would 'vary in accordance with the extent to which the father is or has been actively engaged in the care, nurture, education and upbringing of the child'.[25] Fennelly J was anxious to assert the court's 'power to regulate and control the scope and ambit of that relationship in an application for guardianship or custody on the part of the natural father'.[26] The success rate is apparently relatively high, albeit not as high as in England and Wales: orders were not granted in 24 per cent of applications by 'unmarried applicants' in 2015 (Courts Service Ireland, 2018; no figures appear to be available for 2016: Courts Service Ireland, 2018a).

In Scotland in 2014–15, 23 per cent of applications initiated in the Sherriff Courts for parental rights and responsibilities were apparently dismissed (Scottish Government, 2017). In *S v J*, an unmarried father of a 1-year-old child whom she had not seen since she was 6 weeks old sought parental responsibilities and parental rights.[27] There was evidence of the father's violence towards a previous partner and her child, and controlling behaviour towards the mother of the child in issue. The judge acknowledged that 'the law's working hypothesis is that it is normally in the best interests of a child to maintain contact and relations with a natural parent with whom the child is no longer living',[28] subject to the paramountcy of the child's best interests (C(S)A, s 11(7)). He was mindful of the requirements of the ECHR, considered supervised contact appropriate and therefore awarded the father the parental responsibility of contact and the correlative right of contact. The judge did not, however, consider it appropriate to grant other rights and responsibilities, despite his acceptance that, had the father remained in Scotland for one further day following the child's birth, it was likely that both parents would have registered the birth, thereby granting the father full parental rights and responsibilities.

It might be argued that there is little real difference between automatic and other methods of acquiring PR because of the low threshold applied, and that any difference is justified because (consistently with the objections to the compulsory registration proposal considered above) the parents will inevitably be in dispute if the mother refuses consent (eg) to registration and the court is best placed to resolve the dispute. That said, a failure to register could be a matter of inertia (Wright, 2010) and, as argued above, it is undesirable to make PR presumptively dependent on the relationship between the parents. By the time a father makes an application for PR, fundamental decisions might have been taken without his consent or knowledge.

The implications of the difference between automatic and other methods can be illustrated by comparing the English adoption cases of *Re C (A Child) (Adoption: Duty of Local Authority)*[29] and *Re A (Father: Knowledge of Child's Birth)*.[30] *Re C* involved a mother who had become pregnant after a 'one-night stand', and made clear her wish for the resulting child to be adopted shortly after birth. She kept the pregnancy secret from the biological father (lacking parental responsibility), and refused to identify him. The relevant local authority sought judicial guidance on whether it should attempt to identify the father, inform him of the child's birth and possible adoption and assess him as a potential carer. The Court of Appeal ordered the local authority not to take any such steps. The priority was held to be finding a permanent home for the child without further delay. This was the course of action most compatible with the child's best interests, on the court's analysis, and there was no evidence that the father could care for her based on what the mother had said. Arden LJ was somewhat influenced by the fact that the father's consent was not formally relevant to the adoption (Adoption and Children Act 2002, s 52(6)). She held that in 'exceptional situations' such as this it was appropriate for a father to remain ignorant of a child's birth at the time of the adoption.[31] In *Re A (Father: Knowledge of Child's Birth)*,[32] the facts of which many would more readily describe as 'exceptional' compared to those of *Re C*, a mother similarly sought to prevent a father from finding out about the birth and development of their child, whom she intended to relinquish for adoption. The key difference was that the parents were married. The father suffered from 'Severe Depression with Psychotic Symptoms and Post Traumatic Stress Disorder', such that his behaviour was unpredictable and violent. The Court of Appeal nevertheless refused to grant the order sought. A 'very high degree of exceptionality' was required before such secrecy could be justified,[33] and that test was not held to be satisfied. Because he had parental responsibility, the father's consent was *prima facie* necessary before the adoption could proceed, and the first-instance judge (upheld by the Court of Appeal) failed to see 'how the consent could reasonably be dispensed with if it has never actually been sought'.[34] Both may be unusual cases, but they illustrate the difficulties of making PR depend in the first instance on the relationship between the parents.

The presence or absence of parental responsibilities or rights can also be extremely important in Ireland or Scotland. For example, in Scotland, a 'parent' whose consent is *prima facie* required for a child's adoption means a parent who 'has any parental responsibilities or parental rights in relation to the child' or does not have them 'by virtue of a permanence order which does not include provision granting authority for the child to be adopted' (Adoption and Children (Scotland) 2007, s 31(15)). Similarly, in Ireland, the basic position (subject to the ability to dispense with consent) is that an adoption order cannot be made 'without the consent of every person, being the child's mother or guardian or other person having charge of or control over the child' (Adoption Act 2010, s 26), which may exclude a father who is not a guardian, albeit that the relevant Authority is under a basic duty to 'take such steps as are reasonably practicable to ensure that every relevant non-guardian of the child is consulted in relation to the adoption', except in limited circumstances (s 30).

Removal

In England and Wales, where a mother or father has acquired parental responsibility automatically (in the latter case via marriage), only adoption can terminate parental responsibility (and transfer it to the adoptive parents: Adoption and Children Act 2002, s 46). Fathers who have not been in a marriage with the mother are vulnerable to having parental responsibility removed by court order even when they do acquire it.[35] In *Re DW (A Child) (Termination of Parental Responsibility)*, [36] one of few reported cases on removal, it was held that the court would consider the extent to which the criteria for judicially *granting* parental responsibility in the first place are still satisfied and apply the welfare principle even in cases of acquisition by registration. The Court of Appeal rejected any presumption of continuance, but accepted that in general it was 'vitally important to encourage the exercise of parental responsibility by fathers'.[37] On the facts, the father's conviction for sexual abuse of the relevant child's half-sisters, and the resulting emotional harm caused to the whole family, justified the removal of his parental responsibility.

Under the Irish GOIA even as amended, unmarried fathers can similarly obtain guardianship only revocably, while mothers and married fathers cannot be deprived of guardianship short of adoption (s 86) because of what has been described as their 'constitutional right to guardianship' (Department of Justice and Equality, 2015: 14). Unmarried fathers can have their guardianship revoked on the following statutory grounds (GOIA, s 8(7)):

(a) there is another guardian in place or about to be appointed,
(b) the court is satisfied that it is in the best interests of the child that the guardian be removed…,
(c) for substantial reasons that appear to it to be sufficient, the court considers it necessary or desirable to do so, and

(d) the guardian who is to be removed... —

i consents to the removal,
ii is unable or unwilling to exercise the powers, responsibilities and entitlements of guardianship..., or
iii has failed in his...duty towards the child to such extent that the safety or welfare of the child is likely to be prejudicially affected if he...is not removed....

It seems that a court in Scotland may make an order depriving *any* parent of some or all of her parental rights and responsibilities, without that necessarily leading to adoption (C(S)A, s 11(2)(a)). In *AY v MM*,[38] the parental rights and responsibilities of a child's mother were removed after she attempted to smother the child and took a drug overdose. This is a more balanced and child-focused approach than the other two jurisdictions, although it must be borne in mind that automatic PR may be *controlled* by court orders even where it cannot be removed. That said, and particularly given the potentially drastic children's rights implications of adoption (Sloan, 2013), it should not be the sole means of removing PR on the basis of welfare for only some fathers and not for others, or indeed for mothers.

Conclusion

This chapter has shown that, despite recent improvements, married and unmarried fathers are treated differently as regards the allocation of PR in England and Wales, Ireland and Scotland. While there are some important differences between the jurisdictions, so that (for example) only Ireland will in some circumstances confer PR in the absence of both maternal agreement and a court order and only Scotland will contemplate removing it from a married father without adoption, the chapter has argued that general differential treatment is potentially detrimental to children's rights and interests, and therefore potentially incompatible with Article 2 UNCRC and the Convention as a whole. It has been seen that PR is arguably key to Convention rights such as Articles 5 (on parental guidance) and 7 (on care by parents). If the primacy of child welfare is the ultimate goal, its determination as regards PR should arguably be based on an assessment of the child's relationship or potential relationship with her father, rather than on crude assumptions flowing from the father's relationship with the child's mother. The analysis of the UNCRC's requirements undertaken in this paper is by no means beyond question, however, and as ever the Convention has not provided 'a specific and readily ascertainable recipe for resolving the inevitable tensions and conflicts that arise in a given situation among the different rights recognized' (Alston, 1994, p. 2).

Notes

1 Northern Ireland largely mirrors English Law on points within the paper's scope (Children (Northern Ireland) Order 1995).
2 See Family Law Reform Act 1987, s 1 (England and Wales); Status of Children Act 1987, s 3 (Ireland); Law Reform (Parent and Child) (Scotland) Act 1986, s 1.

3 A father married to someone who is *not* the relevant child's mother is also classed as an 'unmarried father' for these purposes.
4 A similar situation can occur where a same-sex partner who is not married to, or in a civil partnership with, the child's mother becomes a parent via assisted reproduction (see, eg, CA, s 4ZA (England and Wales)). For reasons of space, this chapter will focus on fathers.
5 For a broader comparative analysis, see, eg, Scherpe (2009).
6 *R (on the application of SG and others (previously JS and others)) v Secretary of State for Work and Pensions* [2015] UKSC 16. Cf *Dos Santos and others v The Minister for Justice and Equality and others* [2015] IECA 210.
7 *B v UK* [2000] 1 FLR 1, 5; see also *McMichael v UK* (1995) 20 EHRR 205; *Elsholz v Germany* [2000] 2 FLR 486.
8 Cf, eg, Marshall (2012).
9 GOIA, s 10(2)(a). See also the 'guardian of the estate' (s 10(2)(b)). All guardians obtain guardianship of both types 'unless, in the case of a guardian appointed by deed, will or order of the court, the terms of his appointment otherwise provide' (s 10(1)).
10 Indeed, the Law Reform Commission (2010, [1–06]-[1–10]) recommended that the terminology of 'parental responsibility' be adopted in Ireland, though the old terminology is used under the CFRA due to its presence in the new article 42A of the Constitution: see Shannon (2014: [7.2]) for criticism.
11 *O'S & anor v Doyle & ors* [2013] IESC 60 [27] (Macmenamin J).
12 See, eg, *S v J* [2012] CSOH 49.
13 See Parental Responsibility Agreement Regulations 1991/1478, sch 1, as amended.
14 See CA, ss 4(1A), 4ZA(2); Births and Deaths Registration Act 1953, s 10. Cf Welfare Reform Act 2009, sch 6, considered below.
15 Inserted by the Thirty-First Amendment of the Constitution (Children) Act 2012.
16 *G v An Bord Uchtála* [1980] IR 32, 55 (O'Higgins CJ). See, eg, Ryan (2012: 212).
17 *McD v L* [2009] IESC 81 [299] (Fennelly J).
18 See, eg, Shannon (2010:[12–64]-[12–66]). See CFRA, ss 53–57 for a reformulation of the substantive law on custody and access.
19 The existing methods of an unmarried father's acquiring guardianship are broadly retained (CFRA, Part 4).
20 See Children and Family Relationships Act 2015 (Commencement of Certain Provisions) Order SI 2016 12/2016.
21 *Re H (Minors) (Local Authority: Parental Rights) (No 3)* [1991] Fam 151, 158.
22 Compare, eg, *Re S (A Minor) (Parental Responsibility)* [1995] 2 FLR 648 and *M v M (Parental Responsibility)* [1999] 2 FLR 737.
23 *J McB v LE* [2010] IEHC 123.
24 ibid [32].
25 ibid [33].
26 ibid [33].
27 [2012] CSOH 49.
28 ibid [131].
29 [2007] EWCA Civ 1206. See further Sloan (2009).
30 [2011] EWCA Civ 273. See, eg, Sloan (2013: 57–59).
31 *Re C* (n **29**) [24].
32 *Re A* (n **30**).
33 ibid [25].
34 ibid [7].
35 Compare CA, s 2(1) and s 2(1A) with s 2(2)(b) and s 2(2A)(b).
36 [2014] EWCA Civ 315.
37 ibid [33].
38 2012 GWD. 33–674.

References

Alston, P. 1994. The Best Interests Principle: Towards a Reconciliation of Culture and Human Rights. *International Journal of Law and the Family*, 8(1), 1–25.

Bainham, A. 2008. What is the Point of Birth Registration? *Child & Family Law Quarterly*, 20(4), 449–474.

Children's Rights Alliance. 2012. Recognising Children's Rights in the Constitution: The Thirty-First Amendment to the Constitution (Children) Bill 2012.

Clifton, J. 2014. The Long Road to Universal Parental Responsibility: Some Implications from Research into Marginal Fathers. *Family Law*, 44(6), 858–861.

Coalition Government of Ireland. 2011. Government for National Recovery 2011–16. Dublin.

Collins, T.M. 2013. International Child Rights in National Constitutions: Good Sense or Nonsense for Ireland? *Irish Political Studies*, 28(4), 591–619.

Committee on the Rights of the Child. 1995. Consideration of Reports Submitted by States Parties under Article 44 of the Convention – Concluding Observations: United Kingdom (Initial Report). CRC/C/15/Add.34.

Committee on the Rights of the Child. 1998. Consideration of Reports Submitted by States Parties under Article 44 of the Convention – Concluding Observations: Ireland (Initial Report). CRC/C/15/Add.85.

Committee on the Rights of the Child. 2004. Consideration of Reports Submitted by States Parties under Article 44 of the Convention – Concluding Observations: Papua New Guinea. (Initial Report). CRC/C/15/Add.229.

Committee on the Rights of the Child. 2005. Consideration of Reports Submitted by States Parties under Article 44 of the Convention – Concluding Observations: Philippines. (Initial Report). CRC/C/15/Add.259.

Committee on the Rights of the Child. 2006. Consideration of Reports Submitted by States Parties under Article 44 of the Convention – Concluding Observations: Ireland. (Second Report). CRC/C/IRL/CO/2.

Committee on the Rights of the Child. 2013. General Comment No. 14 (2013) on the Right of the Child to Have His or Her Best Interests Taken as a Primary Consideration (art. 3, para. 1). CRC /C/GC/14

Committee on the Rights of the Child. 2016. Consideration of Reports Submitted by States Parties under Article 44 of the Convention – Concluding Observations: United Kingdom. (Fifth Report). CRC/C/GBR/CO/5.

Committee on the Rights of the Child. 2016a. Consideration of Reports Submitted by States Parties under Article 44 of the Convention – Concluding Observations: Ireland. (Third and Fourth Reports). CRC/C/IRL/CO/3–4

Courts Service Ireland. 2018. Topic: Guardianship. Available from: http://www.courts.ie/Courts.ie/Library3.nsf/pagecurrent/969AC9BD2337B7CB8025800C003304B1?opendocument [Accessed 16 May 2018].

Courts Service Ireland. 2018a. Topic: Guardianship. Available from: http://www.courts.ie/Courts.ie/Library3.nsf/pagecurrent/220D2018BA6360438025800C0036FBA?opendocument [Accessed 16 May 2018].

Department for Children, Schools & Families. 2009. The Registration of Births (Parents Not Married And Not Acting Together) Regulations 2010: A Consultation.

Department of Children and Youth Affairs. 2012. Thirty-First Amendment of the Constitution (Children) Bill 2012: Explanatory Memorandum. Dublin.

Department of Children and Youth Affairs. 2013. Ireland's Consolidated Third and Fourth Reports to the UN Committee on the Rights of the Child. Dublin.

Department of Justice and Equality. 2014. General Scheme of a Children and Family Relationships Bill 2014. Dublin.

Department of Justice and Equality. 2015. Children and Family Relationships Bill 2015 Explanatory Memorandum. Dublin.

Erlings, E. 2016. Is Anything Left of Children's Rights? How Parental Responsibility Erodes Children's Rights under English Law. *International Journal of Children's Rights*, 24(3), 624–656.

George, R. 2012. *Ideas and Debates in Family Law*. Oxford: Hart.

Herring, J. 2017. *Family Law*. 8th edition. Harlow: Pearson.

Hodgkin, R. and Newell, P. 2007. *Implementation Handbook for the Convention on the Rights of the Child*. 3rd edition. Geneva: Unicef.

Law Reform Commission. 1982. Report on Illegitimacy. LRC 4. Dublin.

Law Reform Commission. 2010. Legal Aspects of Family Relationships. LRC 101. Dublin.

Marshall, J. 2012. Concealed Births, Adoption and Human Rights Law: Being Wary of Seeking to Open Windows into People's Souls. *Cambridge Law Journal*, 71(2), 325–354.

Ministry of Justice. 2012. Judicial and Court Statistics 2011. London.

National Records of Scotland. 2017. Table 3.02: Live Births, Numbers and Percentages, by Marital Status of Parents and Type of Registration, Scotland, 1974 to 2016.

Norrie, K. M. 2013. *The Law Relating to Parent & Child in Scotland*. 3rd edition. Edinburgh: W. Green.

Office for National Statistics. 2017. Statistical Bulletin: Births by Parents' Characteristics in England and Wales: 2016. London.

Ryan, F. 2012. Out of the Shadow of the Constitution: Civil Partnership, Cohabitation and the Constitutional Family. *Irish Jurist*, 48, 201–248.

Scherpe, J. M. 2009. Establishing and Ending Parental Responsibility: A Comparative View. In: R. Probert, S. Gilmore and J. Herring, eds. *Responsible Parents and Parental Responsibility* (pp. 43–62). Oxford: Hart.

Scottish Government. 2018. Review of Part 1 of the Children (Scotland) Act 1995 and creation of a Family Justice Moderation Strategy. A Consultation. (May 2018). Available at: https://www.gov.scot/binaries/content/documents/govscot/publications/consultation-paper/2018/05/review-part-1-children-scotland-act-1995-creation-family-justice/documents/00535359-pdf/00535359-pdf/govscot%3Adocument?forceDownload=true

Scottish Government. 2017. Civil Justice Statistics in Scotland 2015–16. Edinburgh.

Shannon, G. 2010. *Child Law*, 2nd edition. Dublin: Round Hall.

Shannon, G. 2014. *The Children and Family Relationships Bill 2014*. Dublin: Children's Rights Alliance.

Sloan, B. 2009. Re C (A Child) (Adoption: Duty of Local Authority) – Welfare and the Rights of the Birth Family in 'Fast Track' Adoption Cases, *Child & Family Law Quarterly*, 21(1), 87–103.

Sloan, B. 2013. Conflicting Rights: English Adoption Law and the Implementation of the UN Convention on the Rights of the Child. *Child & Family Law Quarterly*, 25(1), 40–60.

Treoir. 2014. Submission to the Oireachtas Committee on Justice, Defence and Equality on the General Scheme of a Children and Family Relationships Bill 2014. Available at: https://www.treoir.ie/wp-content/uploads/2018/03/Submission-Oireachtas-Committee.pdf

UK Government. 2014. The Fifth Periodic Report to the UN Committee on the Rights of the Child United Kingdom. London.

United Nations General Assembly. 2010. UN Guidelines on the Alternative Care of Children. A/RES/64/142.

Wallbank, J. 2009. 'Bodies in the Shadows': Joint Birth Registration, Parental Responsibility and Social Class. *Child & Family Law Quarterly*, 21(3), 267–282.

Wright, O. 2010. I'll register both births this time, vows Miliband. *The Independent*, 3 November 2010. Available at: https://www.independent.co.uk/news/uk/politics/ill-register-both-births-this-time-vows-miliband-2123549.html [Accessed 16 May 2018].

6 The non-discrimination principle in child protection

A snapshot on a seemingly trivial practice of transitions in care

Tarja Pösö

Introduction

Child protection aims to promote children's rights in situations in which children need protection from public authorities. The vulnerability of children is then viewed, in general terms, by considering either the needs of children (as is commonly done in family-service orientated child protection systems) or the risks (as is commonly done in protection orientated child protection systems, e.g. Gilbert et al. 2011, Burns et al. 2017). Vulnerable situations as met in child protection are often related to a variety of social inequalities, poverty in particular (Saarikallio-Torp et al. 2010; Davidson et al. 2017), and therefore the issues of equality and inequality are inevitably embedded in child protection. The United Nations Convention on the Rights of the Child (CRC), Article 2 especially, directs child protection to act in a non-discriminatory manner when tackling children's vulnerabilities. This principle is in practice further supported by social workers' professional commitment to individual rights and social justice (Clark 2002).

However, practising rights and justice requires constant contextual interpretations of what rights and justice mean in each case (Banks 2016). In the literature on children's rights, it is stated that children's rights are not easily translated from principle into effective practice (Tisdall and Davis 2004). Nevertheless, exactly the way the rights are practised – that is to say, put into effective practice – matters a lot to children in vulnerable situations. While there is already some body of research on children's rights for participation in practice, with a clear reference to Art 12 (Gal and Duramy 2015), the non-discrimination principle of Art 2 CRC has been explored to a lesser extent, leading to a gap in the knowledge base in child protection. According to Besson (2005), children require special measures of protection that take into account their particular vulnerability vis-à-vis the State, but also vis-à-vis their families and other individuals; further, they may also be discriminated against by their families and the State. Can child protection be practised so that it protects children without discrimination in a way that it ensures 'that the child is protected against all forms of discrimination or punishment on the basis of the status, activities, expressed opinions, or beliefs of the child's parents, legal guardians, or family members' (Art 2)?

This chapter provides an explorative reading of how the non-discrimination principle is materialized in child protection practice. The focus is on one specific practice within out-of-home care in child protection: children's transitions into substitute homes. Transitions materialize the formal removal decisions, with the consequence of children leaving their familiar relations and environments to enter a set of new social relations, customs and spaces of foster homes or residential institutions. Although removal decisions should be made in the children's best interest, transitions may be highly stressful events for children in vulnerable situations, as will be highlighted later in this chapter. Transitions are studied here through one empirical snapshot on transport services. These are outsourced services to bring children to and from the substitute homes in certain situations, carried out by profit-making agencies. This snapshot is a reminder that children's rights should be included in every element of child protection and that every local interpretation and practice of rights matter (Ife 2001, pp. 127–301). Such a reminder is important in societies such as Finland in which child protection legislation and other legislation defining human and basic rights in general are strongly against discrimination of any kind. As a Nordic welfare state, Finland aims to provide sufficient welfare for all and to minimize inequality of welfare among its people. A focus only on legislation and the ambitions of policy would give a limited picture, if not even a misleading one, of the rights of children and their equality in the child protection system. The snapshot highlights complex relations between children's rights and needs in practice and demonstrates how children with complex needs are justified to be treated differently from those with lesser needs, and how a narrower spectrum of practice principles may be employed with them (e.g. safety vs. relationship-based care) in transitions.

The first section of this chapter describes the conceptual approach to study discrimination in child protection practice, informed by social rather than by legal studies on rights, followed by sections about the context (transitions in child protection) and findings of the chosen empirical snapshot (transport services). The conclusions highlight the contradictions between rights-based child protection and other rationales guiding child protection which influence the implementation of the non-discrimination principle.

Child protection, vulnerabilities and discrimination at intersections

In child protection, children's needs and risks are viewed mainly in the frame of the nature of parental care (or the lack thereof). Although most Western societies provide assistance and support to parents to look after their children, children grow up in vulnerable situations and sometimes need to be taken into state care to be provided with less harmful conditions for everyday life and growing up. The removal is inevitably a reflection of a variety of inequalities as well as socio-economic and psychosocial problems children and their families encounter in their lives (Davidson et al. 2017). According to Bessell and Gal (2009), the principle of non-discrimination is of particular relevance in child protection for children with special needs – as many children entering the child protection system are – as well as for children from culturally and linguistically diverse backgrounds.

When taking children into state care, the intention is to give children better opportunities to grow up and to compensate them for the shortcomings of care given by their parents, sometimes addressed as 'tailored counteracting against inequalities' (Heino and Bardy 2014). Although much is expected from child protection, a common feature of child protection across countries is that the services are reported to lack enough material and human resources to meet the needs and rights of children properly (Bessell and Gal 2009). As a consequence, children may experience shortcomings of material, educational and psychological well-being both in care and after care (Fernandez 2009; Sallnäs et al. 2012; Cameron et al. 2018). However, children's well-being, either overall or in part, may also improve as a result of care (Fernandez 2009). The former type of findings often compare children in the child protection system with their peers outside the system (interpersonal comparisons), whereas the latter type of findings come from studies looking at the changes in individual life-courses (intrapersonal comparisons) (Devaney 2004; Coman and Devaney 2011; Brady and Gilligan 2018). The understanding of equality and inequality is thus influenced by the designs and methodologies the studies employ.

In a similar way, the exploration of the principle of non-discrimination in child protection is far from being straightforward, conceptually or methodologically. Even the very concept of 'rights' is contested (Bessell and Gal 2009). Child protection very rarely focuses on one social category only (e.g. as 'children'), rather the focus is on multiple categories (e.g. children, neglect, disability and poverty). To address situations in which multiple forms of inequality, vulnerabilities and grounds of discrimination operate at the same time – as is typically the case in child removals – the term 'intersectional discrimination' has been proposed (Ravnbøl 2009). The concept allows the analysis of the dynamics of parallel forms of discrimination (e.g. structural/political/external/internal) (ibid.). It echoes the term 'intersectionality' which 'alerts us to the fact that social inequality cannot be fully understood if only one social category is considered' (Phoenix 2016). In this view, social categories (related to ethnicity, age, social class, for example) are dynamic and changing rather than fixed. They are also provisional, often related to other social categories (ibid.). When such constructs as discrimination, power, and social inequalities are addressed from the point of view of intersectionality, the recognition of multiple, multifaceted and diverse realities of individuals, groups and interventions in a variety of systems should somehow be included in the research designs (Murphy et al. 2009). This is a relevant remark for studies on child protection as those services operate at the intersections of legislation, policy, organizations, professional theories and methods as well as practitioners' interaction with children and families and their agency, each employing their own understandings of children's and families' lives and the equality therein. Discrimination may thus be complex to spot, if not even be hidden, in the many practices and layers of child protection and in the multiple and changing categories of children and vulnerabilities.

Transitions in child protection

For a child, the very decision to remove her into public care is materialised by the placement in a substitute home, either a foster home or a residential institution (or an adoptive home in some countries). For a practitioner, the removal is an outcome of a series of formal decisions, including the decisions to match a child with a particular substitute home (Zeijlmans et al. 2018; Pösö and Laakso 2016). The new home is expected to give the child a safe environment for everyday life as well as to provide services, e.g. educational support, healthcare or a therapeutic environment (Whittaker et al. 2015). Transitions from the birth parents' home to a substitute home involve changes in children's close relations and social environments, and affect the children's interpersonal world, and potentially mark a significant turning point in their lives (Mitchell and Kuczynski (2010). Transitions may be experienced as highly stressful events (Baugerud and Melinder 2011; Goodyer 2016, Scott and Anglin 2016; Mitchell et al. 2010). They also mark the changes in the child's formal position in society: while the birth parents' rights are restricted by the removal decision, she is looked after by the State (Bullock et al. 2006). Transitions also occur when the child exits care either when ageing out of care or when the needs for the placement expire. For care leavers, the mechanisms of transitions are away from the system, not into the system, and often into adulthood (Bengtsson et al. 2018).

In Finland, as elsewhere, the landscape of substitute care has been transformed several times during the history of child protection. The ideology of what is 'good substitute care' has changed, as have the ways that substitute care is provided, organised and funded. According to the present Finnish Child Welfare Act (417/2007), children and families should be supported in their own environment as much as possible, and a care order and out-of-home placement is an option only if the in-home services are not sufficient enough from the point of view of the child's best interest. Although in-home services make up the majority of child protection services, a good number of children still enter care, either by a care order decision, as part of voluntary supportive services, or as emergency cases. In 2016, 1.4 per cent of children (N=17,330) under the age of 18 were in out-of-home care, of whom 10,424 children were there based on a care order decision (Lastensuojelu 2016).

Although removals should always aim for a family reunification, as legislation does not recognise permanent placements, one third of children in out-of-home care in 2016 had been in out-of-home care at least half their lives (Forsell et al. 2018). During such long placements, children are likely to experience multiple removal decisions. Multiple removal decisions means multiple placements in different substitute homes, and eventually multi-local residency as suggested by some scholars (Forsberg and Ritala-Koskinen 2016). As family contact is important during the placements, children in out-of-home care visit their birth parents' (or other close people's) homes on a regular basis – sometimes weekly – which adds to the multiplicity of homes which children have in their everyday life (Pösö 2016). The multiplicity of homes has both sequential features as a result of different removal decisions, as well as parallel features as a result of the family contact principle. This all means multiple transitions into different homes.

In addition to the transition decisions made by the child protection agencies, there may also be unauthorized transitions in child protection due to children's own initiatives: for example, when children run away from their substitute homes and eventually are taken back there. These transitions are sensitive in many ways as children have very personal reasons for running away (Hoikkala and Kemppainen 2015). They may run away in order to escape the conditions in the substitute home or in order to look after their parents in their birth homes or to meet their friends.

If we revisit the terminology used for addressing the placements, as suggested by Andenaes (2011), the multiplicity of homes and transitions becomes a rights-based issue. As 'placement' is an administrative term, grounded in legislation, it easily invites further passive and depersonalizing vocabulary (Andenaes 2011). Such language about placements 'constructs the child as an object to be handled as a kind of parcel' (ibid.). The language hides the everyday experiences of children when they move from one home to another. When the gaze moves from 'parcels' closer to children and their lived experiences on the move, their rights, needs and wishes become topical. Consequently, the practices which exist to move the child from one home to another become important due to the recognition of the sensitive and intimate nature of the transitions. Children are, after all, in a very vulnerable situation when they are moved from their parents' care into public care, and, more concretely, when they enter a new substitute home, and when they move between different homes. They need adults to accompany them in these transitions. Most often the adults are parents or other family members, social workers or other carers. Sometimes they are accompanied by certain service-providers as will be demonstrated in the following.

Transport services in transitions

The transitions into and from substitute homes are examined here in a mundane, material way: how are children transported to and from the homes? Empirically the task is even narrower: how do transport services view children and their rights during transitions? The empirical analyses rests on the public presentation of these services, that is their web-based sites to present and market their services, the data of which is cross-read with some findings from our empirical work with children in care (Enroos et al. 2017). This is done because it is highly consequential for the service provision, and the service-users in particular, how the human service agencies put together the particulars of their clients and themselves in order to dispense the agency's services (Spencer 2001).

This particular choice of the empirical case of transport services was made for two reasons. First, the view on transport services highlights an on-going privatization tendency in child protection, well known in Finland, Sweden, Norway and the United Kingdom (Meagher et al. 2016). It is, in principle, the task of the public authorities to provide child protection services in Finland, therefore certain decisions of services, such as taking a child into care, can only be made by (certain) public authorities. The municipalities can, however, outsource services in child protection. This has resulted in a situation in which the majority of residential care institutions for children, among other services, have been outsourced in Finland. In 2018, 90 per cent of child protection residential units are provided by private (profit-making) enterprises (Porko et al. 2018). Privatization means a change in the way the public authorities consider their obligations in taking care of children in vulnerable situations as new rationalities in addition to the professional, legal and bureaucratic ones emerge to serve the logic of the markets (Forkby and Höjer 2018). The contracts between the municipalities and service providers follow competitive bidding in which factors such as the quality measurements and the costs of services play their part. This change has been addressed in research as being a 'dysfunctional service chain', which, according to Kouvonen (2012), means the following: first, 'partnership' provision of services as the public duties/ tasks to provide child protection services is outsourced to private agencies; second, contracts and competitive bidding shape services; and third, a fragmentation of services for children needing protection from the State. The concrete focus of this chapter, the transport services as one outsourced service, allows us to speculate how such services meet the rights of children.

Second, the choice to explore the public websites of the transport services needs to be explained. This approach rests on a public image of a *good* service provided for information and marketing purposes.[1] The websites exist to inform the child protection practitioners and administrators making contracts with service providers about the availability and nature of the services. Undoubtedly, the websites have been carefully put together to interact with different interest groups so as to (re) present the key elements of the transport service as a product to be included into the contracts and to be purchased in child protection. The websites do not inform how transports are carried out or what kind of other information is used when contracts between the municipalities and these service-providers are made. The empirical view can be said to be a limited snapshot. Snapshots of this kind can be relevant to cast light on the constantly changing services in which child protection legislation, policy principles and the needs and rights of children are negotiated.

In more concrete terms, the website material comes from two agencies: Agency A and Agency B. Agency A was introduced by social workers in a previous study as an example of the new – and in their view, contested – features in child protection. This agency 'Kultainen noutaja' (translation: 'Golden Retriever') has a public website (https://www.kultainennoutaja.fi/). For its part, Agency B, 'Turvallinen kuljetus' (translation: 'Safe Transport'), was found on the internet through a search engine, and its website (http://turvallinenkuljetus.fi/) is equally included in the data for analysis. The internet search did not result in any other agencies marketing their transport services for child protection. As there still may be other transport agencies for child protection not yet found for this explorative study, this analysis should not be treated as exhaustive. In addition, there is no information available as to how many children meet outsourced transport services in their transitions or how many municipalities use outsourced transport services. The analysis concentrates on the written representation of the services, and exclude the visual images on the websites presenting the staff members (e.g. the pictures of friendly, smiling men in their cars). The textual representation of the services is very condensed, with the messages being crystallized in short sentences and paragraphs. The written texts are read in a naturalistic way (Gubrium and Holstein 1997, pp. 19–37), taking them as they are, excluding the analysis of their rhetorical tools. The findings are grouped under two questions: how do the transport services profile themselves in the field of child protection, and how do they profile the child in their services?

Fragmentation: a service to support other services

The agencies 'A' and 'B' profile themselves as being clearly the agencies in and for child protection. They both state that their main task is to provide transport services to child protection, which the agency 'A' defines as being 'child protection work' and 'B' as a service to child protection actors.

More specifically, the situations in which transport services will be provided are presented in the following way. Agency 'A' provides services in runaway situations: if a child runs away from his/her substitute home, 'A' will find the child and bring him/her back home. The agency also mentions that they may provide other types of transition services as well, such as taking a child to the substitute home when requested by the child protection agency. Agency 'B' provides a wider range of services: first, they transport children to their home visits, hobbies and similar destinations, if the carers in the substitute home are too busy; second, they provide transport services in especially challenging situations (e.g. when the child's behaviour is violent or when the child has run away); and third, they provide safety training to the carers. In the latter services, the aim is to train carers to act well in situations which involve violence or the threat thereof.

Both agencies provide their services nationwide, 24/7 and they are registered as service-providers at the supervisory authority of private services in social welfare and health. Their staff have experience in child protection and/or training in social care and other competences (e.g. personal achievements in sport), as informed on the websites. The approach to work is not only based on safety principles, as described by the agency 'B', but also on crisis work and social guidance as stated explicitly by agency 'A'. 'A' also lists the laws which regulate their work. Indeed, the agencies' profiles include established professional and legal elements, well recognised in any child protection service.

It is clear that the website information positions these agencies on the continuum of child protection services: transporting children is framed as being very much about intense child protection, requiring special expertise. The situations in which their services would be required are distinctive due to the child's behaviour (violent or unpredictable behaviour and harmful behaviour are listed as examples on the websites), but their services may also be required due to the acute shortage of staff and carers in the substitute homes. This is to say that the substitute homes would not always have carers who have competences to work with children's problematic behaviour, or that the homes would not have enough carers. Private transport services are needed to fill both gaps. The presentation of the service profile includes, in fact, a statement about the fragmentation of child protection services: when taken into public care, children's care can be fragmented into little pieces due to the shortage of human resources and competences. Even the transitions into and from substitute care may be isolated as 'products' which can be bought and delivered.

Fragmentation, for its part, may treat children in care differently. The transport services target 'difficult situations'. From the children's point of view, those situations may mean that they are at their most vulnerable. The extract below, based on the study mentioned earlier (Enroos et al. 2017), describes a teenage girl's description of her transition from her previous substitute home into her present one. She was transferred by transport services. It cannot be known whether they are the agencies 'A' or 'B' but that is not important. She told the interviewer that she was not feeling well at the moment of the transition, she tried to run away, and she was aggressive, that is to say that she met the description of the target groups of 'A' and 'B' well. She objected to her removal to the particular new home. She was also in need of psychiatric care and was taken to hospital soon after the transition. The transition into the new substitute home was done by people other than those taking care of her (social workers, parents, carers at the substitute home); indeed, she could be seen as a parcel delivered to the substitute home.

> Young person: I didn't want to switch because I'd found good friends there. I'd just got used to being there, and changing is always so hard for me.... You have to go to a new place and start everything from scratch, and all that.
>
> Interviewer: Can you tell me about when you came here, to this unit?
>
> Young person: I don't know who I came with, it was some sort of transport service thing.... Some sort of men... I can't remember much about it. I did stay here for a little bit and then I had to go into that psychiatric hospital for four days. I could calm down a bit there then because it came so suddenly a couple of hours before I was supposed to leave.

Consequently, the practice to treat her as a 'parcel' in her very vulnerable state positions her differently from other children in the care system who might not be 'aggressive or runaways', as she described herself, or who are placed into homes which have a sufficient number of staff and carers. She was a difficult teenager and she was transported accordingly. Art. 2 CRC gives obligations to 'ensure that the child is protected against all forms of discrimination'. The extract above suggests that fragmentation of services may include elements which fragment the responses to children's needs and, accordingly, fragment their needs and rights.

The child to be delivered

Agencies 'A' and 'B' state on their websites that they aim to give good care to children who need to be accompanied to and from the substitute homes. Their high standard of service is described in different ways. Agency 'B' uses the term 'safe' to describe the good quality of transport 'even in difficult situations' which could mean, according to the website, 'risks to run away', 'the child's violence towards herself or others' and 'unpredictable behaviour'. Agency 'A' instead emphasises the situations being 'crisis', 'acute' and 'surprising' and including the factor of the child 'seriously harming her own life, health or development or those of others'. The descriptions by 'A' and 'B' do not address children in much detail, but emphasise the challenges the children's behaviour bring to transitions and transport. Children's rights are not mentioned. 'Safety' is important as children need to be safely moved from one place to another and the transport agencies help the child protection authorities to do that.

In research literature, there are calls to establish more agency-oriented and rights-based language in child protection (Goodyer 2016; Bessell and Gal 2009) in which the talk about children as parcels, as referenced earlier to Andenaes (2011), would not be taken for granted. The websites of the transport services do, however, employ such language. When doing that, they describe children as parcels so 'difficult' that their services and special competences become justified. As the parcels are 'difficult', the expectations for transport focus on safety: safe delivery of the parcel is the key criterion for good service. The categorization of children in the child protection system, in residential care especially, as being difficult and, in fact, more and more difficult, is a common way to address children in Finland (Hoikkala 2006) and this way of talking is employed on the 'A' and 'B' agencies' websites as well.

The representation of children as parcels to be delivered is, in fact, closely related to the fragmented services as approached in the websites. The representation of transport services as part of child protection does not include the other features of substitute care such as upbringing, care, looking after or support but just the transition moment into the homes. If the children become constructed as being 'difficult', it is likely that transitions into care will be difficult as well and the special input by the transport services would be needed. In consequence, parcel deliveries become an unavoidable element of child protection, and safety a taken-for-granted main criterion for those deliveries.

Fragmented services, children as parcels and discrimination

The images of services, service-users and service-providers are not meaningless; rather they powerfully influence different levels of child protection as they channel emotions and related moral judgements; that is, they contribute to the emotional politics of child protection (Warner 2015). In the case of transport services, the images of the services and children justify the very existence of such services, and make them unquestionable. Why should one be critical of any service using the metaphor of the friendliest and kindest dog (golden retriever) and which promises to take care of the safety of children? Such criticism would be even more difficult because the transport services build on the existing features of the present child protection system. Although the fragmentation of child protection into separate services and interrupted relations between practitioners and service-users has been critically described for a while in the reviews of the quality of child protection (e.g. Tuloksellisuuskertomus 2012), the privatisation tendency in general utilizes that fragmentation. Above we have seen how transport services do the same.

From the point of view of equality, however, the very construction of 'difficult' children and that of the shortages of human resources in child protection as legitimate grounds for the use of transport services is problematic. Those children who are difficult – who behave poorly and, for example, protest against the transition, as the girl in the previous extract did – are seen as the target group of fragmented transport services. These services are not for any child in child protection but for the 'difficult' ones, and for those who are placed in those substitute homes which have shortages of staff and competences to deal with the transitions of 'difficult' children.

If 'difficult children' are termed as children with complex needs (Thoburn 2010), the analysis above suggests that children with complex needs make up the target for outsourced services. This suggests that those children with very complex needs could be treated differently from children with less complex needs. Those children with lesser needs may be supported by their own social workers and carers in transitions and they may be placed in substitute homes which are staffed more sufficiently. Relations and relationship-based work is highly appreciated in child protection as the professional ideal (e.g. Ruch et al. 2010). When matching children, parents and substitute carers, for example, lot of attention is paid to the nature of the relations between them, and children, parents and the new substitute carers are ideally given enough time to learn to know each other before the transition into care (Pösö and Laakso 2016). Thus, the separation of the transition transport from other care relations of child protection is against that ideal.[2] Consequently, the imaginary platform created by the transport service websites indicates that children with complex needs *may* be treated in a less professional way because of their complex needs: safety matters more than caring relations. In other words, children with complex needs may be discriminated against compared to those with less complex needs. This is indeed against the very philosophy of child protection, which aims to protect the rights of (the most) vulnerable children.

The agencies 'A' and 'B' have been in the market already for several years so there must be a demand for such services. Obviously, there is reason to think that the images of services and children needing the services mirror the expectations of those child protection practitioners who make the decisions about whether to use their services or not. Indeed, the snapshot of the websites of the transport agencies thus informs us that a likelihood of discriminatory practices exists. This likelihood may, however, remain hidden in the midst of fragmented services and dynamics of outsourced service-provision in child protection and the overall vocabulary of delivering 'safe care' for children in transitions.

Concluding remarks

The Convention on the Rights of the Child, national child welfare legislation and universal professional codes of social work would make one assume that children with the most complex needs would invite the most alert and careful consideration of their rights (also) in the sensitive situations of transitions into/in public care. Unfortunately, the snapshot provided above suggests that this might not be necessarily the case: the children with most complex needs are portrayed for information and marketing purposes as being entitled to a narrower kind of service than other children, and the shortage of human resources of public care to support these children in transitions is taken for granted. The snapshot also highlights how transitions become distinctive segments of service, although for children themselves transitions may mean a holistic change of the everyday environment and social relations, including the care by adults. Transport services, a seemingly trivial matter among the complex legal, social and psychological matters of child protection, demonstrate how important it is that the non-discrimination principle is included in every part of child protection practice – even in the textual practices to communicate about the practices.

The very existence of the transport services builds on the fragmentation of child protection services and an on-going shift between the responsibilities of the state and the market (Meagher et al. 2016). Consequently, we have seen above that the implementation of the non-discrimination principle recognised in this empirical snapshot is related to the structure of service provision (e.g. the fragmentation of the services, the shift between the public and private responsibilities) and to policy (e.g. the privatisation of child protection services, a shortage of human resources in public child protection services) and it may be experienced as a lack of respect towards one's wishes, rights and needs in transitions. In order to abolish discrimination and the likelihood of discriminative practices in child protection, the mundane practices – including even the textual practices of websites – but also legislation and policy on the national and local levels, and related values, organisations and resources should be taken into account. Intersectional discrimination (Ravnbøl 2009), as recognised in the analysis above requires changes in many layers of the child protection system and beyond. This is to say that when children's rights to non-discrimination are to be fully implemented, the task should be shared by everyone and every practice involved directly or indirectly in child protection. The challenge is to strengthen rights-based child protection within other rationales and interests embedded in present child protection.

Notes

1 The methodological choice was influenced by cultural criminology (e.g. Ferrell et al. 2008) which emphasizes the role of representations – public images, pictures, films, social media – in our understanding of crimes and criminality, and thereby, the importance of studying the cultural representations of crime. In that view, ethnography, for example, could be a kind of 'instant ethnography' – instead of a long-lasting participation in a community – to capture the moments and images in which crime is culturally represented. In a similar way, public websites of social services can be used to capture the moments of the constantly changing provision of services.

2 As I have conducted earlier ethnographic studies in some residential care institutions, I remember vividly the practices to look after runaways in the early 1990s: it was the runaway's closest staff member plus other carers who went out to find the child who had run away. The understanding was that you had to know the child very well to make informed guesses where the child could be found. In addition, the moments of travelling back to the institution were seen as being very important for the child and the staff as the journey provided a good opportunity to discuss the reasons for running away. Indeed, if there was a word to describe the approach of that time, it was 'therapeutic', based on the relations between the child and staff.

References

Andenaes, A. 2011. From 'placement' to 'a child on the move': Methodological strategies to give children a more central position in Child Welfare Service. *Qualitative Social Work*, 11(5), 486–502.

Banks, S. 2016. Everyday ethics in professional life: Social work as ethics work. *Ethics and Social Welfare*, 10(1), 35–52.

Baugerud, G. and Melinder, A. 2011. Maltreated children's memory of stressful removals from their biological parents. *Applied Cognitive Psychology*, 26, 261–270.

Bengtsson, M., Sjöblom, Y. and Öberg, P. 2018. Young care leavers' expectations of their future: A question of time horizon. *Child & Family Social Work*, 23(2), 188–195.

Bessell, S. and Gal, T. 2009. Forming partnerships: The human rights of children in need of care and protection. *International Journal of Children's Rights*, 17, 283–298.

Besson, S. 2005. The principle of non-discrimination in the Convention on the Rights of the Child. *The International Journal of Children's Rights*, 13, 433–461.

Brady, E. and Gilligan, R. 2018. The life course perspective: An integrative research paradigm for examining the educational experiences of adult care leavers? *Children and Youth Services Review*, 87, 69–72.

Bullock, R., Courtney, M., Parker, R., Sinclair, I. and Thorburn, J. 2006. Can the corporate state parent? *Children and Youth Services Review*, 28, 1344–1358.

Burns, K., Pösö, T. and Skivenes, M. 2017. *Child Welfare Removals by the State*. Oxford: Oxford University Press.

Cameron, C., Hollingworth, K., Schoon, I., van SantenE., Schröer., W., Ristikari, T., Heino, T. and Pekkarinen, E. 2018. Care leavers in early adulthood: How do they fare in Britain, Finland and Germany? *Children and Youth Services Review*, 87, 163–172.

Clark, C. 2002, Identity, Individual Rights and Social Justice. In R. Adams, L. Dominelli and M. Payne. (eds) *Critical Practice in Social Work* (pp. 38–45). Basingstoke: Palgrave Macmillan.

Coman, W. and Devaney, J. 2011. Reflecting on outcomes for looked-after children: An ecological perspective. *Child Care in Practice*, 17(1), 37–53.

Davidson, G., Bunting, L., Bywaters, P., Featherstone, B. and McCartan, C. 2017. Child welfare as justice: Why are we not effectively addressing inequalities? *British Journal of Social Work*, 47(6), 1641–1651.

Devaney, J. 2004. Relating outcomes to objectives in child protection. *Child and Family Social Work*, 9, 27–38.

Enroos, R., Heino, T. and Pösö, T. (eds) 2017. *Huostaanotto. Lastensuojelun vaativin tehtävä* [Care Order. The Most Challenging Task in Child Protection]. Tampere: Vastapaino.

FernandezE. 2009. Children's well-being in care: Evidence from a longitudinal study of outcomes. *Children and Youth Services Review*, 31, 1092–1100.

Ferrell, J., Hayward, K. and Young, J. 2008. *Cultural Criminology*. London: Sage.

Forkby, T. and Höjer, S. 2018. Placering I köpt vård – Om rationell styrning och kontrakstproblem på den sociala barnavårdsmarknaden [Placement in purchased care]. In M. Sallnäes and S. Wiklund (eds) *Socialtjänstmarknden*. [The Social Service Market] (pp. 160–182). Stockholm: Liber.

Forsberg, H. and Ritala-Koskinen, A. 2016. Multi-local residency of children through the case descriptions of Finnish child welfare social workers. *European Journal of Social Work*. doi:10.1080/13691457.2016.1185699.

Forsell, M., Heino, T. and Kuoppala, T. 2018. Kodin ulkopuolelle sijoitettujen lasten sijoitusten kestot 2016 [The lengths of the out-of-home placements of children in

2016]. *Tilastoraportti*, 9. Helsinki: THL. Retrieved May 24, 2018 from: http://urn.fi/URN:NBN:fi-fe2018042318219.

Gal, T. and Duramy, B. (eds) 2015. *International Perspectives and Empirical Findings on Child Participation*. New York: Oxford University Press.

Gilbert, N., Parton, N. and Skivenes, M. 2011. *Child Protection Systems: International Trends and Orientations*. New York: Oxford University Press.

Goodyer, A. 2016. Children's accounts of moving to a foster home. *Child and Family Social Work*, 21, 188–197.

Gubrium, J. and Holstein, J. 1997. *The New Language of Qualitative Method*. New York: Oxford University Press.

Heino, T. and Bardy, M. 2014. Lastensuojelu on räätälöityä eriarvon tausta [Child protection is tailored counteracting against inequalities]. In: *Eriarvoistuva lapsuus. Lapsiasiavaltuutetun vuosikirja*. [Inequalizing childhood. The Year Book by the Children's Ombudsman]. Retrieved on May 29, 2018 from: http://lapsiasia.ssthosting.fi/wp-content/uploads/2014/12/Vuosikirja-2014.pdf

Hoikkala, S. 2006. Onko lastensuojelun laitoshuollon asiakkaista tullut vaikeahoitoisia ja erityisen huolenpidon tarpeessa olevia lapsia? [Have the children in child protection residential care become difficult to treat and at need of special care?] *Nuorisotutkimus*, 24(2), 83–87.

Hoikkala, S. and Kemppainen, M. 2015. Running away from children's residential care: The Finnish case. *International Journal of Child, Youth and Family Studies*, 6(3), 466–477.

Ife, J. 2001. *Human Rights and Social Work. Towards Rights-Based Practice*. New York: Cambridge University Press.

Kouvonen, P. 2012. Foster care partnerships in Finland 1990–2010: From social task to ensuring better market share? *Law and Childhood Studies. Current Legal Studies*, 14, 487–506.

Lastensuojelu [Child Welfare]. 2016. Tilastoraportti 43. Suomen virallinen tilasto [Official Statistics Finland]. Helsinki: Terveyden ja hyvinvoinnin laitos.

Meagher, G., Lundström, T., Sallnäs, M. and Wiklund, S. 2016. Big business in a thin market: Understanding the privatization of residential care for children and youth in Sweden. *Social Policy & Administration*, 50(7), 805–823.

Mitchell, M. and Kuczynski, L. 2010. Does anyone know what is going on? Examining children´s lived experience of the transition into foster care. *Children and Youth Services Review*, 32, 437–444.

Mitchell, M., Kuczynski, L., Tubbs, C. and Ross, C. 2010. We care about care: Advice by children in care for children in care, foster parents and child welfare workers about the transition into foster care. *Child & Family Social Work*, 15(2), 176–185.

Murphy, Y., Hunt, V., Zajicek, A., Norris, A. and HamiltonL. 2009. *Incorporating Intersectionality in Social Work Practice, Research, Policy, and Education*. Washington: NASW Press.

PhoenixA. 2016. Diversity, difference and belonging in childhood: Issues for foster care and identities. *Social Work and Society*, 14(2).

Porko, P., Heino, T. and Eriksson, P. 2018. Selvitys yksityisistä lastensuojelun yksiköistä [Report about the private child protection units]. *Working paper 28*. Helsinki. THL. Retrieved on June 8, 2018 from http://urn.fi/URN:ISBN:978-952-343-131-7.

Pösö, T. 2016. Managing Complexity of Family Contact in Child Welfare. In J. Gubrium, T. Andreassen and P. Solvang (eds). *Reimagining the Human Service Relationship* (pp. 178–194). New York: Columbia University Press.

Pösö, T. and Laakso, R. 2016. Matching children and substitute homes: Some theoretical and empirical notions. *Child & Family Social Work*, 21(3), 307–316.

Ravnbøl, C. 2009. Intersectional discrimination against children: discrimination against Romani children and anti-discrimination measures to address child trafficking. *Innocenti Working Paper No. IDP 2009–2011*. Florence: UNICEF Innocenti Research Centre.

Ruch, G., Turney, D. and Ward, A. 2010. *Relationship-based Social Work*. London: Jessica Kingsley.

Saarikallio-Torp, M., Heino, T., Hiilamo, H., Hytti, H. and Rajavaara, M. 2010. Lapset huostassa, vanhemmat ahdingossa [Children in care, parents in trouble]. In: U. Hämäläinen and O. Kangas (eds) *Perhepiirissä* [In Family Circles] (pp. 178–194). Helsinki: Kela.

Sallnäs, M., Wiklund, S. and Lagerlöf, H. 2012. Welfare resources among children in care. *European Journal of Social Work*, 15(4), 467–483.

ScottA. and Anglin, J. P. 2016. *We Don't Feel that Love: Retrospective Reflections on the Experiences of Removal, Transition and Trauma*. Victoria, BC: University of Victoria.

Spencer, J. W. 2001. Self-Presentation and Organizational Processing in Human Service Agency. In J. Gubrium and J. Holstein (eds). *Institutional Selves. Troubled Identities in a Postmodern World* (pp. 158–175). New York: Oxford University Press.

Thoburn, J. 2010. Towards knowledge-based practice in complex child protection cases: A research-based expert briefing. *Journal of Children's Services*, 5(1), 9–24.

Tisdall, K. and Davis, J. 2004. Making a difference? Bringing children's and young people's views into policy-making. *Children & Society*, 18(2), 131–142.

Tuloksellisuuskertomus. Lastensuojelu [Performance Management Report. Child Welfare]. 2012. *Report 6*. Helsinki: National Audit Office of Finland.

Warner, J. 2015. *The Emotional Politics of Social Work and Child Protection*. Bristol: Policy Press.

Whittaker, J., del Valle, J. and Holmes, L. 2015. *Therapeutic Residential Care For Children and Youth. Developing Evidence-Based International Practice*. London: Jessica Kingsley.

Zeijlmans, K., Lopez, M., Grietens, H., and Knorth, E. 2018. 'Nothing goes as planned': Practitioners reflect on matching children and foster families. *Child & Family Social Work*, 23(3), 458–465.

7 That time of the month

Discrimination against girls who cannot afford sanitary health care

Lize Mills and Comine Howe

Introduction: a monthly reality

Poverty is a harsh reality for many South Africans. According to a 2011 Report by Statistics SA, 45.5 percent of South Africans are considered "poor" and as such unable to purchase necessary food items. 32.3 percent live under the Lower Bound Poverty Line, which means that they can afford essential food items, but in order to afford necessary non-food items, they would have to sacrifice the purchase of certain food items (Statistics South Africa 2014). Even harsher a reality is that poverty appears to discriminate between the two sexes and has a disproportionate impact on women: in the most recent SANHANES study, it was reported that more women (15.5 percent) than men (4.7 percent) fell into the monthly income level of less than R800 (€50) (Shisana et al. 2014).[1] One of the consequences of this reality is that a large number of women and girls cannot effectively manage their health care in respect of menstrual hygiene (APHRC 2010, p. 3). It is estimated that a third of South African females are unable to afford sanitary towels and are forced to use alternatives which are often unhygienic (Ramathumba 2015, p. 5). This has the effect that, on a monthly basis, an estimated one-third of female learners in South African schools do not attend school when they are menstruating since they cannot afford sanitary pads or tampons. If it is borne in mind that women use an average of 25 sanitary towels during their menstruation, and that the average price of a packet of 16 sanitary pads is R23 (€1.50), it is estimated that the 15.5 percent of women whose monthly income is approximately R800, spends about 5 percent of their income on their period.[2]

An additional factor which causes an increase to the cost of sanitary health care products, lies in the fact that such products are subject to Value Added Tax (VAT).[3] As of April 2018, VAT in South Africa is levied at 15 percent, even though certain – mostly food – items that are considered necessary goods, are not taxed.[4] On 24 October 2018, the South African Minister of Finance, Mr Tito Mboweni, announced in his medium-term budget policy statement that from 1 April 2019, sanitary pads will be zero-rated for purposes of VAT (National Treasury 2018, p. 23). The VAT exemption, however, will only apply to sanitary pads and not other products such as tampons or menstrual cups.

The lack of sufficient sanitation and sanitary wear is not unique to South Africa. Many studies have proven that girls in Ethiopia (Tegegne and Sisay 2014),[5] Kenya

(APHRC 2010), Nepal (Oster and Thornton 2011), Cambodia (Sperling and Winthorp 2016, p. 133),[6] and several other developing countries are absent from school during their menstruation period.[7] Girls who do not have access to sanitary pads, tampons or menstrual cups experience a great deal of anxiety, discomfort and embarrassment. A pilot study in Kenya identified stigmatisation of menstruation as a barrier to accessing information regarding menses. In Zimbabwe it was found that only 18 percent of women used conventional sanitary pads, whilst 45 percent indicated that they would use old clothes and rags to manage their period. Many girls stipulated the reasons for not using conventional sanitary pads were a lack of knowledge as to how to use them, the shame they experienced when purchasing pads from shops, and in particular, high cost.[8] In addition to the fact that girls do not attend school due to a lack of sanitary wear, the problem is further exacerbated by the fact that many schools do not have private, working sanitation facilities (The South African Human Rights Commission 2014, p. 57).[9]

This lack of facilities, as well as the lack of adequate sanitary supplies, seem to contribute to the absenteeism of many girls in schools when they feel there is no other option but to remain out of the public eye during menstruation. The reality is that some girls may miss up to 3 months of school per year due to a physical fact unique to females. Because of the biological reality of their sex, as well as their socio-economic status, some girls face a level of discrimination that impacts upon many of their fundamental rights. The lack of access to sanitary wear deters women from making decisions that shape the rest of their lives, such as the choice of attending school and gaining access to education. As a result, when girls do not have access to sanitary wear, it is not merely one right that is infringed, but a plethora of rights.[10] This monthly biological event causes girls, and only girls, to suffer a violation of their rights to, *inter alia*, dignity, bodily integrity, health and education. Discrimination based on sex or any other status is explicitly forbidden in terms of Article 2 of the Convention on the Rights of the Child.[11]

A framework of rights

The right to non-discrimination

To discriminate means to treat differently, to distinguish or single out certain people because of certain characteristics which they possess.[12] In terms of Article 2 of the CRC and Article 3 of the African Charter on the Rights and Welfare of the Child,[13] State Parties must ensure and respect children's rights without discrimination of any kind. Phrased differently, the CRC and the ACRWC provide that Member States must guarantee that all the rights that all children have, are effected, without denying one group certain rights because this group experiences a monthly biological reality.

At para 20 of its General Comment No 20, the UN Committee on Economic, Social and Cultural Rights (CESCR) explains that "[n]on-discrimination and equality are fundamental components of international human rights law and essential to the exercise and enjoyment of economic, social and cultural rights"

(CESCR 2009). In fact, discrimination is prohibited in terms of The Universal Declaration of Human Rights, 1948, the International Covenant on Civil and Political Rights, 1966, the International Covenant on Economic, Social and Cultural Rights, 1966 (ICESCR), the European Convention for the Protection of Human Rights and Fundamental Freedoms, 1971, the American Convention on Human Rights 1969, and the African Charter on Human and Peoples' Rights 1981. Another important instrument of international law, namely the Convention on the Elimination of Discrimination against Women,[14] at Article 1, describes "discrimination against women" as:

> [A]ny distinction, exclusion or restriction made on the basis of sex which has the effect or purpose of impairing or nullifying the recognition, enjoyment or exercise by women, irrespective of their marital status, on a basis of equality of men and women, of human rights and fundamental freedoms in the political, economic, social, cultural, civil or any other field.

This treaty furthermore provides for the enactment of legislation that will eradicate discrimination against women, and in particular calls for the recognition of particular circumstances which only women may face in order to effect their right to equality.[15] In addition, it must be emphasised that one of the cornerstones of the South African democracy is the right to equality, enshrined in section 9 of the Constitution.[16] It provides that "[e]quality includes the full and equal enjoyment of all rights and freedoms"[17] and that no one, including the state, may "unfairly discriminate directly or indirectly against anyone on one or more grounds, including … sex".[18] It also provides that, in order to "promote the achievement of equality, legislative and other measures designed to protect or advance persons, or categories of persons, disadvantaged by unfair discrimination may be taken". Therefore, it is clear that the South African Constitution also enshrines the principle of substantive equality.[19]

Indeed, it has been accepted worldwide that the obligation not to discriminate is not a passive one (Committee on the Rights of the Child 2013, p. 11) but that, in order to achieve equality, differences must be recognised and understood, in order to remove factors that may cause the dissimilar treatment of people. Substantive equality requires the elimination of barriers which exclude certain groups from participation in the workplace or, in the case of children, from school and other activities. The CESCR has explained that "[m]erely addressing formal discrimination will not ensure substantive equality as envisaged and defined by article 2 (of the ICESCR) but that discrimination in practice requires paying sufficient attention to groups of individuals which suffer historical or persistent prejudice instead of merely comparing the formal treatment of individuals in similar situations" (CESCR 2009). This will require States parties to adopt special measures, both on a permanent or semi-permanent basis, to diminish conditions that perpetuate discrimination.

In South Africa, the Constitutional Court has confirmed the importance of substantive equality on numerous occasions, rather notably in the decision of

President of the Republic of South Africa v Hugo where O'Regan J explained it in the following way:

> [A]lthough the long term goal of our constitutional order is equal treatment, insisting upon equal treatment in established inequality may well result in the entrenchment of that inequality.
>
> (*President of the Republic of South Africa v Hugo* 1997)

As a result, it must be realised that the equal treatment of people in different circumstances may perpetuate inequality. In certain circumstances, different or additional mechanisms may have to be put into place in order to create equality and justice. Therefore, the South African Constitutional Court has developed a transformative approach to substantive equality in terms of which one has to locate an understanding of disadvantages within systemic inequalities, develop new normative interpretations of equality and pragmatic remedies which will eradicate social and economic disadvantage which will, in the end, establish "real change" (Albertyn 2007, p. 258).

Although Article 2 of the CRC does not explicitly promote substantive equality to the extent that some of the other legal documents mentioned above do so, it is submitted that the provision of the CRC cannot be interpreted in any other way. The inference must be drawn that special and additional measures have to be introduced to ensure that all of the rights contained in the CRC are effectively implemented for all children. This may have the effect that additional services be provided to one vulnerable group, in order to eradicate the effect that biology has on the realisation of rights.

The right to social security

In addition to the above, it is submitted that this interpretation is in line with Article 26 of the CRC which provides that measures of social security and social insurance must be used to achieve the full realisation of children's rights. The CRC prescribes that the resources and circumstances of the child (as well as those persons responsible for the care of the child) be taken into account in considering an application for benefits made by or on behalf of the child.

The right to education

In terms of Article 28 of the CRC, Article 11 of the ACRWC and section 29 of the South African Constitution, every child has the right to education. It is particularly important to note that in terms of Article 28(1)(*e*) of the CRC, Member States are obliged to "[t]ake measures to encourage regular attendance at schools and the reduction of drop-out rates".[20] Article 11(1)(*e*) of the ACRWC places emphasis on the distinct needs of girls in that it requires Member States to "take special measures in respect of female, gifted and disadvantaged children, to ensure equal access to education for all sections of the community". In this respect, it is significant to note one of the statements made by the Committee on the Rights of the Child in its General Comment 1 of 2001: *The Aims of Education*. It reads as follows:

> Discrimination on the basis of any of the grounds listed in article 2 of the Convention, … offends the human dignity of the child and is capable of undermining or even destroying the capacity of the child to benefit from educational opportunities. … To take an extreme example, gender discrimination can be reinforced by practices such as a curriculum which is inconsistent with the principles of gender equality, by arrangements which limit the benefits girls can obtain from the educational opportunities offered, and by unsafe or unfriendly environments which discourage girls' participation. … All such discriminatory practices are in direct contradiction with the requirements in article 29 (1)(a) that education be directed to the development of the child's personality, talents and mental and physical abilities to their fullest potential.
>
> (Committee on the Rights of the Child 2001)

Fifteen years later, the Committee on the Rights of the Child reiterated this imperative by expressing their concern at the inability of many Member States to keep girls in school beyond primary education (Committee on the Rights of the Child 2016). The Committee once again called for investment in strategies and effective measures "that promote positive gender relations and social norms; … including within schools; and … the economic empowerment of women, to overcome the legal, political, cultural, economic and social barriers that represent barriers for girls" (Committee on the Rights of the Child 2016). The Committee, in its General Comment, listed a number of contributing factors, which it observed contributes to the absenteeism of girls. This list includes "fees and associated costs; … lack of adequate and safe sanitation facilities for girls; … [and] environments not conducive to girls' inclusion and safety" (Committee on the Rights of the Child 2016). Unfortunately, the Committee fails to specifically mention the effect which a lack of sanitary pads and tampons may have on girls.[21]

The right to health

From the amount of international instruments that enshrine the right to health, it is clear that an explicit and shared normative framework exists in this regard.[22] One of the general comments by the Committee on Economic, Social and Cultural Rights (CESCR) explains that right to health does not merely refer to the right to not be sick, but rather that the right encompasses an array of socio-economic factors that are conducive to promoting a safe and healthy environment in which people can lead a healthy, sanitary and dignified life.[23] The right to health entitles persons to a health care system that provides the enjoyment of a variety of facilities and goods.[24] Therefore, it may be deduced that a right to sanitary wear emanates from the right to health care, due to the detriments that arise to health in the absence of sufficient sanitary wear. The General Comment by the CESCR emphasises the special attention that must be given to children, especially young girls, in providing them with health care in the promotion of their physical and mental development.[25] It is also important to note that the CESR is of the view that one of the core obligations in terms of the ICESCR is that governments must ensure "the right of access to health facilities, goods and services on a *non-discriminatory* basis, especially for *vulnerable* or marginalized groups" (CESCR 2000).[26]

In addition, the Committee on the Rights of the Child emphasises that the right to health should not be undermined as a result of discrimination, which is a factor that contributes to vulnerability (Committee on the Rights of the Child 2013). In its General Comment on the implementation of the rights of the child during adolescence, the Committee makes reference to the importance of having access to "free, confidential, adolescent-responsive and non-discriminatory sexual and reproductive health services, information and education, available both online and in person, including on … menstrual hygiene", emphasising that "unequal access by adolescents to such information, commodities and services amounts to discrimination" (Committee on the Rights of the Child 2016).

The right to dignity and bodily integrity

Another immediate harm is due to the shame and indignation experienced by teenage girls in a school environment where many of their peers will ridicule and mock them, due to their own lack of knowledge about menstruation. As is evident from the above, the right to health, both in its realisation, as well as a means of realising other human rights, is closely related to rights such as the right to dignity, the right to privacy, education and equality.[27] The right to dignity is a source of all other personal rights in the Bill of Rights of the South African Constitution and when this right is infringed, it cuts at the core of the founding constitutional principles (*S v Makwanyane* 1995).

The best interests of the child

Over and above these rights, Article 3 of the CRC provides that the best interests of the child shall be a primary consideration in all matters affecting children. The Committee on the Rights of the Child has explained that the concept of the best interests of the child is a multifaceted one existing as (a) a substantive right; (b) a fundamental, interpretative legal principle and; (c) as a rule of procedure (Committee on the Rights of the Child 2013, p. 4). It has also stressed that at all stages of the adoption of laws, policies, strategies, programmes, plans, budgets, legislative and budgetary initiatives and guidelines concerning children, due consideration must be given to their best interests (Committee on the Rights of the Child 2013, p. 5). Such an assessment and determination of the best interests of the child require procedural guarantees. The justification for a decision must show that the right has been explicitly taken into account (Committee on the Rights of the

Child 2013, p. 4). This means that the child's best interests must be appropriately integrated and consistently applied in all implementation measures. Furthermore, it must be explained how the right has been respected in the decision, that is, what has been considered to be in the child's best interests; what criteria it is based on; and how the child's interests have been weighed against other considerations, be they broad issues of policy or individual cases (Committee on the Rights of the Child 2013, p. 4).

Realising rights by recognising difference

South Africa ratified the CRC on 16 June 1995 and the ACRWC in 2000 (UN Human Rights Office of the High Commissioner 2018). In terms of section 39(1)(*b*) of the Constitution, when interpreting the Bill of Rights of the Constitution, a court, forum or tribunal must take international law into account. As a result, provisions of, for example, the CRC and ACRWC[28] must be considered when giving effect to rights contained in the South African Constitution, including the rights to dignity, bodily integrity, health and education. Despite the fact that the South African government has promised to uphold, *inter alia*, Article 2 of the CRC in ensuring that all children, without discrimination based on the child's sex, are entitled to implementation of their rights, the State is not giving effect to the rights of girls by failing to provide sanitary health care products to girl children who cannot afford to buy it for themselves. As a result, it is submitted that the South African government is discriminating against girls by failing to take reasonable legislative and other measures to ensure that the rights set forth in the CRC are realised, and as a result failing in its international obligations. The State is failing to provide products to girls that will encourage their school attendance. In fact, the government is adding to the cost of such products, increasing its unavailability, by charging VAT for these monthly necessities but that are only used by one sex. If it is furthermore borne in mind that in June 2017 the National Department of Basic Education of South Africa introduced a policy of providing free condoms and HIV-testing at all schools but not for sanitary health care products, the level of discrimination is increased.[29] Whilst it is true that condoms and programmes of sex education may prevent pregnancies of school going girls, it is also a fact that all girls who have reached puberty menstruate on a monthly basis, while not all girls are sexually active.

One of the immediate health implications young girls will suffer when they do not have access to sanitary wear, is that, since they are still developing physically, they are more susceptible to infections that may render them incapable of healthy physical development. Therefore, it is submitted that the South African government, by failing to provide indigent girls with sanitary health care products and facilities, is violating the right to health, enshrined in the Constitution in sections 27 and 28.

Section 27(1)(*a*) of the South African Constitution provides for the qualified right of access to health care whilst section 28(1)(*c*) grants all children the unqualified right to health care and social services. Section 27 provides that the state must take reasonable legislative and other measures to provide access to health care, "within its available resources" but s 28(1)(*c*) does not restrict a child's right to basic health care services in this way. As a result, it may not hide behind an excuse of a lack of financial resources as to why sanitary health care products are not provided to school girls. The failure of the state to effect the socio-economic rights of adults due to limited resources and budgetary constraints may only be deemed justified if it can be proven to be reasonable (*Minister of Health v Treatment Action Campaign (2)* 2002).[30] However, a higher standard of reasonableness exists in adjudicating state action regarding the socio-economic rights of children (Currie and De Waal 2008, pp. 610–613). In *Minister of Health v Treatment Action Campaign (2)* it was found that the vulnerability of children in society necessitates greater consideration for the realisation of their socio-economic rights by the state.[31] The enforcement of children's socio-economic rights require greater expediency in their implementation, as well as development of programmes to realise such rights, considering the pernicious nature of harm induced during childhood by a lack of socio-economic rights (Creamer 2002, p. 17).

The effects of a lack of sanitary products not only manifest as violations of the child's immediate well-being, but they also have a detrimental impact on the child's development and future capacity for autonomy. The future implications are to be found in young girls' inability to attend school during menstruation, which places them in a far more vulnerable group as education being undertaken by adults is not necessarily of a primary or basic nature, resulting in disadvantages for both future education and employment. In the instance that the sex of a child and the bodily functions that accompany only that sex, are not catered for and it leads to an inability to attend school, it cannot be seen as anything but discrimination and a violation of a girl's right to education. In its statement provided above, the Committee on the Rights of the Child explained that any discrimination in relation to the right to education also violates one of the aims of education, contained in Article 29(1) of the CRC. Girls, who cannot afford to manage their menstrual cycles effectively, in this way, are also denied the opportunity to develop their personalities, talents and mental and physical abilities.

In South Africa, the right to basic education enshrined in the Constitution, is an unqualified right to which all persons are entitled to.[32] Moreover, the right to education has to take equity into account in order to be fulfilled.[33] In the South African National Gender Framework it is stipulated that in order for any policy regarding the education of women to be deemed effective in the promotion of gender equality, special consideration of the difficulties encountered by women in attending school should be taken into consideration (The Office on the Status of Women 2000, pp. 5, 12). It can thus be said that the principle of substantive equality must also be effected in this sphere. Therefore, when women are granted access to education but without taking into account the factors that deter them from having the same learning experience as their male counterparts, it cannot be considered an equal fulfilment of the right to education.

Furthermore, it is submitted that the lack of access to sanitary wear limits girls' right to dignity and to be considered as worthy of respect and concern. It was described above that menstruation is the cause of much humiliation and stigmatisation. In many countries and cultures, menstrual blood and menstruating females are regarded as dirty and impure.[34] As a result, girls and women are often embarrassed about menstruation, and adolescent girls attach negative connotations with puberty and growing up. It may also affect their self-esteem.[35] Even when girls do attend school, the stigma and shame associated with menstruation may also affect girls' well-being and performance in school. Girls may be worried about leakage, especially when using alternative sources as sanitary products, and this may affect girls' ability to concentrate and participate in the classroom.[36] Moreover, it must be borne in mind that due to the imbalance in power-relations in many communities, sanitary products are often considered an unnecessary expense at the policy, community, or household level, particularly when finances are limited and/or controlled by men (PATH 2016, p. 3).[37] These discriminatory and degrading attitudes towards women and girls, due to stigmatisation of a natural bodily function, violates their right to dignity and bodily integrity.

The South African government is failing to consider the best interests of girl children who cannot afford to buy the necessary products to manage their menstrual health care. It is discriminating against girls by ignoring the rights of girls to receive the same level of uninterrupted education as boys, to develop their personalities, talents and mental and physical abilities in the same way that those of boys are being developed. By ignoring the monthly reality which adolescent girls have to face, the State is disregarding the simple necessities that they require to live a life of dignity and self-worth. It is failing to implement laws, policies, strategies, programmes, plans, and legislative and budgetary initiatives and guidelines which consider the best interests of girl children who cannot afford to buy sanitary health care products. The South African government has never explained why it chose to rather provide free condoms to schools, instead of sanitary health care products, and by failing to do so, the South African government has never explained how girl children's interests have been weighed against other considerations.

It is submitted that with respect to the provision of sanitary wear to girls who cannot afford to buy it themselves, it is definitely time that the executive and legislative arms of the South African government too need to understand these systemic inequalities and implement pragmatic remedies which will effect real change. There finally needs to be delivery on the number of promises made that indigent girls will be provided with sanitary health care products which will enable them to attend school. The first public notice given to the need for free sanitary pads, for poor women and girls, was in January 2011. The then president of South Africa, Jacob Zuma, at the Peter Mokaba Stadium in Polokwane, insisted that government would be promoting a campaign supporting free sanitary towels for poor women (Mathlala 2011). A month later, during the State of the Nation address, president Zuma reiterated the government's concern for poor women and girls and stipulated that health rights of women should be broadened to include sanitary towels for the poor (Zuma 2011). The only other glimmer of support was found in a speech by Buti Manamela, then Deputy Minister in the Presidency, at the launch of a non-government organisation, Dignity Dreams, in 2015 (Manamela 2015). Unfortunately, little tangible change has been effected in promoting access to sanitary wear (Sefali 2015). There has been no legislative or policy reform to guarantee sanitary health care products, and only one provincial department of education has introduced a measure of relief. In January 2017 the KwaZulu-Natal Department of Education launched a project for the provision of sanitary pads to indigent girl learners in selected quintile 1–4 schools in grade 4–12 (Staff Reporter 2017). This project has been praised and lauded for the initiative that explicitly "seeks to reduce the drop-out rate of girl learners, caused by missing out on school, due to not being able to afford sanitary pads" (Department of Education Kwa-Zulu Natal 2017). It can only be hoped that the National Department of Education will soon follow with a nationwide policy that will also seek to remove the barriers that prevent substantive equality in South African schools. Apparently this wish will not be soon fulfilled, however, if the statement by the Western-Cape Education department, explaining that there "are no plans to roll out free sanitary pads for schoolgirls in the Western Cape" is to be believed (Thembo 2017).

Conclusion

Approximately every 28 days, most women and some girl children experience the shedding of the lining of their uterus (Chamberlain 2017). For most of these females, this experience is uncomfortable and sometimes painful (Crosta 2017). For a number of indigent women and girls, however, the experience is completely debilitating, often due to a lack of sanitary health care products and safe and clean sanitation services, and also due to social discriminatory attitudes and stigmatisation.

This chapter has shown that the lack of access to adequate sanitary wear not only affects girl children's dignity and self-worth, but exacerbates the feminisation of poverty by infringing their right to education and health and negatively affects the realisation of gender equality. Article 2 of the CRC and other instruments of international law clearly require that governments ensure that all rights are effectively implemented without discrimination. In some instances, in order to eliminate conditions which perpetuate discrimination, special measures have to be adopted to achieve substantive equality. In the case of children, the obligation is even more urgent: children should be afforded special consideration, over and above adults in the realisation of their rights, due to their vulnerability and dependence on adult care, and as children have limited capacity in identifying, realising and enforcing their socio-economic rights (Nolan 2011, pp. 14–16). Girl children, who cannot afford sanitary wear, are afforded an unqualified right in terms of section 28(1)(*c*) of the South African Constitution. They have a direct and immediate claim upon the State for the fulfilment of their right to health care, which is not dependent on the progressive realisation of the State's ability within its means, as can be argued is the case for adult women. It is our argument that the South African government must treat girls differently but with the purpose to enable them to manage their menstrual health effectively and attend school. The State must provide girls, who cannot afford to do so themselves, with the monthly necessities which will empower them to develop to their full abilities, in the same way that boys are allowed to do.

Notes

1 The SANHANES study explains further that 14.9 percent of males, but 9.2 percent of females earned R3 201 to R12 800 per month, whereas 5.2 percent of men and 2.2 percent of women's monthly income ranged between R12 801 to R51 200. A total of 32.5 percent of respondents reported no income. The reported source of income showed further disparity between sexes where more males (45.5 percent) as opposed to females (32.4 percent) received salaries and wages and where more females (27.4 percent) relied on pensions, grants and UIF than males (14.6 percent).

2 Furthermore, the monthly child care grant in South Africa currently amounts to R400, whilst pensioners receive R1 690 and disability and care dependency grants stands at R1 600. 16.5 million people from a population of 51.8 million are recipients of social assistance grants.

3 This chapter will not focus on the discriminatory nature of imposing "luxury taxes" on necessary items such as sanitary health care products that are only used by women. For an insightful contribution in this regard, see (Crawford and Spivack 2017).

4 These goods include brown bread, dried mealies and beans, lentils, tinned pilchards or sardinella, rice, fresh fruit and vegetables, vegetable oil, milk, eggs, and illuminating paraffin (The South African Institute of Chartered Accountants 2008).

5 Ethiopian research indicated that in a pilot study of rural girls in Northeast Ethiopia 55.6 percent of girls used rags and underwear as soak ups, which they would wash and re-use. Many stipulated the reason for not using conventional sanitary pads was due to high cost, lack of knowledge how to use them and the shame they experienced purchasing them from shops.

6 The authors explain that in Cambodia 31 percent of schools do not have a toilet on school grounds, suggesting that post pubescent girls must leave school in order to effectively manage their period. This information was gathered by (Connolly and Marni 2013).

7 See further studies referred to by (Sperling and Winthorp 2016) and (Tamiru et al. 2015), as cited by (PATH 2016). Some studies, however, found that the provision of sanitary products does not necessarily cause an improvement in school attendance. See in this regard (Ackerman 2015).

8 In a pilot study done in 2015 in the rural Vhembe district in Limpopo, South Africa, girls were interviewed in respect of their practices surrounding their menstruation period. Only 37 percent of the girls stipulated that they used conventional sanitary pads and changed them twice a day, even though sanitary pads should be changed every 4 to 8 hours to prevent infection (Ramathumba 2015, p. 4). 55 percent of the girls admitted to using cloths and rags which they would wash, but due to embarrassment they felt because of stigmatisation in their community, they would not hang these items outside to dry, but would rather hide them in their homes. Others would use hand towels filled with sand as a replacement for sanitary pads (Ramathumba 2015, pp. 4–9). Some girls confessed to "recycling" tampons, sanitary pads and even nappies (Bernardo 2016).

9 The urgent need for sanitation facilities at certain schools was recently illustrated by the tragic deaths of two young children who drowned in pit toilets in the Eastern Cape. President Cyril Ramaphosa called upon the Department of Basic Education to address the dire situation as a matter of grave importance (Etheridge 2018).

10 The notion of interdependence and indivisibility of all human rights is firmly established in international law. See, for example, Tobin 2006, p. 281 explaining how this guiding principle is derived from the Vienna Declaration and Programme of Action adopted at the World Conference on Human Rights in 1993. In (*Khosa v Minister of Social Development* 2004) the Constitutional Court emphasised the interconnectedness of the rights in the Bill of Rights of the Constitution of the Republic of South Africa, 1996 and that in determining whether a right should be provided for, special consideration must be given to the impact on other rights.

11 1989, hereafter the CRC. Art 2 provides that "1. States Parties shall respect and ensure the rights set forth in the present Convention to each child within their jurisdiction without discrimination of any kind, irrespective of the child's or his or her parent's or legal guardian's race, colour, sex, language, religion, political or other opinion, national, ethnic or social origin, property, disability, birth or other status. 2. States Parties shall take all appropriate measures to ensure that the child is protected against all forms of discrimination or punishment on the basis of the status, activities, expressed opinions, or beliefs of the child's parents, legal guardians, or family members."

12 See, for example, the definition of discrimination in *The Oxford English Dictionary*: (https://en.oxforddictionaries.com/definition/discrimination).

13 1990, hereafter the ACRWC. Art 3 reads: "Every child shall be entitled to the enjoyment of the rights and freedoms recognized and guaranteed in this Charter irrespective of the child's or his/her parents' or legal guardians' race, ethnic group, colour, sex, language, religion, political or other opinion, national and social origin, fortune, birth or other status."

14 1979, hereafter the CEDAW.

15 See in this regard, Arts 10, 11, 12 and 14 in particular.

16 The Constitution of the Republic of South Africa, 1996, hereafter the Constitution.

17 S 9(2) of the Constitution.

18 S 9(3) provides that the "state may not unfairly discriminate directly or indirectly against anyone on one or more grounds, including race, gender, sex, pregnancy, marital status, ethnic or social origin, colour, sexual orientation, age, disability, religion, conscience, belief, culture, language and birth."

19 S 9(2) of the Constitution.

20 A similar provision is found in Art 11(3)(*d*) of the ACRWC.

21 The fact that the CRC has never specifically mentioned the effect which a lack of menstrual health care products has on the lives of children, also not in any of its Concluding Remarks – as to the knowledge and research of the authors – must also be bemoaned.

22 These documents include the Universal Declaration of Human Rights of 1948 of which Art 25.1 provides that "[e]veryone has the right to a standard of living adequate for the health of himself and of his family, including food, clothing, housing and medical care and necessary social services"; the International Covenant on Economic, Social and Cultural Rights ("ICESCR") of 1966: Art 12.1 of the ICESCR recognises "the right of everyone to the enjoyment of the highest attainable standard of physical and mental health", while Art 12.2 provides a number of "steps to be taken by the States parties … to achieve the full realization of this right"; Art 11.1 (f) of the International Convention on the Elimination of All Forms of Racial Discrimination of 1965; Art 12 of the Convention on the Elimination of All Forms of Discrimination against Women of 1979; Art 11 of the European Social Charter of 1961; Art 16 of the African Charter on Human and Peoples' Rights of 1981; Art 10 of the Additional Protocol to the American Convention on Human Rights in the Area of Economic, Social and Cultural Rights of 1988; Art 24 of the CRC of 1989, discussed below; Art 14 of the ACRWC of 1990, discussed below; and Art 25 of the Convention on the Rights of Persons with Disabilities of 2006.

23 Para 4 of the General Comment (CESCR 2000). See also (Office of the United Nations High Commissioner for Human Rights 2008); and para 2 of the General Comment No 15 (2013) (Committee on the Rights of the Child 2013a) 4.

24 Para 9 of the General Comment 14.

25 At para 22.

26 At para 43(a), own emphasis.

27 See also para 3 of the CESCR General Comment 14. It is interesting to note that the CRC does not explicitly enshrine the child's right to dignity or bodily integrity but refers to the dignity of the disabled child; those who are accused of, or found guilty of offences; and of child victims. On a strict reading of Art 2 of the CRC, requiring that the "rights set forth in the present Convention" be ensured on a non-discriminatory

basis, the right to dignity and bodily integrity are not included in the rights to be respected in terms of Art 2.

28 1990, hereafter the ACRWC. The ACRWC entered into force in November 1999 and South Africa ratified this convention on 7 January 2000.

29 The department allocated R245 million towards the policy for the 2017 financial year (Hlatshaneni 2017).

30 It is submitted that even if girls' right to sanitary wear should be enforced as a qualified right, it is evident that the government's action regarding this cannot be deemed reasonable, as it has failed to realise this right by taking legislative and other measures, so as to achieve the progressive realisation of the right, within available resources.

31 At para 68.

32 S 29 reads: "(1) Everyone has the right (a) to a basic education, including adult basic education; and (b) to further education, which the state, through reasonable measures, must make progressively available and accessible.

(2) Everyone has the right to receive education in the official language or languages of their choice in public educational institutions where that education is reasonably practicable. In order to ensure the effective access to, and implementation of, this right, the state must consider all reasonable educational alternatives, including single medium institutions, taking into account: (a) equity; (b) practicability; and (c) the need to redress the results of past racially discriminatory laws and practices. (3) Everyone has the right to establish and maintain, at their own expense, independent educational institutions that: (a) do not discriminate on the basis of race; (b) are registered with the state; and (c) maintain standards that are not inferior to standards at comparable public educational institutions. (4) Subsection (3) does not preclude state subsidies for independent educational institutions."

33 S 29(2)(*a*) of the Constitution.

34 See Path 2016, p. 2 citing research conducted in Ethiopia, Uganda, South Sudan, Tanzania, Zimbabwe, India and Nepal.

35 See Path 2016, p. 2 citing research conducted especially in Kenya, Tanzania, Ethiopia, Uganda, South Sudan and Zimbabwe.

36 Studies in Kenya, for example, found that girls were unable to focus on their teacher because they were concerned about blood leaking on their clothes. They were also afraid of standing up to answer questions in case blood had seeped onto their uniforms (PATH 2016, p. 5).

37 It is submitted that this is clearly evident on a policy level since sanitary health care products are subject to tax, as discussed above.

References

Ackerman, X. 2015. Innovation and action in funding girls' education. *Global Economy & Development Working Paper 84.* [Online] Available at: http://www.ungei.org/Ackerman_Girls_Education_v2.pdf [Accessed 23 January 2017].

Albertyn, C. 2007. Substantive Equality and Transformation in South Africa. *South African Journal on Human Rights*, 23(01), 253–276.

APHRC. 2010. Experiences & problems with menstruation among poor women and schoolgirls in Nairobi, Kenya. *Policy Brief No. 20.* Nairobi, Kenya: The African Population and Health Research Center.

Bernardo, C. 2016. The case for tax free tampons, pads in SA. *IOL.* [Online] Available at: http://www.iol.co.za/lifestyle/the-case-for-tax-free-tampons-pads-in-sa-2012494 [Accessed 21 April 2016].

CESCR. 2000. General Comment 14: The right to the highest attainable standard of health. E/C.12/2000/4. [Online] Available at: http://www.refworld.org/pdfid/4538838d0.pdf [Accessed 15 March 2017].

CESCR. 2009. General Comment No. 20: Non-discrimination in economic, social and cultural rights (art 2, para 2, of the International Covenant on Economic, Social and Cultural Rights). E/C.12/GC/20.

Chamberlain, K. 2017. What is menstruation – definition and cycle. [Online] Available at: https://study.com/academy/lesson/what-is-menstruation-definition-cycle.html [Accessed 20 March 2018].

Committee on the Rights of the Child. 2001. General Comment 1: The aims of education. CRC/GC/2001/1. Geneva: United Nations.

Committee on the Rights of the Child. 2013. General Comment No 14 on the right of the child to have his or her best interests taken as a primary consideration (art 3, para 1). CRC/C/GC/14. Geneva: United Nations.

Committee on the Rights of the Child. 2013a. General Comment No 15 on the right of the child to the enjoyment of the highest attainable standard of health (art 24). CRC/C/GC/15 4. Geneva: United Nations.

Committee on the Rights of the Child. 2016. General Comment No 20 (2016) on the implementation of the rights of the child during adolescence. CRC/C/GC/20. Geneva: United Nations.

Connolly, S. and Marni, S. 2013. Cambodian Girls' Recommendations for Facilitating Menstrual Hygiene Management in School. *Journal of Water, Sanitation and Hygiene for Development*, 3(4), 612–622.

Crawford, B. J. and Spivack, C. 2017. Tampon Taxes, Discrimination, and Human Rights. *Wisconsin Law Review*, 491, 491–549.

Creamer, K. 2002. The impact of South Africa's evolving jurisprudence on children's socio-economic rights in budget analysis. *Occupational Paper*, IDASA Budget Information Service.

Crosta, P. 2017. What's to know about menstrual cramps. *Medical News Today.* [Online] Available at: https://www.medicalnewstoday.com/articles/157333.php [Accessed 20 March 2018].

Currie, I. and De Waal, J. 2008. *The Bill of Rights Handbook.* 5th edition. Cape Town: Juta.

Department of Education Kwa-Zulu Natal. 2017. Distribution of sanitary pads to schools. *Circular No 02 of 2017.* [Online] Available at: http://www.kzneducation.gov.za/Portals/0/Circuiars/KZN/2017/KZN%20CIRCULAR%20NO.%2002%20OF%202017-DISTRIBUTION%20OF%20SANITARY%20PADS%20TO%20SCHOOLS.pdf [Accessed 9 March 2017].

Etheridge, J. 2018. Following pit toilet death, Education department to implement sanitation audit. *Mail & Guardian.* [Online] Available at: https://mg.co.za/article/2018-03-22-following-pit-toilet-death-education-department-to-implement-sanitation-audit [Accessed 22 March 2018].

Hassim, A., Heywood, M. and Berger, J. 2007. *Health and Democracy: A Guide to Human Rights, Health Law and Policy in Post-apartheid South Africa.* Cape Town: Siber Ink CC.

Hlatshaneni, S. 2017. Free contraceptives and HIV tests at primary and high schools is coming soon. *The Citizen.* [Online] Available at: https://citizen.co.za/news/south-africa/1545897/school-condom-plan-may-blow [Accessed 17 July 2017].

Khosa v Minister of Social Development, 2004. (6) SA 505 (CC).

Kukathas, C. 2015. Do children have interests?London: Department of Government, London School of Economics. [Online] Available at: https://www.academia.edu/12516733/Do_children_have_interests [Accessed 15 July 2015].

Manamela, B. 2015. Launch of Dignity Dreams Nelson Mandela Day campaign speech. [Online] Available at: http://www.gov.za/speeches/keynote-address-deputy-minister-buti-manamela-dignity-dreams-nelson-mandela-day-campaign [Accessed 19 April 2016].

Mathlala, A. 2011. Zuma promises free towels for women. *Sowetan Live.* [Online] Available at: http://www.sowetanlive.co.za/news/2011/01/10/zuma-promises-free-towels-for-women [Accessed 19 April 2016].

Mills, L. 2016. *Considering the best interests of the child when marketing food to children: an analysis of the South African regulatory framework* (LLD thesis). Cape Town: Stellenbosch University.

Minister of Health v Treatment Action Campaign (2), 2002. SA.

National Treasury Republic of South Africa, 2018 *Medium Term Budget Policy Statement 2018.* [Online] Available at: http://www.treasury.gov.za/documents/mtbps/2018/mtbps/FullMTBPS.pdf [Accessed 25 October 2018].

Nolan, A. 2011. *Children's Socio-Economic Rights, Democracy and the Courts.* Oxford: Hart Publishing.

Office of the United Nations High Commissioner for Human Rights. 2008. Fact Sheet No. 31: The Right to Health. [Online] Available at: http://www.ohchr.org/Documents/Publications/Factsheet31.pdf [Accessed 2 April 2014].

The Office on the Status of Women. 2000. South Africa's National Policy Framework for Women's Empowerment and Gender Equality. [Online] Available at: https://www.gov.za/sites/default/files/gender_0.pdf [Accessed 15 March 2017].

Oster, E. and Thornton, R. 2011. Menstruation, sanitary products, and school attendance: Evidence from a randomized evaluation. *American Economic Journal: Applied Economics,* 3(1), 91–100.

Oxford English Dictionary. 2015. 'Interest', noun. [Online] Available at: https://en.oxforddictionaries.com/definition/interest. [Accessed 15 July 2015].

PATH. 2016. Outlook on reproductive health – girls' and women's right to menstrual health: Evidence and opportunities. [Online] Available at: https://www.path.org/publications/files/RH_outlook_mh_022016.pdf. [Accessed 23 February 2017].

President of the Republic of South Africa v Hugo, 1997. SA.

Ramathumba, D. 2015. Menstrual knowledge and practices of female adolescents in Vhembe district, Limpopo Province, South Africa: Original research. *Curationis,* 38(1), 1–6.

S v Makwanyane (1995) 1995 (3) SA 391 (CC), 1995 (6) BCLR 665 (CC).

Sefali, P. 2015. Presidency silent on sanitary pad promise. *GroundUp.* [Online] Available at: http://www.groundup.org.za/article/presidency-silent-sanitary-pad-promise_2930. [Accessed 19 April 2016].

Shisana, O., Labadarios, D., Rehle, T., Sombayi, I., Zuma, K., Dhansay, A., Reddy, P., Parker, W., Hoosain, E., Naidoo, P. et al. 2014. *South African National Health and Nutrition Examination Survey (SANHANES-1): 2014.* Cape Town: HSRC Press.

The South African Human Rights Commission. 2014. Report on the right to access sufficient water and decent sanitation in South Africa. Cape Town: South African Human Rights Commission.

The South African Institute of Chartered Accountants. 2008. Zero rating of foodstuff. [Online] Available at: https://www.saica.co.za/integritax/2008/1671_Zero_rating_of_foodstuff.htm [Accessed 20 March 2018].

Sperling, G. and Winthorp, R. 2016. *What Works in Girls Education.* Washington: The Brookings Institution.

Staff Reporter. 2017. KZN health department applauded for free sanitary pads programme. *The Mail and Guardian* [Online] Available at: https://mg.co.za/article/2017-02-01-kzn-health-department-applauded-for-free-sanitary-pads-programme [Accessed 9 March 2017].

Statistics South Africa. 2014. Poverty trends in South Africa: An examination of absolute poverty between 2006 & 2011. [Online] Available at: http://www.statssa.gov.za/publications/Report-03-10-06/Report-03-10-06March2014.pdf [Accessed 20 April 2016].

Tamiru, S., Kuribachew, M. and Acidria, P. 2015. Towards a sustainable solution for school menstrual hygiene management: Cases of Ethiopia, Uganda, South Sudan, Tanzania and Zimbabwe. *Waterlines*, 34(1), 92–102.

Tegegne, T. and Sisay, M. 2014. Menstrual hygiene management and school absenteeism among female adolescent students in Northeast Ethiopia BMC Public Health. [Online] Available at: http://bmcpublichealth.biomedcentral.com/articles/10.1186/1471-2458-14-1118 [Accessed 20 April 2016].

Thembo, T. 2017. No free sanitary pads yet for Cape girls. *IOL*. [Online] Available at: https://www.iol.co.za/news/south-africa/western-cape/no-free-sanitary-pads-yet-for-cape-girls-7889908 [Accessed 9 March 2017].

Tobin, J. 2006. Beyond the supermarket shelf: Using a rights based approach to address children's health needs. *International Journal of Children's Rights*, 14(3), 275–306.

UN Human Rights Office of the High Commission. 2014. Statement by the United Nations Special Rapporteur on the human right to water and sanitation (Visit to Kenya, 22–28 July). OHCHR. [Online] Available at: http://www.ohchr.org/EN/NewsEvents/Pages/DisplayNews.aspx?NewsID=14912&LangID=E [Accessed 22 February 2018].

UN Human Rights Office of the High Commissioner. 2018. Ratification Status for CRC. [Online] Available at: http://tbinternet.ohchr.org/_layouts/TreatyBodyExternal/Treaty.aspx?Treaty=CRC&Lang=en [Accessed 20 March 2018].

Wolfson, S. 1992. Children's Rights: The Theoretical Underpinning of the Best Interests of the Child. In: M. Freeman & P. Veerman (eds). *The Ideologies of Children's Rights* (pp. 1–21). Dordrecht: Martinus Nijhoff Publishers.

Zuma, J. 2011. State of the Nation Address by His Excellency Jacob G. Zuma, President of the Republic of South Africa, at the Joint Sitting of Parliament, Cape Town. [Online] Available at: http://www.thepresidency.gov.za/pebble.asp?relid=3498 [Accessed 19 April 2016].

8 Collateral damage

Discrimination in failure-to-protect laws for children's well-being

D. Kelly Weisberg

Introduction

Millions of women are victimized by an intimate partner annually – making it one of the most common crimes against women (Black et al. 2011). Children in these families are the invisible victims. According to a comprehensive nationwide survey of the prevalence of children's exposure to violence, about one in five children in the United States are "exposed" to intimate partner physical violence during their lifetimes (Hamby et al. 2011, p. 6). Children who are exposed to domestic violence witness the abuse of their mothers but are not physically abused themselves (Edleson 2001, p. 91). The act of witnessing domestic violence encompasses auditory, visual and inferred impressions (Children's Bureau 2016), such as children seeing or hearing their mother's physical abuse, viewing the setting of the violence, including any property damage, and seeing the after effects of the assault on their mother in the form of her bruises and/or broken bones.

A common child welfare practice, historically, in the United States is the removal of children from the home based on the mother's status as a victim of domestic violence. This practice was the subject of a famous New York law suit discussed herein. The practice appears to violate Article 2 of the United Nations Convention on the Rights of the Child (CRC) that prohibits discrimination against children "based on the child's or, alternatively, a *parent's* race, color, sex, language, religion, political or other opinion, national, ethnic or social origin, property, disability, birth or *other status*" (UNCRC 1989). Although United States law does not have a similar provision and has not ratified the CRC, Article 2 sets forth an aspirational principle of respect for the child that all nations should strive to meet.

These children, in being removed from the home, are being discriminated against through no fault of their own or that of their mothers. The crux of the matter is the placement of children based on the parent's behavior. Normally, placement in foster care stems from a finding of abuse or neglect. However, these children are removed from the care of mothers, who were victims of domestic violence, without any judicial finding that their mothers were abusive or neglectful. This child welfare practice has serious implications for the children's well-being. Removal to foster care necessitates separation from the home and siblings, and also may subject children to multiple foster care placements. The lifetime consequences of early trauma are well-known and often severe.

The U.N. Committee on the Rights of the Child has long been concerned with the issue of children's right to be protected from all forms of physical and mental violence in the home. This concern is reflected in the Committee's General Comment No. 13 on Article 19 of the Convention, requiring States parties to take appropriate measures to protect children from parental abuse and neglect. The General Comment highlights the need for all States parties to act expeditiously to fulfil their obligations under the Convention to protect children against all forms of parental mistreatment (UNCRC 2011).

The issue of children's exposure to domestic violence evokes a legal response by the civil law (the family courts, the child protection system) and also the criminal justice system in the United States. This paper is largely concerned with the civil system of child protection. Cases of children's exposure to intimate partner violence come to the attention of child welfare authorities when law enforcement is summoned to provide emergency assistance in the aftermath of an assault. In such cases, the agency sometimes charges the mother with "failure to protect" – the act of permitting the child to witness domestic violence. The unfortunate consequence is that the mother loses custody of her child when the state removes the child from the home and places the child in foster care.

Several rationales underlie this child welfare practice. The "official" rationale is child protection – a desire to protect children from physical or psychological harm by their caretakers. Case workers' actions in the domestic violence context are based on certain assumptions (Block 2007). First, case workers assume that the existence of domestic violence means that child maltreatment is likely to occur. Second, they assume that all children are harmed by their exposure to domestic violence. Third, they assume that domestic violence compromises battered mothers' ability to parent their children (ibid., p. 3). Case workers remove children from these mothers – but without taking into account the mothers' individual circumstances, without determining whether parental unfitness exists in fact, and, if so, whether it rises to the level of imminent danger that justifies child removal (*Nicholson v. Scoppetta* 2004).

The "unofficial" rationale for the child's removal is institutional leverage. Social workers' invocation of the ground of "failure to protect" gives them (together with legal personnel) the necessary leverage to force the battered mother to comply with requirements to "improve" her parenting. This institutional leverage is a common occurrence in child protection interventions generally: child protective service workers have the leverage to make parents comply with conditions prior to reunification. In the case of a battered woman, the conditions might require her to end the intimate relationship, undergo counseling for domestic violence, or seek alternative housing. "Once a battered woman is involved in services,… child protection workers generally take control away from her by mandating that she leave the batterer and comply with services" (Block 2007, p. 4).

However, this coercive rationale *presumes* that the battered mother is unfit. She has never been adjudicated "unfit" or admitted any parental unfitness. Therefore, the court technically has no basis for asserting its jurisdiction. Under the Due Process

Clause of the Fourteenth Amendment (*U.S. Const., Amend.* XIV) of the federal Constitution, parents have a constitutional right to the care, custody, and control of their children. This principle was first recognized in two United States Supreme Court cases in the 1920s that upheld the rights of parents to control the upbringing of their children (*Meyer v. Nebraska* 1923; *Pierce v. Society of Sisters* 1925). However, the principle is not absolute. The state can intervene to restrict parental authority in the interest of child welfare (*Prince v. Massachusetts* 1944) provided, however, that the state first proves that the parent is unfit (*Roe v. Conn* 1976).

The "unofficial" rationale for the child's removal from the home in the domestic violence context, explained above, is based on misguided expectations about battered mothers. Case workers believe that battered mothers must conduct themselves in certain ways to demonstrate that they are exercising a minimum degree of care as a parent (Lansner 2008). Case workers contend that battered mothers must achieve safety for their children by leaving the abuser. Yet, exit from an abusive relationship is a dangerous process. Too often, separation from the abuser merely enhances the danger to battered mothers (DeKeseredy et al. 2017; Hotton 2001; Mahoney 1991). For example, in a sample of approximately 250,000 people who experienced post-separation intimate partner violence, 24 percent reported that the violence continued and became more serious after separation, and 39 percent indicated that the violence first started after separation (Hotton 2001, p. 2). Exit from an abusive intimate relationship is so dangerous that sometimes it triggers homicide. The percentage of female homicide victims who were separated or divorced from their intimate partners ranges from approximately 40 percent to 75 percent, depending on the study (DeKeseredy et al. 2017, p. 42; Hotton 2001, p. 6). Battered women are aware that, paradoxically, sometimes staying with their abusers is less dangerous than leaving them. Therefore, case workers who insist that battered women leave their abusers are not taking into account the danger that departure evokes.

When children are involuntarily removed from the home, they suffer "collateral damage." They are often torn from the custody of a non-abusive mother and placed in out-of-home care with strangers. The children are traumatized by the child welfare system (Greeson et al. 2011) through no fault of their own or their mothers.

> Although it may be assumed that children living in violent homes are safer when placed in out-of-home care, the act of being separated from one or both parents may be more traumatic than or just as traumatic as experiencing DV.
>
> (Ogbonnaya and Pohle 2013, p. 1401)

This child welfare practice of removing children from the home penalizes, rather than protects, children as well as their mothers. A famous New York case in 2004 (*Nicholson v. Scoppetta* 2004), held out hope of putting an end to this harmful child welfare practice. This paper explores this landmark decision and its legacy.

Nicholson case: changing the tide

In 2004, New York's highest state court announced its decision in *Nicholson v. Scoppetta*. The case began in 1999, when Sharwline Nicholson, the 32-year-old single mother of two young children, was the victim of a vicious assault by her boyfriend, who was the father of her youngest child. The father had never resided with her and did not have a key to her residence. He lived out of state and visited once per month. According to the mother, he had never assaulted her before. The assault took place when the mother attempted to terminate their intimate relationship.

During the altercation, Nicholson suffered a broken arm, fractured ribs, and head injuries. Neither of her two children witnessed the assault. Her 8-year-old son was at school at the time. Her 3-year-old daughter was in a crib in an adjacent room. Because of the seriousness of her injuries, Nicholson decided to go to the hospital for treatment. Before she left in an ambulance, she arranged for a neighbor, who had cared for the children in the past, to pick up her son at his bus stop when he returned from school. She asked the neighbor to care for both children until her return.

In New York, as elsewhere in the United States, social workers investigate cases of child abuse and neglect, and then refer appropriate cases to the courts. While Sharwline Nicholson was hospitalized, New York child welfare authorities removed her children from her neighbor's home, without her consent, and took them to a detention center. A state social worker notified Nicholson that the agency had possession of her children. Case workers then placed her children in foster care. The social workers did not require proof that the children had actually witnessed the violence or that the violence had had an adverse effect on the children. Foster care placement occurred automatically by virtue of the fact that the mother had been battered – even though she herself had committed no wrong.

Nicholson's troubles were just beginning. Child welfare authorities filed a petition with the family court against Nicholson and her former boyfriend, charging them both with neglect for engaging in domestic violence in the presence of children. The petition made no distinction between the victim and the abuser – labeling them both equally responsible. Moreover, the social worker who was assigned to oversee the case testified at trial that, before the filing of the petition, he did not believe that Ms. Nicholson was actually neglectful (*Nicholson v. Williams* 2002, factual history). The case manager who had placed the children in foster care admitted that it was routine practice in domestic violence cases to remove children from battered mothers and to delay returning them as coercive measures. He conceded that "after a few days of the children being in foster care, the mother will usually agree to ACS's conditions for their return without the matter ever going to court" (ibid., p. 170).

It took 21 days for Nicholson to be reunited with her children. Because of her experience, Nicholson filed a class-action lawsuit on behalf of herself and several other battered mothers and their children. She challenged the constitutionality of the practice of removing children from the custody of their battered mothers. The plaintiffs alleged that they were deprived of substantive and procedural due process, and that their children were removed based on constitutionally inadequate investigations, without probable cause, and without the case workers' receiving adequate training and supervision.

At the federal district court trial, experts established that children do not presumptively suffer severe harm from witnessing domestic violence (*Nicholson v. Williams* 2002, p. 170). Rather, children suffer a wide range of effects that are mitigated by such factors as age, frequency and content of the observations, the child's proximity to the event, the victim's relationship to the child, and the presence of the non-abusive parent to mediate the intensity of the event (Edleson 2001; Lansner 2008; *Nicholson v. Williams* 2002, pp. 197–198). The federal district court made written findings that the city's child welfare department routinely removed children from battered mothers without a court order and then charged the mothers with neglect. The court found that the child welfare department failed to ensure that battered mothers received necessary social services, the agency provided inadequate training for case managers, and failed to consider alternatives short of removal that might have been less harmful to the children.

As a remedy, the court enjoined these practices. The court concluded that the government had violated the mothers' and children's constitutional rights by infringing on their substantive due process rights as well as the procedural due process rights of mothers and children not to be separated by the government *unless the parent was proven unfit* (*In re Nicholson* 2002, p. 185).

The Second Circuit Court of Appeals upheld the preliminary injunction. However, before reaching the merits on the constitutional issues, the federal appellate court referred the matter to New York's highest state court, certifying questions of statutory interpretation to the court in asking whether the practice of removal in such cases violated state law. In response, the New York Court of Appeals held that the child welfare practice policy violated *state* law. The court ruled that child welfare authorities cannot take children from non-abusive parents and place them in foster care merely because the children have been exposed to domestic abuse. Permitting a child to witness domestic violence was insufficient, without more, to satisfy the state statutory definition of a "neglected child." The court thereby rejected a blanket presumption that permitted removal of children from the home of battered mothers.

The decision is important because the state court went far beyond holding that the child welfare policy violated state law. The court crafted specific standards to govern the removal of children. A judge must do more than speculate about the *risk of serious harm*. A court must identify facts supporting the existence of such a risk. A court must determine that the threat to the child's health or welfare is *imminent*. A court must make efforts to *avoid removal* by weighing whether the imminent risk to the child can be mitigated by reasonable efforts to avoid removal. In determining the outcome, the court must balance the risk against the harm engendered by removal. Emergency removal without a court order should be rare. Prior to removal, welfare authorities must establish by proof of particularized evidence that removal is in the child's best interests. A finding of neglect must be based on the mother's actions (i.e., her failure to exercise a minimum degree of care) and not merely on her status as a victim of domestic violence or her children's exposure to it. The actual or threatened harm to the children must be clearly attributable to the mother's inaction.

In addition, in evaluating the mother's actions, the court must consider the risks that she faced as a victim of domestic violence as well as the resources available to her. For example, an assessment of the reasonableness of a battered mother's actions must take into account:

> risks attendant to leaving, if the batterer has threatened to kill her if she does; risks attendant to staying and suffering continued abuse; risks attendant to seeking assistance through government channels, potentially increasing the danger to herself and her children; risks attendant to criminal prosecution against the abuser; and risks attendant to relocation.
>
> (*Nicholson v. Scoppetta* 2004, p. 847)

The court cautioned that recognition of the many factors that *might* affect a mother's decision whether to leave a household or relationship was insufficient to justify the practice of removing children. Such an approach rests on negative stereotypes of battered women as unfit mothers.

Positive legacy of *Nicholson v. Scoppetta*

State child welfare reform

The *Nicholson* case had important implications for child welfare practice in the city and state of New York (Kohler 2009–2010, pp. 262–263). Its primary significance was the change in the definition of "neglect" by holding that the state could no longer presume that battered mothers were neglectful solely because of their children's exposure to domestic violence. The case recognized that removal of children from a non-abusive parent unfairly punishes battered mothers and, on balance, may cause more harm than good in terms of children's welfare.

The lawsuit forced New York City welfare authorities to revise the practice of removal and to change their attitudes toward battered mothers. Emergency removals of children stemming from intimate partner violence were more closely scrutinized by the courts (Weinstein 2008, p. 85). The city's child welfare department charged fewer battered mothers with neglect and removed fewer children. At the time of *Nicholson*, welfare authorities charged about 234 mothers annually with neglect for failing to protect their children from witnessing domestic violence (Mandel 2005). In the first year after the injunction in *Nicholson*, there were only 13 complaints of agency noncompliance and only two complaints during the second year, as documented by the *Nicholson* Review Committee that was established by the federal district court to oversee the agency's compliance with the principles of *Nicholson v. Williams* (Copps 2009, p. 510).

Nicholson also led to a revision of child welfare practices throughout the state. Judges were required to make factual inquiries about the need for removal, including the determination of whether alternative steps, such as removing the *batterer* from the home, would eliminate the need for removing the children. Judges were required to *balance* the need for the removal against the potential trauma to the children from the removal. Thereafter, batterers (rather than non-abusive mothers) were charged more frequently with neglect for exposing children to domestic violence (ibid., p. 511).

Nicholson also led to an emphasis on improving training of child welfare workers statewide. A subsequent New York law (N.Y. Soc. Serv. Law § 17(g)) required domestic violence training for all child welfare workers (Parent Advocates 2004). Increased efforts were made to encourage child welfare agencies, domestic violence advocates, and the courts to address the intersection between child welfare and domestic violence. Within less than a decade, 37 percent of local districts in New York State had adopted a cooperative approach that placed domestic violence advocates within child protective services offices to increase collaboration (Davis 2014).

Nicholson's effects extended beyond the context of domestic violence. The case focused attention on the inadequacy of legal representation for indigents by revealing the plight of battered mothers caught up in the court system. *Nicholson* spurred the New York legislature to increase the rates paid to assigned counsel for all indigent litigants in the family and criminal courts. This change led to greater numbers of qualified counsel participating in the civil and criminal justice processes (Parent Advocates 2004).

National reform

Although *Nicholson* was a New York State decision, its implications reverberated nationwide. In fact, *Nicholson* has been dubbed one of the "top ten cases every child welfare attorney should know." (New York Public Welfare Association 2014) In the wake of *Nicholson*, child welfare authorities nationally reviewed their practices of removing children from battered mothers and charging these mothers with neglect.

Nicholson had relied heavily on the findings of a collaborative project of experts in the fields of domestic violence and child welfare. This influential report posed solutions to problems at the interface of the law's response to child welfare and domestic violence (Green Book 1999). The recommendations specified best practices in the provision of services, such as cultural competency, batterer accountability, an emphasis on the needs of battered immigrant women, and supervised visitation. The proposals advocated a policy disfavoring removal of a child from a non-abusive parent; a priority on the protection of the victim, as well as the child, for all agencies that are involved in a case; and a policy of holding batterers accountable for the damage they inflict on families. The recommendations recognized the need for collaboration between service providers to achieve these goals and set forth guidelines for agencies.

Nicholson also identified best practices regarding treatment of battered mothers by the civil justice system. Mothers could no longer be accused of neglect merely because they were victims of domestic violence. Rather, the court recognized that mothers' inability to prevent the violence stemmed from their lack of resources, not from the lack of desire to protect their children. Therefore, battered mothers should be offered appropriate services. Because removal can cause severe emotional harm, children should be removed only as a last resort when there exists an imminent risk to the safety of the child.

In the wake of *Nicholson*, communities enhanced coordination among courts and social service agencies to better serve needy families. For example, from 2000–2007, the United States Department of Health and Human Services and the Department of Justice provided funding for six demonstration sites (in Colorado, New Hampshire, Oregon, California and Missouri), in which battered women's organizations, child protection agencies, and the courts collaborated to improve child welfare practices (Rose, n.d.). In these ways, *Nicholson* fundamentally changed the approach of child protective services to cases involving domestic violence.

Limitations of *Nicholson v. Scoppetta*

Persistence removals from non-abusive mothers

Despite these impressive reforms, *Nicholson*'s mandate has not been fulfilled either by the child welfare department or the family courts in New York City (Beller 2015; Copps 2009; Perrone 2012; Sirotkin and Fecko 2008). Children of battered mothers still face a substantial risk of being removed from the home as a consequence of their mother's victimization. This is the finding of my research that includes small-scale studies of reported legal cases (Beller 2015; Copps 2009; Perrone 2012; Sirotkin and Fecko 2008); a meta-analysis of the child welfare literature focusing on case outcomes in families that experience domestic violence (Ogbonnaya and Pohle 2013); and a 14-month-long ethnographic study of the child welfare system and family courts involved in domestic violence cases in New York City (Lee 2015).

Child welfare authorities hold mothers accountable for child neglect

Numerous post-*Nicholson* cases reveal that New York child welfare authorities persist in charging mothers' victimization as the basis for neglect and removing children from the custody of non-abusive mothers (Beller 2015; Copps 2009; Perrone 2012; Sirotkin and Fecko 2008). Often these children are then placed in foster care. Sometimes the children are returned to the abusive father's custody (Beller 2015, pp. 237–238). Child welfare workers still condition the return of the children on the mothers' entering a shelter, attending domestic violence counseling, enforcing an order of protection against the father, and cooperating with child welfare supervision by allowing unannounced home visits. In other cases, the court finds the mother neglectful solely based on her refusal to leave the abusive relationship. Sometimes, the court blames the mother for her own abuse (Beller 2015, p. 238).

A meta-analysis of 16 articles in the child welfare literature on the outcomes in families experiencing domestic violence reports that in half of the cases, the existence of domestic violence increased the likelihood of children's out-of-home placement when compared to children referred for other reasons (Ogbonnaya and Pohle 2013, p. 1403). That study reviewed 2,000 randomly selected CPS cases, 3,129 children investigated for child maltreatment, 747 children with CPS involvement receiving in-home or out-of-home services, and 1,035 families in initial CPS investigation.

An ethnographic study of the child welfare system and family courts in New York City concluded that courts continue to blame non-abusive mothers and assume that they are equal participants in the abuse (Lee 2015, pp. 68–69). That 14-month study was based on interviews with 13 attorneys, two judges, 13 child welfare workers, two social workers and 24 parents involving 254 cases that included 24 domestic violence cases (ibid., p. 69).

Cases fail to implement Nicholson*'s principles governing removals*

Research also confirms that child welfare practices fail to fully implement the principles of *Nicholson*. *Nicholson* specified the importance of strict guidelines governing removals, such as adopting a standard of imminent risk for removal of children from the custody of the non-abusive parent. Nonetheless, family courts continue to hold neglect hearings involving battered mothers where child welfare authorities fail to meet the requisite "imminent risk" standard (Copps 2009, p. 512–513; Perrone 2012, p. 663). In some cases, child welfare authorities inappropriately presume that the child is at risk based on the mother's *possible* actions. Sometimes, child welfare authorities remove children based on mere speculation that the mother *might* return to her abuser (Perrone 2012, pp. 663–664).

Child protection agencies base removal decisions on other inappropriate criteria. Sometimes they assume that the mother is unfit based on the *father's* actions. Some child welfare authorities remove children from non-abusive mothers based on the fact that the father had violated an order of protection (ibid.). One judge found that a child was neglected because the batterer ransacked the mother's apartment looking for money (ibid., pp. 664–665). Another court found a battered mother liable for neglect because of the father's drug use coupled with the mother's alleged "lack of awareness" of the impact of the father's actions on the child (ibid., p. 665). Child protection workers continue to allege pretextual reasons for a child's removal from the home (Copps 2009, pp. 514–515). In some cases, the pretext concerned the presence of a dirty home. Case workers conceal the fact that removal stems from the mother's victimization or her refusal to receive services (ibid., pp. 515–516).

Child welfare authorities rely on the same assumptions and unsupported predictions that *Nicholson* rejected. The agencies' treatment of battered mothers reveals a lack of understanding of the dynamics of domestic violence, by blaming mothers for the violence and undermining mothers' efforts to create a better life for their families (Beller 2015, pp. 237–238).

Nicholson's vision has not been fulfilled in other ways. Child welfare authorities still fail to offer adequate services to victims of domestic violence prior to removal of children (Block 2007, p. 4; Copps 2009, pp. 519–520; Lee 2015, p. 79; Perrone 2012, p. 664). Best practices dictate offering such services as shelter assistance, family and individual therapy, legal advocacy, medical advocacy, social service referrals and advocacy, parenting skills classes, employment referrals and housing assistance. Instead, child welfare workers are quick to blame victims and remove children (Lee 2015, pp. 79–80; Perrone 2012, pp. 663–668). Moreover, many child welfare case workers still lack adequate training regarding domestic violence (Block 2007, p. 5; Copps, 2009, p. 519; Ogbonnaya and Pohle 2013, p. 1401; Perrone 2012, pp. 660–661). As a result, they often fail to conduct a comprehensive assessment of the family situation before removing children (Copps 2009, pp. 512–513; Lee 2015, p. 79; Perrone 2012, p. 668).

Criminal implications

Even more serious ramifications occur. Following *Nicholson*, many states criminalized battered mothers' failure to protect their children from abuse. Currently, at least 29 states have such criminal laws (Campbell 2014a). The offense goes by different names, such as "permitting child abuse" (*Ark. Code Ann.* §5–27–221); "enabling child abuse" (*Okla. Stat.* § 7115(B)); or "injury to a child by omission" (*Texas Penal Code* § 22.04). Even if specific criminal laws do not exist, prosecutors in other states use more general laws to the same effect (Campbell 2014a). For example, many states have laws that prohibit criminal negligence in the care of a child or placing a child in a dangerous situation.

Battered women, who are non-abusive parents, have been sentenced to lengthy prison sentences (in some cases, 10 years or more) for failing to protect their children who died from injuries inflicted by an abusive intimate partner (Campbell 2014b). In these cases, the battered mother's only "crime" was failing to stop the abusive partner from harming the child – not commission of the abuse herself. In some states, a non-abusive mother has received *lengthier* prison sentences than the abusive father who perpetrated the actual crime (ibid.).

Persistence of discriminatory child welfare practices

Many countries have policies that apply to removals of children from the home. The removal decision generally is accomplished through an interaction of administrative and judicial systems with the collaboration of social workers and legal personnel (Burns et al. 2017). Removal of a child from the home, without the consent of the parent, is a significant interference in family life. This intervention is such a serious threat to the privacy and autonomy of the family unit that international human rights documents apply to it.

For example, the European Convention on Human Rights (ECHR) Article 8 requires a strict justification for interferences in family life, such as children's removals from the home (Council of Europe 1950). Article 8 requires that there shall be no interference with family life except in accordance with law, and provided that it is necessary in the interests of public safety and for the protection of health.

In addition, the Council of Europe passed a resolution in 2015 on the removal of children from the home (Council of Europe 2015). According to that resolution, children "have the right not to be separated from their parents against their will, except when competent authorities subject to judicial review determine that such separation is necessary in the best interests of the child." The resolution reflects the idea that removals should be undertaken only when the child's welfare is at stake and also should be subject to judicial review. The threshold for removal is high: the child is judged to be at risk or imminent risk of suffering serious harm.

Given the international consensus that removal from the home is a serious infringement on family privacy and autonomy, the question arises: why do discriminatory child welfare practices, such as those enshrined in *Nicholson v. Scoppetta*, persist? The answer lies in combination of institutional constraints and the phenomenon of mother blaming.

First, structural constraints impose various pressures on the child welfare system. These consist of the need for institutional accountability, limited financial resources, and political pressures. In New York the child welfare agency has an overwhelming task of investigating an average of 60,000 reports of child abuse and neglect annually (Fermino 2016).

In the decade after *Nicholson*, the New York child welfare agency oversaw 30 cases in which children died from child abuse (ibid.). Subsequently, a battle waged over whom to hold accountable for the deaths of these children. According to an audit of the child welfare agency by the state controller, agency workers were so overworked that they could not handle their caseloads (ibid.). Because of their limited resources, the agency had failed to conduct required checks of troubled homes and omitted domestic violence evaluations (ibid.). Case workers were blamed for failing to remove children from the homes of abusive parents or returning them too quickly. Political pressure mounted for child protective services to take a more interventionist approach. Case workers were encouraged to place more children in foster care to minimize the risk of agency liability (Mays 2016).

Another institutional constraint is the fundamental tension in the philosophy of the child welfare department about goals. Child welfare practices unfold within the context of "risk-oriented" systems or "service-oriented" systems (Burns et al. 2017). Risk-oriented systems set a high bar for government intervention in the family and focus on mitigating serious risks to the child's well-being. In contrast, service-oriented systems set a lower threshold for intervention. They focus on the prevention of harm and the provision of services in order to rehabilitate family members to prevent future harm. Norway, Sweden, and Finland have been categorized as service-oriented systems. In contrast, England, Ireland and Switzerland have been categorized as risk-oriented systems similar to the United States (ibid.).

However, in both systems, social workers have unbridled discretion to make decisions about children's welfare. *Nicholson* is an example of a social welfare practice that permitted the exercise of vast discretion in the removal process. The exercise of that discretion enables the perpetuation of decision making based on stereotypes about mothers, especially poor women of color, that contribute to the persistence of removing children from the homes of battered women (Lee 2015, p. 80; Perrone 2012, pp. 655–660).

The theme of mother-blaming runs through the law's response to battered mothers and child welfare practices (Moulding et al. 2015; Murphy 1998, pp. 741–766). Victim blaming is common in the domestic violence context. This gendered discourse has implications for child welfare practitioners who have the task of safeguarding children in homes where domestic violence occurs (Moulding et al. 2015). Child welfare agencies investigate reports of abuse and neglect, provide services to families to keep children safe, remove children from unsafe homes when the circumstances are warranted, make recommendations for children's short-term and long-term care, and place children in foster care when appropriate. They make these decisions with virtually no oversight.

Case workers and judges hold mothers responsible for their children's protection regardless of the harms that the mothers may have experienced. Beginning in the 1990s, several prominent feminist scholars criticized such gender bias in the law's response to child abuse. In several famous cases, battered women who were mothers of children and who were abused by their batterers were prosecuted, themselves, for child abuse and neglect (Johnson 1990; Schneider 1992, p. 552 n. 135). Gender bias resulted in the enhanced likelihood of these mothers being charged with failure to protect (Becker 1995, p. 14; Roberts 1993, pp. 109–115; Schneider 1992). As one feminist legal scholar explained:

> This phenomenon compounds the harm from which battered women suffer, for where a child is beaten by her father or even just exposed to violence, the mother is likely to be held responsible for any harm that the child suffers.
> (Schneider 1992, p. 551)

The battered woman's victimization is minimized by the child welfare system. Mother blaming comes to the forefront particularly when a child dies from the child abuse perpetrated by the man in the household.

The battered woman's role as mother overshadows her role as victim. The law holds mothers to an unrealistic high standard: "We expect mothers to transcend their victimization, to act on behalf of their children regardless of their own situations" (ibid., p. 552). Mothers are expected to overcome all obstacles to protect their children – even in the face of their own victimization. Gender bias operates as a double standard.

> In legal proceedings, this bias operates as an unspoken and unconscious double standard for mothers and fathers, such that mothers are expected to be much better and more powerful parents than fathers, always putting their children's needs above their own and protecting their children from all harm.
> (Becker 1995, p. 15)

These beliefs are premised on the myths that the battered mother has the power to attain safety from her abuser and that she, alone, has the responsibility to end the abuse (Kitchen 2015, p. 376).

Nicholson v. Scoppetta changed the approach of child welfare authorities involving domestic violence. *Nicholson* suggested a number of theoretical and practical improvements in welfare practices for children exposed to domestic violence. Yet, the experience of the child welfare system in the post-*Nicholson* era emphasizes the troubled legacy of the case. The child protection system continues to hold battered mothers accountable for their victimization and for the impact of domestic violence on children. Far too often, the response of the child welfare system is the removal of the child from the home of the non-abusive parent. In this way, the child protection system serves as another source of victimization for the adult victims of domestic violence and their children. Even though the focus of the *Nicholson case* concerned the issue of removal, the underlying child welfare practice affects children in a manner that should be regarded as discrimination. The state continues to place these children in an unfavorable situation due to the mother's status.

References

Ark. Code Ann. §5-27-221.

Becker, M. E. 1995. Double Binds Facing Mothers in Abusive Families: Social Support Systems, Custody Outcomes, and Liability for Acts of Others. *University of Chicago Law School Roundtable*, 2: 13–33.

Beller, L. F. 2015. When in Doubt, Take Them Out, Removal of Children from Victims of Domestic Violence: Ten Years after *Nicholson v. Williams. Duke Journal of Gender Law and Policy*, 22: 205–239.

Black, M. C., Basile, K. C., Breiding, M. J., Smith, S. G., Walters, M. L., Merrick, M. T., Chen, J., and Stevens, M. R. 2011. National Intimate Partner and Sexual Violence Survey (NISVS): 2010 Summary Report. Atlanta, GA: National Center for Injury Prevention and Control, Centers for Disease Control and Prevention. Available at: https://www.cdc.gov/violenceprevention/pdf/NISVS_Executive_Summary-a.pdf.

Block, S. B. 2007. How the Illinois Department of Children and Family Services Responds – on Paper – to Domestic Violence. *The Family Defender*, 2(01). 3–5.

Burns, K., Pösö, T. and Skivenes, M. 2017. *Child Welfare Removals by the State: A Cross-Country Analysis of Decision-making Systems.* Oxford: Oxford University Press.

Campbell, A. 2014a. Battered, Bereaved, and Behind Bars. *Buzzfeed.* Available at: https://www.buzzfeed.com/alexcampbell/how-the-law-turns-battered.

Campbell, A. 2014b. These Mothers Were Sentenced to at Least 10 Years for Failing to Protect their Children from a Violent Partner (survey of cases in 11 states). *Buzzfeed.* Available at: https://www.buzzfeed.com/alexcampbell/these-mothers-were-sentenced.

Children's Bureau. 2016. Child Witnesses to Domestic Violence. Washington, DC: U.S. Department of Health and Human Services. Available at: https://www.childwelfare.gov/pubPDFs/witnessdv.pdf.

Copps, K. A. 2009. The Good, the Bad, and the Future of *Nicholson v. Scoppetta*: An Analysis of the Effects and Suggestions for Further Improvements. *Albany Law Review*, 72: 497–526.

Council of Europe. 1950. *Convention for the Protection of Human Rights and Fundamental Freedoms (European Convention on Human Rights, as Amended) (ECHR) Art 8 (as amended).* Available at: https://www.echr.coe.int/Documents/Convention_ENG.pdf.

Council of Europe. 2015. *Resolution 2049 (2015). Social services in Europe: Legislation and Practice of the Removal of Children from their Families in Council of Europe member States.*

Davis, L. 2014. The Co-Occurrence of Domestic Violence and Child Maltreatment, *Children's Bureau Express*, 14(07). Washington, DC: U.S. Department of Health & Human Services. Available at: https://cbexpress.acf.hhs.gov/index.cfm?event=website.viewArticles&issueid=159&articleid=4259.

DeKeseredy, W. S., Dragierwich, M. and Schwartz, M. D. 2017. *Abusive Endings: Separation and Divorce Violence Against Women*. Oakland, CA: University of California Press.

Edleson, J. L. 2001. Studying the Co-Occurrence of Child Maltreatment and Domestic Violence in Families. In: S. A. Graham-Bermann, and J. L. Edleson (eds) *Domestic Violence in the Lives of Children: The Future of Research, Intervention, and Social Policy*. Washington, DC: American Psychological Association.

Fermino, J. 2016. Audit Finds NYC Administration for Children's Services Fails to Perform Check-ins, Skips Domestic Violence Evaluations. *N.Y. Daily News*. Available at: http://www.nydailynews.com/new-york/audit-shows-major-failures-nyc-children-services-agency-article-1.2676451.

Green Book. 1999. *Effective Intervention in Domestic Violence and Child Maltreatment Cases: Guidelines for Policy and Practice*. Available at: http://www.thegreenbook.info/documents/Greenbook.pdf (popularly known as the "Green Book" because of the color of its cover).

Greeson, J. K., Briggs, E. C., Kisiel, C. L., Layne, C. M., Ake, G. S.3rd., Ko, S.j., Gerrity, E. T., Steinberg, A. M., Howard, M., Pynoos, R. S. and Fairbank, J. A. 2011. Complex Trauma and Mental Health in Children and Adolescents Placed in Foster Care: Findings from the National Child Traumatic Stress Network. *Child Welfare*, 90(6): 91–108.

Hamby, S., Finklehor, D., Turner, H., and Ormrod, R. 2011. *Children's Exposure to Intimate Partner Violence and Other Family Violence. National Survey of Children's Exposure to Violence*. Washington, DC: Office of Justice Programs.

Hotton, T. 2001. Spousal Violence after Marital Separation, *Juristat*, 21(7). Canadian Centre for Justice Statistics. Available at: http://www.violenceresearch.ca/system/files/files/HOTTON%20%282001%29%20SPOUSAL%20VIOLENCE%20AFTER%20MARITAL%20SEPARATION_0.pdf.

Johnson, J. 1990. *What Lisa Knew*. New York: Putnam Adult.

Kitchen, R. K. 2015. Constrained Choice: Mothers, The State, and Domestic Violence. *Temple Political & Civil Rights Law Review*, 24: 375–399.

Kohler, A. 2009–2010. The Battered Mother's Struggle in New York: The Laws and Policies that Led to the Removal of Children from their Abused Mothers Based on the Child's Exposure to Domestic Violence. *University of Pennsylvania Journal of Law and Social Change*, 13(2): 243–264.

Lansner, D. 2008. The Nicholson Decisions: New York's Response to "Failure to Protect" Allegations, ABA Commission on Domestic Violence. *ENewsletter*, 12. Washington, DC.

Lee, T. 2015. Child Welfare Practice in Domestic Violence Cases in New York City: Problems for Poor Women of Color. *Women, Gender, and Families of Color*, 3(1): 58–87.

Mahoney, M. 1991. Legal Images of Battered Women: Redefining the Issue of Separation. *Michigan Law Review*, 90: 1–94.

Mandel, B. A. 2005. Comments and Casenotes, The White Fist of the Child Welfare System: Racism, Patriarchy, and the Presumptive Removal of Children from Victims of Domestic Violence in *Nicholson v. Williams*. *University of Cincinnati Law Review*, 73(3): 1131–1163.

Mays, J. 2016. Mayor's Plan for ACS Monitor Was Actually Mandated by State Officials. Available at: https://www.dnainfo.com/new-york/20161213/gramercy/de-blasio-carrion-acs-independent-monitor.

Meyer v. Nebraska, 262 U.S. 390(1923). US Supreme Court.

Moulding, N. T., Buchanan, F. and Wendt, S. 2015. Untangling Self-Blame and Mother-Blame in Women's and Children's Perspectives on Maternal Protectiveness in Domestic Violence: Implications for Practice. *Child Abuse Review*, 24: 249–260.

Murphy, J. C. 1998. Legal Images of Motherhood: Conflicting Definitions from Welfare "Reform," Family, and Criminal Law. *Cornell Law Review*, 83: 688–766.

New York Public Welfare Association. 2014. Top Ten Cases Every Child Welfare Attorney Should Know. Available at: http://nypwa.com/HANDOUTS%20for%20WEBSITE%20SC14/Top%20Ten%20Cases%20Every%20Child%20Welfare%20Attorney%20Should%20Know/10%20CASES%20EVERY%20CHILD%20WELFARE%20ATTORNEY%20SHOULD%20KNOW-FINAL.pdf.

Nicholson, In re. 2002. 181 F.Supp.2d 182.

Nicholson v. Scoppetta. 2004. 820 N.E.2d 840 (N.Y.).

Nicholson v. Williams. 2002. 203 F. Supp. 2d 153 (E.D.N.Y.).

N.Y. Soc. Serv. Law § 17(g).

Ogbonnaya, I. N. and Pohle, C. 2013. Case Outcomes of Child Welfare-Involved Families Affected by Domestic Violence: A Review of the Literature. *Children & Youth Services Review*, 35: 1400–1407.

Okla. Stat. § 7115(B).

Parent Advocates. 2004. Nicholson v. Scoppetta Sets Precedent Protecting Children of Battered Women from Being Taken Away from Their Mothers (Press Release). Available at: http://www.parentadvocates.org/nicecontent/dsp_printable.cfm?articleID=6839.

Perrone, J. 2012. Failing to Realize *Nicholson*'s Vision: How New York's Child Welfare System Continues to Punish Battered Mothers. *Journal of Law and Policy*, 20: 641–675.

Pierce v. Society of Sisters, 268 U.S. 510(1925).

Prince v. Massachusetts, 321 U.S. 158(1944).

Roberts, D. 1993. Motherhood and Crime. *Iowa Law Review*, 79: 95.

Roe v. Conn, 417 F. Supp. 769 (M.D. Ala. 1976).

Rose, J. n.d. Lessons Learned from the Green Book Initiative. Resource Center on Domestic Violence, Child Protection and Custody. Available at: https://www.rcdvcpc.org/the-greenbook-initiative/lessons-learned.html.

Schneider, E. M. 1992. Particularity and Generality: Challenges of Feminist Theory and Practice in Work on Woman-Abuse. *New York University Law Review*, 67: 520–568.

Sirotkin, J. N. and Fecko, C. M. 2008. Expert Insights: A Case Study in Post-Nicholson Litigation, ABA Commission on Domestic Violence. *eNewsletter*, 12. Available at: www.americanbar.org/content/newsletter/publications/cdv.../vol12_expert2.html.

Texas Penal Code § 22.04.

UNCRC. 1989. United Nations Convention on the Rights of the Child, Article 2. Available at: http://www.un.org/documents/ga/res/44/a44r025.htm.

UNCRC. 2011. General Comment No. 13. The Right of the Child to Freedom from all Forms of Violence. Available at: http://docstore.ohchr.org/SelfServices/FilesHandler.ashx?enc=6QkG1d%2FPPRiCAqhKb7yhsqIkirKQZLK2M58RF%2F5F0vFKtnY3RFBX0eVOrGEVYuIm9CsHNwh1HrjED9fVmGn%2BaZ1TGy6vH1Iek6kukGyB%2FFCGBbSOP0uwpKf24vcxkEnv.

U.S. Const., Amend. XIV.

Weinstein, J. B. 2008. The Role of Judges in a Government of, by, and for the People: Notes for the Fifty-Eighth Cardozo Lecture. *Cardozo Law Review*, 30: 1–244.

9 Citizen children and unauthorized immigrant parents

Linda D. Elrod[*]

Introduction

> Please do not deport my parents because you will also deport a girl who only has a year left in high school and a dream to become something more than the daughter of illegal immigrants.[1]

The United States Constitution and the United Nations Convention on the Rights of the Child offer citizen children arguments for protection from immigration laws and policies that seek to deport their parents, and often them. Children born in the United States are citizens protected by the Constitution.[2] Eighty-two percent of children in families with an unlawfully present parent are citizens (see Thronson 2013). The Constitution also protects parental rights and the sanctity of the family.[3] The primacy of the parent-child relationship, the importance of family unity and the best interest of the child standard are bedrock principles in family law.[4] Children have the right to live with their parents unless a judge determines by clear and convincing evidence that there is harm by remaining in the parents' custody.[5] Over four million citizen children in "mixed status" families[6] also have a right to protection of their family relationship.[7]

The UN Convention on the Rights of the Child (1989) (CRC) clearly articulates a "Bill of Rights" for children (see Nicholson 2006). Article 2 requires state parties to:

> respect and ensure the [Convention] rights to each child within their jurisdiction without discrimination irrespective of parent's... race, color, sex, language, religion, political or other opinion, national, ethnic or social origin, property, disability, birth or other status. State parties shall take all appropriate measures to ensure that the child is *protected against all forms of discrimination or punishment on the basis of the status*, activities, expressed opinions or beliefs of the child's parents [Emphasis added].

While the United States has not ratified the CRC, it can be considered international customary law because 196 countries have enacted it. The CRC can be used to argue that, regardless of the parent's undocumented status, children should be protected and respected.[8]

This chapter argues that current immigration law and enforcement-only policies discriminate against citizen children based on their parents' unauthorized status, violating the children's right to a family under both the Constitution and the UN Convention on the Rights of the Child.[9] Enforcement-only policies unnecessarily separate, sometimes permanently, otherwise fit-but-for-status parents from their citizen children without due process of law (see Stief 2010; Kaskade 2009). The detention and potential deportation of an immigrant parent harms citizen children by destroying their family unit and their sense of security. The trauma of involuntary separation may cause lifelong emotional, psychological and physical harm to children (see Henderson and Baily 2013; Capps et al. 2007). Even voluntarily separations place children at greater risk of developing anxiety and depression symptoms.[10]

Part II discusses briefly the importance of the UN Convention on the Rights of the Child as a global standard for children's rights. Part III briefly explains the current immigration system and discrimination against children based on their parent's status. Part IV discusses the due process rights of parents and children and the interplay of immigration, parental fitness and best interest of the child determinations. Part V urges the adoption of a child-centered best interest of the child standard in all immigration proceedings that may deport a parent. The chapter concludes that to avoid discrimination based on the parent's status, immigration law should be reformed to include a best interests analysis when parents are detained or deported.

The UN Convention: recognizing rights for children

> The Convention… establishes new standards by codifying for the first time a child's right to be heard… in all proceedings that affect the child. This right to participate, together with the nondiscrimination in Article 2 and provision for the child's best interest in Article 3, form the guiding principles of the Convention.
>
> (Kilkelly 2001, p. 311)

The UN Convention on the Rights of the Child (CRC), acknowledged as the most important international document recognizing rights for children, has been adopted in all countries except the United States (see Middleton 2016). The core principles of the CRC are Article 2 which prohibits discrimination based on the parent's status; Article 12 which gives children a voice in proceedings about their custody (see Elrod 2011), and Article 3 which provides that the best interests standard will be the primary consideration in all matters.[11] Article 5 protects the right to grow up in a family. Article 9 protects the right to remain with parents unless removal is in the child's best interests and if parents are detained, children have a right to know where and to have contact so long as such contact is not contrary to the child's best interest.[12]

Many of the CRC rights are imbedded in American family law, such as the protection of family unity and the use of the best interests of the child standard (Elrod and Dale 2008). Unfortunately, these rights as well as the right of children to have their voices heard and to know where a detained parent is and have contact, are currently missing in immigration law. Children are discriminated against based on their parent's unauthorized status. If the United States would enact the CRC, children would have broader human rights protection than under current law.[13] A federally ratified treaty would require immigration judges to comply with the spirit of the CRC which would mean following the principles of nondiscrimination. The CRC would support family unity, require hearing and giving weight to children's voices and considering the best interest of children in the deportation decision.[14]

Even though ratification of the CRC is not in the political future, American delegates did help draft the CRC and proposed many of its foundational principles, including the protection of families and use of the best interests of the child standard. More importantly, the CRC is international customary law (Fox 1997) which lawyers can argue in American courts.[15] The United States Supreme Court cited the CRC in deciding a juvenile death penalty case.[16]

The United States has ratified other international documents which support protection of the family unit. The International Covenant on Civil and Political Rights (ICCPR) states that the "family is the natural and fundamental group unit of society and is entitled to protection by society and the State."[17] One federal judge found that summary deportation violates the ICCPR's guarantee against arbitrary interference with one's family.[18] The United States adopted the Universal Declaration of Human Rights in 1948 which states that the "family is the natural and fundamental group unit of society and is entitled to protection by society and the State."[19] The American Convention on Human Rights (ACHR), which the United States signed, also protects generally the right to, and protection of, a family.[20] The Vienna Convention on Consular Relations gives consular officers the right to assist their nationals regarding guardianship determinations of minors and requires the United States to notify the consulate of certain matters pending against a foreign national.[21] There are other international conventions that support family unity and children's rights although the United States is not a party to them.[22] None, however, provide for children the substantial bundle of rights and protections of the UN Convention on the Rights of the Child.

Enforcement-only immigration policies discriminate against children

> Exploiting the fear of family separation should not be the lynchpin of modern immigration enforcement.
>
> (Thronson 2008, p. 417)

Federal immigration policy undermines state family policy by unnecessarily separating families. Immigration law discriminates against citizen children in several ways. First, discrimination against children occurs when their families are torn apart by surprise immigration raids on homes and workplaces that result in immediate detention of the undocumented parent. If the parent is summarily deported, these citizen children may never be reunited with the parent as they are left with relatives or placed in state foster care (Molina and Kohm 2013). Second, immigration law provides no avenue for children to petition for their parents to become lawful residents until the child is 21. Although citizens and legal permanent residents may petition for immigrant visas for select relatives including children,

children cannot extend the possibility of immigration status to other family members.[23] Immigration law currently gives no special consideration to the parents of citizen children and fails to make family preservation a priority (Thronson 2010). Once detention and deportation of an unauthorized parent has commenced, the immigration court is not required to try to reunify the family, to consider the best interest of the children or to hear the children's voices.

The federal government holds plenary power over immigration law (Lindsay 2010). Immigration policy prior to 1996 generally adhered to international legal norms, including the concept of family unity.[24] The Illegal Immigration Reform and Immigrant Responsibility Act of 1996 (IIRIRA) and Antiterrorism and Effective Death Penalty Act of 1996 (AEDPA)[25] changed the rules considerably. AEDPA expanded the definition of aggravated felony to include nonviolent crimes.[26] The repeal of waivers once removal has begun effectively took away the ability for judges to consider family unification in deportation and removal proceedings. The law also provided for expedited removals allowing deportation without a hearing unless the immigrant can prove presence for 2 years and a claim to legal status or credible fear of persecution if returned to the home country. The law also provided state and local partnerships for raids and substantial bars on reentry if a person has remained unlawfully in the United States.[27] Parents who either entered illegally or became unlawful (overstayed a visa) may have resided in the United States for decades and have citizen children who have no legal means available to get legal status to keep their family intact.

The U.S. Department of Homeland Security (DHS) by its U.S. Citizenship and Immigration Services (USCIS) and Immigration and Customs Enforcement (ICE) divisions enforce immigration laws with Customs and Border Protection (CBP) agents being on the front line of enforcement. An immigration case involves two steps: a petition to classify an individual as eligible for a benefit or classification, and an application to obtain a visa based on that eligibility. If sought in the United States, USCIS can grant the visa, called "adjustment of status." An applicant must be "admissible" – mentally and physically healthy, have no criminal background, and not be barred due to past unlawful presence. If a visa is issued, the person has the right be present in the United States, either temporarily (nonimmigrant visa for students or tourists) or permanently – an immigrant visa, or green card. A green card holder who has legal permanent resident (LPR) status can remain indefinitely and may apply for citizenship. Immigrants without visas are undocumented, unlawful or illegal aliens.

Numerous attempts to come up with comprehensive immigration reform over the past 22 years have failed. President Obama ameliorated some of the harsh impacts by directing DHS to use its prosecutorial discretion to refrain from deporting people who had more favorable factors than negative. ICE then prioritized arrests based on the severity of the immigrants' criminal records.[28] The 2016 election of Donald Trump, however, with his "Build the wall" and "America first" platforms radically changed the picture. On January 25, 2017, President Trump signed an executive order "Enhancing Public Safety in the Interior of the United States" [29] requiring ICE to (1) identify and deport removable aliens; (2)

increase enforcement of laws; (3) punish sanctuary jurisdictions; (4) speed up removal proceedings; and (5) empower local and state enforcement officials to act as immigration officers. The order targeted thousands more immigrants, including those who have been convicted of a crime, have been charged with a crime, committed an act that could constitute a crime, have engaged in fraud or willful misrepresentation on an application or other business with a government agency, have abused any program related to receiving public benefits, or pose a risk to public safety as determined by an immigration officer. Any crime is a deportable offense, even if the person is not a threat to others or to national security. Most deportations are for nonviolent crimes, such as overstaying a visa.

The number of immigrant arrests by ICE surged 40 percent between January and September 2017. An example of the difference in policy is illustrated by the story of Syed Jamal, a 55-year-old scientist in Lawrence, Kansas. On January 24, 2018, ICE agents, based on a deportation order from May 2013, arrested and handcuffed Syed in his front yard as he was getting his three children off to school. Syed had lived peacefully in the United States for 30 years after coming on a nonimmigrant student visa in 1987 from Bangladesh. He earned several degrees, overstayed his visa, but was allowed to voluntarily depart in July 2002. He left, married and legally reentered the country on another nonimmigrant visa later that year to work at a hospital. He changed his visa to pursue a doctorate and again overstayed, resulting in an order to leave the country. Syed worked continually as a chemist to support his wife and three citizen children, was active in the community, paid taxes, and had no criminal record. He was taken to a jail in Missouri, within days transferred to a detention center in Texas, and placed on a plane that, fortunately for him, stopped in Hawaii. An incredible outcry from the Lawrence community, local immigration lawyers and a couple of congresspersons led to a federal judge issuing a stay of removal pending review and Syed was returned to a Missouri jail. By March 20, 2018, there was a hearing and a bill proposed in Congress to grant him and his wife permanent resident status (Krug 2018; Wang and Sacchetti 2018). No final decision has been made, but in August 2018 a federal judge granted his request for a hearing.

Under Obama's policy, Syed was the type of person who was a nonpriority – a good family man who worked hard, posed no threat to national security, and was not a flight risk. If he had been deported, likely his wife also would have been deported. Once deportation proceedings have commenced, it is difficult to stop them. One exception to cancel a removal is "exceptional and extremely unusual hardship" to a child but the standard is almost impossible to achieve. Courts have found that family separation is "simply one of the common results of deportation… insufficient to prove extreme hardship."[30] Syed Jamal's teenage son wrote a letter on his father's behalf which explains the hardship from the child's view:

> Hello, my name is Taseen Jamal, and my father has recently been arrested… and is being considered for deportation. My little brother cries every night, my sister can't focus in school, and I cannot sleep at night. My mother is in trauma and because she is a live organ donor, she only has one kidney, so the stress is very dangerous.… If my father is deported, my siblings and I may

> never get to see him again. He is an older man and due to conditions in his country, he might not be able to survive... we are requesting on behalf of our family for your kind help to get back our father. A home is not a home without a father.
>
> (Wang and Sacchetti 2018)

Deporting this father for overstaying his visa will harm his three citizen children who will be without their father, perhaps forever. Syed would be returning to a country where he has no close ties, might be in danger from the current political factions, and may be unable to obtain work. These children are "punished" for the parent's overstaying his student visa by either having to live in the United States without their father or going with him to a nonnative country.[31] Additionally, hardship waivers for reentry to the United States only consider adult hardship, not the hardship to children.[32]

Discrimination: lack of due process for parents and children

> [O]ur immigration system doesn't allow immigration judges to consider... whether or not there are U.S. citizen children who are dependent.... We must afford a minimum level of due process consistent with our national values.
>
> (Senator Coons, 2013)[33]

Federal immigration enforcement is a civil, not criminal, proceeding.[34] Border patrol agents (CBP) conduct expedited removals largely free from the restrictions of due process and without concern for dependent children. In one case a 4-year-old citizen child was deported to Guatemala because her grandfather and parents were unauthorized. ICE gave the father on the telephone an hour to decide whether to allow deportation or placement with a Virginia adoption agency (Rogerson 2013).

Immigrant detention happens suddenly, without notice, and for an indefinite period of time, often months and years. As in Syed's case, when ICE raids a home or workplace and determines a parent is unauthorized, ICE immediately places the parent in a local jail before transferring him or her to immigration detention, often thousands of miles away. Deportation can happen within weeks. The detainee has little ability to seek assistance in defending against the removal process as access is limited to phone calls and language services. The detainee may appear before the Immigration Judge by telephone or video.[35] Lacking a "civil Gideon,"[36] there is no right to counsel, no right to challenge a final order through a habeas corpus petition,[37] no right to a fair and speedy trial, no right to a jury of their peers, and no protections against cruel and unusual punishment, retroactive penalties, and disproportionate sentencing (see Noferi 2012).

When unauthorized parents are "picked up" without notice and without them having the opportunity to make care arrangements,[38] their children can end up in the state child welfare system. Placing thousands of children, who are not abused or neglected, in state child welfare systems for indefinite periods of time[39] puts a tremendous burden on already underfunded, understaffed systems (Rogerson 2013; Rabin 2011). It also triggers use of state child welfare laws whose primary goal is generally family reunification. The Adoption and Safe Families Act (ASFA),[40] the federal law that supports state welfare programs, requires that agencies create case plans for reintegration of a child with the family members, and supply services to help make that happen. ASFA requires that permanency hearings be held no later than 12 months after the child enters foster care and that the state initiate a termination of parental rights proceeding when a child has been in foster care for 15 out of the past 22 consecutive months.[41] ASFA also excuses states from making "reasonable efforts" to reunite parents and children under certain circumstances, which can include parental incarceration.[42] When unauthorized parents are detained often thousands of miles away from where the children may have been placed, the parent faces almost insurmountable obstacles to finding and having contact with their children, meeting any case plan requirements, or attending a hearing to defend a challenge to their parental rights (Bui 2012). The parental deportation often creates permanent chaos. Where the parent and children have had a strong relationship, failure to provide reasonable efforts to reunite the family discriminates against children based on the parent's status, violates the core values of a right to family life, and is contrary to the children's best interests (see Rogerson 2013).

While state law forbids depriving parents and children of access to each other without due process of law, immigration law has trumped. To terminate parental rights requires a state to show by clear and convincing evidence not only that the parent has abused, abandoned or neglected the children, but also that termination is in the children's best interests. A parent's unauthorized status, even with potential for detention or deportation, should not be unfairly and disproportionately counted against parental fitness.[43] Some trial judges have considered the future possibility of deportation of an authorized parent in terminating parental rights (see Thronson 2006; Yablon-Zug 2012; Hall 2011). Fortunately, several appellate courts have noted that the lack of immigration status itself is not maltreatment, nor is it clear and convincing evidence of unfitness.[44] States must carefully balance the unauthorized parent's rights and the best interest of children. States should consider enacting a statutory presumption against termination of parental rights based solely on the potential deportation of an immigrant parent.

In 2012, the American Bar Association (ABA) issued model standards for the immigration detention system and urged due process protections for detained immigrant parents.[45] An ABA House of Delegates resolution states that immigrant detainees who are "parents, legal guardians and primary caregivers of children" should be provided with access to an attorney to help them understand the legal issues and referred to an attorney who can represent their interests in state court custody, dependency, and other legal actions. They should be allowed meaningful participation in all state judicial proceedings involving their children's custody and welfare.[46] Adopting these resolutions would further the best interests of citizen children by supporting family reunification.

When parents are separating or divorcing, one parent may attempt to use the other parent's unauthorized status to argue for placement with the citizen parent.

Judges discriminate against children if they unfairly weigh the unauthorized immigrant parent's status. (see Fata et al. 2013). Most courts use a list of factors to determine "best interests" (see Elrod and Dale 2008). Immigration status is not a listed statutory factor, nor is it relevant as to which parent was the primary caregiver or which parent has the strongest relationship and ability to care for the child. As in a relocation case, the potential for deportation may be relevant as to the safety of the child if placed with a parent who is being deported to a potentially dangerous country. Immigration status may be relevant as it relates to the best interests of the child and its effect on a child's physical, intellectual, moral and spiritual well-being.[47]

Due process for citizen children would require the immigration system to recognize the children's right to family life and protect the relationship. It would also require judges to appoint lawyers for children in not only immigration cases, but also in other custody cases in which the issue of a parent's unauthorized status might be relevant. Due process would require that children be allowed to express their views as to the case and have those views taken into account. The judge should take the best interests of the child into account in any decision that impacts their custody.

Child-centered best interests considerations prevent discrimination

> Each decision made, considers the individual child's development and psychological needs. Rather than focusing on parental demands, societal stereotypes, cultural tradition, or legal precedent, the best interests standard asks the decision makers to consider what this child needs at this point in time, given his family and its changed nature.
>
> (Kelly 1997, p. 385)

Overall, the best interest of the child standard has been successful in protecting children (Carr 2009). A child-centered best interest standard is an inherently individualized standard that should be incorporated into procedural and substantive changes to immigration law. Family unity is a goal of child welfare law and international law, but not current immigration law. Unfortunately, there has been a serious lack of federal planning for the best interests of children left behind because of a parent's deportation. Children end up in chaos, sometimes in the custody of relatives, friends, or often the child welfare system.

A child-centered best interest standard would include a family focus in immigration enforcement (see Fagden and Prescott 2016; Thronson 2006; Schoenholtz 2012; Zug 2011). ICE should place a parent detainee as close as possible to the where the children are placed and give the children an opportunity to communicate with their parents. For example, Syed Jamal's "crime" was overstaying his visa. He was picked up, detained, moved to another state, and not allowed to talk to anyone until an immigration lawyer became involved.

Immigration courts should have discretion to issue a "hardship" suspension of removal in cases where the unauthorized parent has been in the United States for a substantial period of time, has been a "good citizen" and it is in the best interests of their children to stay with them in the United States. In Syed's case, an immigration judge should have been able to consider the 30-year history of good conduct and hard work in the United States, and that it would be in the best interests of three minor citizen children to continue living with a fit and loving father. Those considerations might tip the scale against deportation and toward family reunification because the removal of a parent may result in a greater violation of the rights of citizen children than the state's interest in deportation.

The 112th Congress considered, but did not pass, a Child Citizenship Protection Act that would prioritize the best interests of the child in ICE and immigration courts to prevent unnecessary separation from parents in removal proceedings (see Molina and Kohm 2013). It should be reconsidered. Judges should have the discretion to take into account the best interests of the children affected by a parent's potential deportation in rendering a final decision on the merits of the parent's immigration case. The child should have a lawyer or a child advocate to ensure the best interests are presented to the judge. Among the factors that could be considered and can vary considerably are:

- the child's age and maturity
- the child's vulnerability
- the child's preference of country
- level of dependency of the child on the unauthorized parent
- length of time and degree of child's establishment in the United States
- the likelihood the child would have to leave the United States
- the child's identity with a particular culture
- the importance to the child of preservation of this family unit
- care, protection and safety of the child in the United States
- care, protection and safety issues in the parent's native country
- the availability of an alternative caregiver in the United States
- the child's health concerns that can be treated better in one location
- impact on the child's educational needs and opportunities
- presence of siblings, other close relatives in the United States or other country

The court should examine the underlying conduct that led to a parent's detention and whether it is related to their fitness as a parent or the best interests of the child. For example, in Syed's case, the "crime" was overstaying a student visa. By all accounts, however, Syed was an upstanding member of the community, worked hard, paid taxes, and, perhaps most importantly from the best interest standpoint, was a good father to his three children.

A child's best interests would include not being separated from the parent unless the parent poses a threat to the children. If the parent and children are separated, the separation should be the least detrimental available alternative, such as in a close location, not thousands of miles away so that they can speak with, see, and touch each other. In most cases, the best interest of the child would be better served by being reared by their parents, rather than being placed with strangers. Lingering in foster care is not in the best interests of any child.

Part of the best interests is hearing the voice of the child. Hearing children is important and children want to be heard. One of the best ways to do that is to ensure that the citizen child has an attorney who represents the child (see Elrod 2007; O'Neill et al. 2015). At the least, the child should have a best interests advocate or child advocate to ensure that the children's voices are heard and considered by anyone making a decision about whether the children stay in the United States or go with the parent.[48] Citizen children whose immigrant parents are detained or deported should have a court-appointed counsel; be allowed contact with their detained parents; allowed meaningful participation in immigration and family court proceedings that impact the parent-child relationship; and have a voice in all proceedings affecting their custody and care.

Conclusion

> Bias against children's interests that characterizes immigration law also distances it from mainstream family law values.
>
> (Thronson 2013, p. 660)

The best interests of citizen children should be at the center of immigration law reform. Current enforcement-only immigration policies discriminate against citizen children based upon their parents' unauthorized status, destroy families without due process and consideration of the children's best interest, and harm children in violation of both domestic and international law (see Starr and Brilmayer 2003). Good immigration policy would safeguard and protect the interests of families in being together and not punish children for the unauthorized status of their parents. The policy would include a child-focused best interest consideration which would allow the unauthorized parent to prove that his or her children's best interests outweigh the state's interest in deportation. It would give immigration judges discretion to consider the totality of circumstances of the family. Immigration reform is essential to protect children.

Notes

* Richard S. Righter Distinguished Professor of Law and Director of Children and Family Law Center, Washburn University School of Law.

1 *Memije v. Gonzales*, 481 F.3d 1163, 1167 (9th Cir. 2007) (letter from 16-year-old Ruby Arcos, a U.S. citizen child of undocumented parents who were being deported with their four citizen children to Mexico after 11 years in the United States).

2 U.S. Const. Am. XIV § 1. See Immigration and Nationality Act (INA), 8 U.S.C. § 1401. See *Brown v. Topeka Board of Educ.*, 347 U.S. 483 (1954); *Planned Parenthood of Cent. Mo. v. Danforth*, 428 U.S. 52, 74 (1976) ("constitutional rights do not mature and come into being magically only... [at] the state-defined age of majority.").

3 *Meyer v. Nebraska*, 262 U.S. 390, 399 (1923); *Moore v. City of East Cleveland*, 431 U.S. 494, 503–504 (1977); M.L.B. v. S.L.J., 519 U.S. 102, 116–117 (1996) ("Choices about marriage, family life, and the upbringing of children are... sheltered... against the State's unwarranted usurpation, disregard or disrespect."); *Nicholson v. Williams*, 203 F. Supp. 2d

153, 235 (E.D. N.Y. 2002) ("rights of family integrity are fundamental liberty interests entitled to due process protections").

4 *Troxel v. Granville*, 530 U.S. 57, 68–69 (2000) (if parents are fit, there will normally be no reason for the State to inject itself into the private realm of the family). See also Elrod 2018, §1:2; §4:6; §§7:1, 2.

5 *Santosky v. Kramer*, 455 U.S. 745 (1982).

6 American Immigration Council 2018. In 2016, 17, 997,000 children had one immigrant parent. See http://migrationpolicy.org/programs/data-hub (88.2 percent of these children were born in the United States).

7 *Plyler v. Doe*, 457 U.S. 202, 210 (1982) (constitutional protections of the Fourteenth Amendment are not confined to the protection of citizens… "an alien is surely a 'person'"). See also *Newton v. INS*, 736 F.2d 336, 343 (6th Cir. 1984) (immigrants also have protected parental interests).

8 United Nations, Joint general comment No. 3 (2017) of the Committee on the Protection of the Rights of All Migrant Workers and Members of Their Families and No. 22 (2017) of the Committee on the Rights of the Child on the general principles regarding the human rights of children in the context of international migration, available at https://tbinternet.ohchr.org/_layouts/treatybodyexternal/Download.aspx?symbolno=CRC/C/GC/22&Lang=en.

9 Many of the same arguments can extend to unaccompanied minors seeking asylum and to the 2,300 noncitizen children separated from their parents between May 7, 2018 and June 20, 2018, by Attorney General Sessions's zero-tolerance policy. Federal judges have ordered reunification, but many parents were summarily deported and 500 remain in foster care.

10 See Post-deportation Human Rights Project 2013, (a child's relationship with familiar caregivers is a "necessary foundation for developing social, cognitive, and emotional regulation skills that are fundamental throughout life"). See also UCLA-Duke U. National Center for Child Traumatic Stress 2012.

11 CRC, art. 3. The right of the child to have his or her best interest taken into account is a substantive right, an interpretative legal principles and a rule of procedure. General Comment No. 14, para. 6. Conflicts between the child's best interests and other interests or rights (the public or parents) have to be decided on a case by case basis.

12 CRC, art. 9: "a child shall not be separated from… parents against their will, except when competent authorities subject to judicial review determine that such separation is necessary for the best interests of the child." See also art. 9(3) (4). Art. 19 states that children have the right to be protected from all forms of physical or mental violence, injury or abuse, neglect or negligent treatment, maltreatment, including sexual abuse.

13 *Lopez v. Richardson*, 647 F. Supp. 2d 1356, 1366 (N.D. Ga. 2009).

14 "Best interest" is mentioned in the Child Torture Convention and the Special Immigrant Juvenile Status (SIJS) that allows for humanitarian relief for unauthorized migrant children who have been abused, neglected or abandoned. INA § 101(a)(27)(J)(iii)(I) as amended, 8 U.S.C. §1101(a)(27)(J).

15 President Clinton signed the CRC on February 16, 1995, arguably acknowledging it as customary international law which should not be disregarded when creating and interpreting legislation. *Murray v. The Schooner Charming Betsy*, 6 U.S. 64. 118 (1804).

16 *Roper v. Simmons*, 543 U.S. 551 (2005).

17 International Covenant on Civil and Political Rights, art. 23(1), Dec. 19, 1966, U.N.T. S. No. 14668 (entered into force Mar. 23, 1976). The United States ratified it June 8, 1992.

18 *Beharry v. Reno*, 183 F. Supp. 2d 584 (E.D. N.Y. 2002), rev'd on other ground sub nom., *Beharry v. Ashcroft*, 329 F.3d 51 (2d Cit. 2003) (finding international customary law required allowing those subject to deportation to put on evidence balancing the rights of family and the government).

19 Universal Declaration of Human Rights, art. 16(3), G.A. Res. 217A, at 71, U.N. GAOR, 3d sess., 1st plen. mtg., U.N. Doc A/810 (Dec. 12, 1948).
20 Organization of American States, American Convention on Human Rights, art. 17(1), Nov. 22, 1969, O.A.S.T.S. no. 36, 1144 U.N.T.S. 123 (signed by the United States June 1, 1977).
21 Vienna Convention on Consular Relations, art. 37(b), Apr. 24, 1963, 21 U.S.T. 77, 596 U.N.T.S. 261. If notified, the home country could provide the detained parent with legal counsel or provide consular assistance to aid in information sharing between immigration authorities and the family courts.
22 European Convention for the Protection of Human Rights and Fundamental Freedoms, art. 8, Nov. 4, 1950, 213 U.N.T.S. 222 (entered into force Sept. 3, 1953).
23 See 8 U.S.C. § 1151(b)(2)(A)(i) (for parents, such citizens must be at least 21). A child who obtains legal immigration status through a family petition from one parent may not include the other parent. Children who are parents themselves cannot extend immigration status to their children. INA §§ 207 (c)(2), 208(b)(2), 8 U.S.C. § 1151 (b)(2)(A)(i); § 1153(d).
24 Human Rights Watch 2007.
25 Pub. L. No. 104–208, 110 Stat. 3009–546 (1996) (codified in scattered sections of 8 U.S.C.) (expedited removals).
26 INA § 101(a)(43); AEDPA § 440(d). Expanded deportable offenses were forgery, obstruction of justice and bribery, and an attempt or conspiracy to commit any of those crimes. Noncitizens convicted of aggravated felonies have no right to raise defenses that include consideration of family ties.
27 8 U.S.C. § 1182(a)(9)(B). If a person has remained in the United States unlawfully for more than 180 days and leaves the United States, the person is barred from reentry for 3 years; if the person remained for more than a year, the bar is 10 years; if the person remained more than a year or has been deported and reentered illegally, there is a permanent ban.
28 Morton 2011. By a June 15, 2012 order, President Obama also protected from deportation immigrants who were brought to this country as children (under age 16) before 2007 – the Deferred Action for Childhood Arrivals (DACA).
29 Exec. Order No. 13,768, 82 Fed. Reg. 8,799 (Jan. 25, 2017), reprinted in 8 U.S.C. § 1103 note (Supp. 2017).
30 *Memije v. Gonzales*, 481 F.3d 1163, 1167 (9th Cir. 2007) (lower court did not find "exceptional and extreme hardship" in sending four citizen children back to Mexico with parents who had lived in the United States for 11 years). See also *Olowo v. Ashcroft*, 368 F.3d 692 (7th Cir. 2004) (deporting Nigerian mother of twin girls who claimed the daughters would be subject to genital mutilation, but court found girls did not have to leave the United States).
31 *Plyler v Doe*, 457 U.S. 202, 220 (1982) ("Those who elect to enter our territory… in violation of law should be prepared to bear the consequences… including deportation. But the children of those illegal entrants are not comparably situated").
32 8 U.S.C. § 1182(a)(9)(B)(i)(II).
33 Coons 2013. Werlin 2013.
34 American Immigration Council 2013.
35 8 U.S.C. § 1229a(b)(2)(A)(iii).
36 *Gideon v. Wainwright*, 372 U.S. 335 (1963) requires states to provide the accused in criminal cases with an attorney if the accused cannot afford to hire one. There is no such requirement for civil detentions.
37 A writ of habeas corpus requires a person under arrest to be brought before a judge to secure their release unless lawful grounds are shown for their detention. Under immigration law, a person can be "mandatorily detained" for an uncertain amount of time at a removal facility. 8 U.S.C § 1226(c); § 1231(a)(2).

38 Unauthorized parents need to have all relevant information about the children (birth certificates, travel documents, school records, immunizations) in one place; identify possible alternative caregivers both in the United States and abroad; provide for immediate, and long term, care of children; and draft a power of attorney delegating power to make medical and educational decisions in the event of incarceration.

39 An estimated 5,000 U.S. citizen children in foster care had a detained or deported parent in 2011. American Immigration Council 2018. Under the ICE Detained Parents Directive, ICE should "generally accommodate" the parent's efforts to make child care arrangements before contacting child welfare or law enforcement to take the child into custody. Once the child is in state custody, there are limited mechanisms to safeguard parental rights for those in detention or deportation proceedings.

40 Adoption and Safe Families Act of 1997, Pub. L. No. 105–89, 111 Stat. 2115 (codified in scattered sections of 42 U.S.C.) (reaffirms commitment to family preservation, requires reasonable efforts to reunite, but makes the child's health and safety the paramount concern).

41 *Id.* 42 U.S.C. § 675(5)(E)(i)-(iii).

42 42 U.S.C. § 671(a)(15)(D).

43 See *S.M. v E.M.B.R.*, 332 S.W.3d 793 (Mo. 2011) (reversing termination of mother's parental rights where trial court trivialized illegal immigration as a "lifestyle choice" and presumed the parent was not acting in the child's best interest). Gilger, et al. 2012.

44 *In re* Angelica L., 767 N.W. 2d 74, 93, 96 (Neb. 2009) (reversing the termination of an unauthorized mother's parental rights;she had a constitutional right to raise her children where she was able to provide a stable home and it was in the best interest of the children to be reunited with her in Guatemala); *In re* M.M., 587 S.E.2d 825 (Ga. App. 2003) (reversing termination of parental rights); *In re* B. & J., 756 N.W.2d 234, 236 (Mich. App. 2008) (reversing termination of parental rights as not in the best interests of children where immigrant parents should have had the opportunity to take them to Guatemala).

45 American Bar Association Civil Immigration Detention Standards § III.B.1(d), § VI.B.4 (b), § VI.B.4(g), § VII.D.1, § X.B.4 (Am. Bar Ass'n 2012), http://www.americanbar.org/content/dam/aba/administrative/immigration/abaimmdetstds.authcheckdam.pdf.

46 American Bar Association 2011.

47 *Turrubiartes v. Olvera*, 539 S.W.3d 524 (Tex. App. 2018) (finding mother's immigration status should not have been the determining factor in trial court's denial of her joint conservatorship with the father). See also *Castleman v. Bicaldo*, 2018 WL 2716715 (Fla. Dist. App. June 6, 2018).

48 The American Bar Association Commission on Immigration reported that represented children have a 73 percent success rate in immigration court as compared with only 15 percent of unrepresented children. http:www.americanbar.org/contentdam/aa/administrative/immigration/UACS. An immigration judge stated that a 3 year old did not need a lawyer to understand immigration law. See Leahy 2016.

References

American Bar Association. 2011. Resolution 103C (Aug. 8–9, 2011), Detained Parents, Legal Guardians, or Primary Caregivers are Provided Meaningful Participation at All Judicial Proceedings Involving Their Children's Custody and Welfare. Available at: http://www.americanbar.org/content/dam/aba/directories/policy/2011_am_103c.authcheckdam.pdf.

American Immigration Council. 2013. Two Systems of Justice: How the Immigration System Falls Short of American Ideals of Justice.

American Immigration Council. 2018. U.S. Citizen Children Impacted by Immigration Enforcement (May 23). Available at: https://www.americanimmigrationcouncil.org.

Bui, T. 2012. Battle Scars from the Fight Between Family Law and Immigration Law: Incarcerated Immigrant Parents and Missouri's Response. *UMKC Law Review*,81(1), 183.

Capps, R., Castaneda, R. M. and Ajay Chaudry, R. S. 2007. Paying the Price: The Impact of Immigration Raids on America's Children. *The Urban Institute*. Available at: http://www.urban.org/uploadedpdf/411566_immigation_raids.pdf.

Carr, B. A. 2009. Incorporating a "Best Interests of the Child" Approach into Immigration Law and Procedure. *Yale Human Rights & Development Law Journal*, 12, 120–159.

Coons, Sen. C. 2013. Building an Immigration System Worthy of American Values. Senate Judiciary Committee Hearing, March 20, 2013.

Elrod, L. D. 2007. Client-Directed Lawyers for Children: It is the Right Thing to Do. *Pace Law Review*, 27(4), 869–920.

Elrod, L. D. 2011. "Please Let Me Stay": Hearing the Voice of the Child in Hague Abduction Cases. *Oklahoma Law Review*, 63(4), 663–690.

Elrod, L. D. 2018. *Child Custody Practice and Procedure*. Eagan, MN: Thomson Reuters.

Elrod, L. D. and Dale, M. D. 2008. Paradigm Shifts and Pendulum Swings in Child Custody: The Interests of Children in the Balance. *Family Law Quarterly*, 42(3), 381–418.

Fadgen, T. P. and Prescott, D. E. 2016. Do the Best Interests of the Child End at the Nation's Shores? Immigration, State Courts and Children in the United States. *Journal of the American Academy of Matrimmonal Lawyers*, 28, 359.

Fata, S., Orloff, L. E., Carcamo-Cavazos, A., Silber, A. and Anver, B. 2013. Custody of Children in Mixed-Status Families: Preventing the Misunderstanding and Misuse of Immigration Status in State Court Custody Proceedings. *Family Law Quarterly*, 47(2), 191–242, 244–271.

Foley, E. 2014. Deportation Separated Thousands of U.S. Born Children from Parents in 2013. *Huffington Post*, June 26, 2014. Available at: http:/www.huffintonpost.com/2014/06/26/2014/parents-deportation_5531552.html (stating that 72,410 immigrant parents with one or more children were deported).

Fox, S. J. 1997. Beyond the American Legal System for the Protection of Children's Rights. *Family Law Quarterly*, 31(2), 237–267.

Friedler, E. Z. 1995. From Extreme Hardship to Extreme Deference: United States Deportation of its Own Children. *Hastings Constitutional Law Quarterly*, 22, 491–555.

Gilger, L., Ross, B. and Hill, A. M. 2012. Adoption over 5 Year Old Boy Pits Missouri Couple vs. Illegal Immigrant. *ABA NEWS*, Feb. 1, 2012.

Guggenheim, M. 2005. *What's Wrong with Children's Rights*. Cambridge, MA: Harvard University Press.

Hall, C. E. 2011. Where are My Children … And My Rights? Parental Rights Termination as a Consequence of Deportation. *Duke Law Journal*, 60, 1459–1504

Henderson, S. W. and Baily, C. D. R. 2013. Parental Deportation Families and Mental Health. *Journal of the American Academy of Child & Adolescent Psychiatry*, 52(5), 451–453.

Human Rights Watch. 2007. Forced Apart: Families Separated and Immigrants Harmed by United States Deportation Policy. Available at: http://www.hrw.org/sites/default/files/reports/us0707_web.pdf.

Kanstroom, D. 2012. *Aftermath: Deportation Law and the New American Diaspora X*. Oxford: Oxford University Press.

Kaskade, S. G. 2009. Mothers Without Borders: Undocumented Immigrant Mothers Facing Deportation and the Best Interests of Their U.S. Citizen Children. *William & Mary Journal of Women & Law*, 15(2), 447–467.

Kelly, J. B.,1997. The Best Interest of the Child: A Concept in Search of Meaning. *Family and Conciliation Courts Review*, 35(4), 377–387.

Kilkelly, U. 2001. The Best of Both Worlds for Children's Rights? Interpreting the European Convention on Human Rights in Light of the UN Convention on the Rights of the Child. *Human Rights Quarterly*, 23(2), 308–326.

Krug, N. 2018. Lawrence Father Syed Jamal Freed from Jail as Immigration Case Continues. *Lawrence Journal World*, March 20, 2018. Available at: http://www.2/ljworld.com/news/2018/mar/20/lawrence-father-syed-jamal-faces-hearing-today-dep/.

Leahy, P. 2016. U.S. Courts Should Stop Picking on Immigrant Kids. *CNN Online*, May 9, 2016. Available at: http://www.cnn.com/2016/05/09/opinions/children-need-lawyers-leahy.

Lindsay, M. J. 2010. Immigration as Invasion: Sovereignty, Security and the Origins of the Federal Immigration Power. *Harvard Civil Rights-Civil Liberties Law Review*, 45(1), 1–56.

Meissner, D., Kerwin, D. M., Chishti, M. and Bergeron, C. 2013. *Immigration Enforcement in the United States: The Rise of a Formidable Machinery*. Washington, DC: Migration Policy Institute.

Middleton, M. 2016. The Last Holdout: The ABA Adds its Voice to Calls for the United States to Ratify the Convention on the Rights of the Child. *ABA Journal*, 64 (Mar.)

Miraval, F. 2012. Thousands of Children of Deported Parents Get Stuck in Foster Care. *The Denver Post* (July 5).

Molina, K. E. and Kohm, L. M. 2013. "Are we There Yet?" Immigration Reform for Children Left Behind. *Regent Journal of International Law*, 10(1), 77–108.

Morton, J. 2011. Exercising Prosecutorial discretion Consistent with the Civil Immigrant Enforcement Priorities of the Agency for the Apprehension, Detention and Removal of Aliens (Memorandum from John Morton, June 11, 2011).

Nicholson, A. 2006. The United Nations Convention on the Rights of the Child and the Need for Its Incorporation into a Bill of Rights. *Family Court Review*, 44(1), 5–30.

Noferi, M. 2012. Cascading Constitutional Deprivation: The Right to Appointed Counsel for Mandatorily Detained Immigrants Pending Removal Proceedings. *Michigan Journal of Race & Law*, 18(1), 63–129.

O'Neill, M., Bagheri, P. and Sarnicola, A. 2015. Forgotten Children of Immigration and Family Law: How the Absence of Legal Aid Affects Children in the United States. *Family Court Review*, 53(4), 676–697.

Post-deportation Human Rights Project, Boston Coll. 2013. The Psychosocial Impact of Detention and Deportation on U.S. Migrant Children and Families.

Rabin, N. 2011. Disappearing Parents: Immigration Enforcement and the Child Welfare System. *Connecticut Law Review*, 44(1), 99–160.

Rogerson, S. 2012. Unintended and Unavoidable: The Failure to Protect Rule and Its Consequences for Undocumented Parents and Their Children. *Family Court Review*, 50 (1), 580–605.

Rogerson, S. 2013. Lack of Detained Parents' Access to the Family Justice System and the Unjust Severance of the Parent-Child Relationship. *Family Law Quarterly*, 47(2), 141–172.

Satinsky, S., Hu, A., JeøøerJ. and Farhang, L. 2013. *Family Unity, Family Health: How Family-Focused Immigration Reform Will Mean Better Health for Children and Families.* Oakland, CA. Human Impact Partners. Available at: http://www.family-unityfamilyhealth.org/uploads/images/FamilyUnityFamilyHealth.pdf.

Schoenholtz, A. I. 2012. Developing the Substantive Best Interests of Child Migrants: A Call for Action. *Valapraiso University Law Review*, 46(4), 991–1018.

Shonkoff, J. P., BoyceW. T. and McEwen, B. S. 2009. Neuroscience, Molecular Biology, and the Childhood Roots of Health Disparities: Building a New Framework for Health Promotion and Disease Prevention. *JAMA*, 301(21), 2252–2259.

Starr, S. and Brilmayer, L. 2003. Family Separation as a Violation of International Law. *Berkeley Journal of International Law*, 21(2), 213–287.

Stief, E. 2010. Impractical Relief and the Innocent Victims: How United States Immigration Law Ignores the Rights of Citizen Children. *UMKC Law Review*, 79(2), 477–506.

Thronson, D. B. 2006. You Can't Get Here from Here: Toward a More Child-Centered Immigration Law. *Virginia Journal of Social Policy & Law*, 14, 58–86.

Thronson, D. B. 2008. Creating Crisis: Immigration Raids and the Destabilization of Immigrant Families. *Wake Forest Law Review*, 43, 391–418.

Thronson, D. B. 2010. Entering the Mainstream: Making Children Matter in Immigration Law. *Fordham Urban Law Journal*, 38, 393–413.

Thronson, D. B. 2013. Thinking Globally, Acting Locally: The Problematically Peripheral Role of Immigration Law in the Globalization of Family Law. *Transnational Law & Contemporary Problems*, 22, 655–668.

UCLA-Duke U. National Center for Child Traumatic Stress. 2012. The 12 Core Concepts: Concepts for Understanding Traumatic Stress Responses in Children and Families.

UN Convention on the Rights of the Child, 1989. *Nov. 20, 1989*, 1577 U.N.T.S. 3, 28 I. L.M. 1456.

Wang, A. B. and Sacchetti, M. A. 2018. Chemistry Professor got His Kids Ready for School. Then ICE Arrested Him on his Front Lawn. *The Washington Post*, Feb. 5, 2018.

Werlin, B. 2013. Hearing and Report Highlight Lack of Due Process in Immigration System. *Immigration Impact* (Mar. 22, 2013). Available at: http://immigrationimpact.com/2013/03/22/hearing-and-report-highlight-lack-of-due-process-in-immigration-system/.

Woodhouse, B. B. 1999. Child Custody in the Age of Children's Rights: The Search for a Just and Workable Standard. *Family Law Quarterly*, 33(3), 815–832.

Yablon-Zug, M. 2012. Separation, Deportation, Termination. *Boston College Journal of Law & Social Justice*, 32(1), 63–117.

Zug, M. 2011. Should I Stay or Should I Go: Why Immigrant Reunification Decisions Should Be Based on the Best Interest of the Child. *Brigham Young University Law Review*, 4, 1139–1192.

10 Hidden discriminatory practices in access to education for children with disabilities

A challenge for children's rights*

Trynie Boezaart

Introduction

In South Africa the student-led protest known as '#FeesMustFall' (2015 to 2017) was a response to increased fees at Institutions of Higher Learning. The students demanded free tertiary education and believed that the African National Congress (ANC)-led government has a duty to invest more in tertiary education. It eventually exploded into violent clashes between protesters and police and a vicious cycle ensued with teargas, rubber bullets and stun grenades being answered by massive destruction of property and many young people's arrest. Sadly, some youngsters believed that the government betrayed them because the Freedom Charter promised free education for all.

However, the Freedom Charter that was adopted by the ANC in 1955 promised that 'education shall be free, compulsory, universal and equal for all *children*' [and that] 'higher education and technical training shall be opened to all by means of state allowances and scholarships awarded on the basis of merit' (own emphasis). The promise that materialised into law is articulated in section 29 of the Constitution of the Republic of South Africa, 1996, of which subsection (1) provides:

> Everyone has the right
> (a) to a *basic* education, including adult *basic* education; and
> (b) to *further* education, which the state, through reasonable measures, must make progressively available and accessible (own emphasis).

Section 29 is discussed below but it is clear that the provision does not refer to all accepted education rights.[1] It is limited to basic education and compulsory education is not part of the right. It also does not guarantee a right to free education but most children in South Africa do receive free education. Schools are divided into five categories based on the country's poverty index. All learners in quintile one to three receive free public schooling. In the remaining quintiles the parents of learners that require assistance may apply to be exempted from paying school fees.[2] The South African Schools Act provides that learners are compelled to attend school from the age of 7 years until the age of 15 years, or the ninth grade, whichever comes first.[3]

South Africa is a developing country and even though the largest slice of total expenditure is allocated to education,[4] dividing it between the different sectors in education involves prioritising and agreement on the standards to be applied in that process.[5] In 2014 there were 13,068,855 learners enrolled in all sectors of the basic education system; 12,117,015 (92.7 per cent) were in ordinary public schools and 538,421 (4.1 per cent) were in ordinary independent schools, 295,942 (2.3 per cent) were in early childhood development (ECD) centres and 117,477 (0.9 per cent) were in special schools. There were 10,364 educators in 447 schools involved in the education provided in the special needs education (SNE).[6]

In this chapter the focus will be on children with disabilities. It proposes that international and constitutional standards should be given the force of law when the basic education of children with disabilities is at stake. The South African government's commitment to realise the right to education of children with severe and profound disabilities are tested in case law and hidden discrimination is revealed. The chapter suggests that the way forward comes with clear recognition of international guidance and constitutional imperatives to address discrimination and start with the basic for the most vulnerable in the education system.

The failing funding story

In *Western Cape Forum for Intellectual Disability v Government of the Republic of South Africa*, a body corporate which has as its members non-governmental organisations caring for 1000 children with severe and profound intellectual disabilities (IQ levels of 20–30 or less than 20 respectively) brought an application to the High Court which revealed that these children were not admitted to any government school.[7] Neither the national government nor the provincial government provided schools for such children in that province – rural areas being worst off. The only education available to children with severe and profound intellectual disabilities was at Special Care Centres, run by non-governmental organisations, such as the applicant. The government's only contribution to the education of these children was a subsidy paid to the organisations involved which was less than the funding provided for the education of children who were not so disabled. In the Western Cape the Department of Health at that stage paid an annual subsidy of:

- R5,092.00 (approx. €328) per child for children with severe or profound intellectual disabilities attending Special Care Centres,
- R6,632.00 (approx. €427) per child for children who attend mainstream schools and
- R26,767.00 (approx. €1722) per child for children with mild to moderate intellectual disabilities in special schools.

In this case the court indicated that neither White Paper 6,[8] which embodied the government's response to transform the education system relating to children with disabilities, nor the implementation of government policy makes provision for children with severe or profound intellectual disabilities to be accommodated in special schools. Admission to a special school was on the basis of an assessment of a child's level of educational need. These levels refer to the National Strategy on Screening, Identification, Assessment and Support (the SIAS Strategy) developed by the National Department of Education (in 2005) and in essence entailed that children were admitted to special schools only if they are able to 'acquire sufficient skills' or if they 'achieve the minimum outcome and standards linked to the grade of education' (levels 4 and 5). Children, whose level of need is higher than that, 'receive education through Partial Care Centres' such as those run by the applicant's members with the smallest subsidy.[9] The facts thus revealed that the state's policy and practice excluded children with (severe or profound intellectual) disabilities from basic education (paragraph 19).

A matter of priorities

Unfortunately this is an extremely vulnerable group of children, unable to protest, destroy property or bring institutions to a halt to enforce their rights. They rely on the voice of non-governmental organisations to be heard and taken care of. In the *Western Cape Forum for Intellectual Disability* case the court dealt with the relevant constitutional rights in some depth but only very briefly mentioned a few provisions in international conventions reiterating the rights of children with disabilities. Without detracting any value from a judgment that seeks to improve service delivery to the most vulnerable in the Basic Education sector, the facts in my view clearly called for applying and implementing Article 2 of the 1989 United Nations Convention on the Rights of the Child (CRC).[10]

International standards

Convention on the Rights of the Child

The CRC was the first human rights treaty explicitly prohibiting discrimination against children on the basis of disability.[11] The Preamble to the CRC recognises that in all countries in the world, there are children living in exceptionally difficult conditions, and that such children need special consideration. In South Africa, this treaty has found its way into legislation which guarantees the horizontal effect thereof,[12] and subsequently the Constitutional Court has relied on it in dealing with another general principle of the Convention in a child law matter.[13]

Article 2 of the CRC is prominently placed in the beginning of the Convention and it is also the first of the general principles to be mentioned. It sets out the non-discrimination or anti-discrimination principle[14] as one of the guaranteed rights and thus applies to the interpretation and the application of the entire Convention (Besson 2005, p. 433) and the exact wording is significant.

Article 2(1) obliges ('shall') State Parties (the duty-holders) to 'respect' and 'ensure' that each and every child is afforded all the Convention-rights without any discrimination. The word 'respect' is to heed or regard and does not necessarily require action. But the word 'ensure' is much stronger and requires action:[15] one has 'to secure' or 'make safe'. Note that the principle of non-discrimination is available to 'every' child. It also extends to children whose parents or legal guardians have a disability. Article 2(1) is ground-specific and disability is explicitly mentioned. There are ample reasons to single children with disabilities out in this way, because they are in (at least) 'double jeopardy' because they are at the receiving end of discrimination based both on age and disability. Subsection 2(2) obliges State Parties to be active role-players and put protective measures in place to avoid both discrimination and punishment of children.

The *Western Cape Forum* case exposed the state singling out children with severe and profound disability for manifestly less favourable treatment than other children, and even other children with disabilities, exactly falling within the ambit of Article 2 as explained above. Likewise, the shortage in funds was not imposed on all children (paragraphs 26 and 29). Instead of acting to avoid discrimination against children with severe and profound intellectual disability in line with Article 2, the state failed dismally to provide for their educational needs.[16]

As expected from this child-dedicated human rights instrument which introduced the disability-ground on non-discrimination, Article 23 is specifically dedicated to the rights of children with disabilities, and this article was mentioned and partially quoted in the *Western Cape Forum* case. Article 23 consists of four paragraphs: The first paragraph requires State Parties to recognise that a physically or mentally disabled child should enjoy a full and decent life, in conditions which ensure dignity, promote self-reliance and facilitate the child's active participation in the community. Inclusion is thus core.[17] The second paragraph encapsulates the right of the disabled child to special care and requires State Parties to encourage and ensure the extension of assistance, for which application is made and is appropriate to the child's condition, to the child and those responsible for his or her care or protection. The extension of assistance, however, is made subject to available resources.[18] The third paragraph recognises the special needs of a disabled child and requires that assistance as indicated in the second paragraph, must be provided free of charge – whenever possible – and must be designed to ensure that a disabled child has effective access to and receives education, training, health care services, rehabilitation services, preparation for employment and recreation opportunities in a manner which is conducive to the child achieving the fullest possible social integration and individual development.[19] The final paragraph promotes international co-operation to *inter alia* improve State Parties' capabilities and skills.

Article 23 has been criticised (Combrinck 2008, p. 307 cited Kilkelly 2002, p. 120) as giving children with disabilities no absolute right to assistance, as access to services is made subject to conditions such as whether children are eligible and apply for such services, and is subject to available resources. It has been suggested (Abramson 2008, p. 123) that one way to increase allocations is by adopting 'reasonable accommodation' laws and policies. Reasonable accommodation requires the state to give more social goods to disabled persons, and where this entails material resources, amounts to a type of non-discriminatory affirmative action.[20] Unfortunately none of this could be traced in the facts of the *Western Cape Forum* case. The court did however mention the context-specific right to education confirmed in Article 28. With a view to achieving this right progressively and on the basis of equal opportunity, Article 28(1)(a) requires State Parties to make primary education compulsory and free for all. This has clearly not been the state's response as displayed in the *Western Cape Forum* case. The court also mentioned the right to have education directed to a child's personality, talents and mental and physical abilities to their fullest potential (Article 29(1)(a)).[21]

African Charter on the Rights and Welfare of the Child

South Africa, as a member state of the African Union (or Organisation of African Unity as it was then called), is also a party to the African Charter on the Rights and Welfare of the Child (ACRWC), which came into force in 1999, 10 years after its adoption in 1990. South Africa ratified the ACRWC on 7 January 2000 and submitted its first and second periodic report to the African Committee of Experts on the Rights and Welfare of the Child in 2014.[22] The ACRWC was the first regional human rights instrument which exclusively focused on the rights of the child (Van Bueren 1995, p. 22) and is therefore well worth comparing with the CRC.[23]

Article 3 of the ACRWC sets out the principle of non-discrimination on various grounds – similar to the CRC (in Article 2), but unfortunately omits the aspect of disability as a ground in respect of which a child may not be discriminated against. However, it is doubtful that this means that such children may be the subject of discrimination as the first part of Article 3 confers the right to non-discrimination to 'every child'.

Article 13, conferring rights upon children with disabilities,[24] to a certain extent mirrors the provisions of Article 23 of the CRC, although it is less detailed. Both instruments contain the limitation that protection for disabled children is subject to available resources. On a positive note, assistance under the ACRWC is not dependent on the circumstances of the parent or caregiver – as is the case under Article 23 of the CRC. It has been argued (Combrinck 2008, p. 311) that this could be to the advantage of a disabled child as states are allowed to consider the circumstances of the child's situation and not those of his or her parents. This could imply a higher level of protection, since it widens the group of persons eligible for state assistance.

The list of facilities and services to which a disabled child should have access does not contain education which is provided for in the CRC. Education is, however, dealt with under Article 11 of the ACRWC, but the omission of a reference to education in Article 13 is regrettable (Combrinck 2008, p. 311) because the educational needs of children with disabilities are different from children without disabilities. Article 13 contains an additional provision not found in article 23 of the CRC. Paragraph 3 aims to strengthen mobility for children with disabilities and their access to public institutions and facilities.

United Nations Convention on the Rights of Persons with Disabilities

The CRPD, adopted in December 2006, represents an international response to the long history of discrimination, exclusion and dehumanisation of persons with disabilities. The CRPD does not recognise any new human rights of persons with disabilities, but rather clarifies the obligations and legal duties of states to respect and ensure the equal enjoyment of all human rights by all persons with disabilities.[25] The CRPD also defines (in Article 2) the concept 'discrimination' in relation to disability as:

> any distinction, exclusion or restriction on the basis of disability which has the purpose or effect of impairing or nullifying the recognition, enjoyment or exercise, on an equal basis with others, of all human rights and fundamental freedoms in the political, economic, social, cultural, civil or any other field. It includes all forms of discrimination, including denial of reasonable accommodation[.]

As far as children with disabilities are concerned, the CRPD builds on the provisions of Article 23 of the CRC.

Many of the general principles (mainly in Article 3) governing the operation of the CRPD have a direct bearing on the education context, such as inherent dignity, non-discrimination, participation and inclusion, equality, accessibility and respect for the evolving capacities of the child with disabilities.

Article 24 of the CRPD deals with the right to education in detail.[26] Article 24 (1) obliges State Parties to ensure an inclusive education system at all levels without discrimination and on the basis of equal opportunity.[27] Article 24(2) contains the 'no-rejection clause' and obliges State Parties to ensure that children are not excluded from free and compulsory primary education on the basis of disability (Article 24(2)(a)). They must have access to an inclusive, quality and free primary and secondary education on an equal basis with others (Article 24(2)(b)). Reasonable accommodation of the individual's requirements must be provided for (Article 24(2)(c)). Children with disabilities must receive the support required, within the general education system, to facilitate their effective education (Article 24(2)(d)). State Parties have to provide effective individualised support measures that maximise academic and social development, consistent with the goal of full inclusion (Article 24 (2)(e)). Article 24(3) explores full and equal participation even further setting out the measures to be taken by State Parties in this regard. These measures include *inter alia* facilitating the learning of braille and sign language and the promotion of the linguistic identity of the deaf community (Article 24(3)(a)–(b)). To this end State Parties are required to take appropriate measures to employ teachers, including teachers with disabilities, who are qualified in sign language and/or braille, and to train professionals and staff who work at all levels of education (Article 24(4)).

South Africa ratified the CRPD on the 30 November 2007 and it was extensively quoted in the *Western Cape Forum* judgement. Although the Constitutional Court[28] has emphasised the importance of the CRPD in the promotion of the rights of persons with disabilities, it has not been incorporated into the legislative framework which guarantees enforceable rights in South Africa[29] and may therefore have mere interpretative effect in furthering the rights of children with disabilities.[30]

The legislative framework in South Africa

The Constitution of the Republic of South Africa, 1996

Equality and non-discrimination

Equality before the law and equal protection of and benefit from the law are guaranteed in section 9(1) of the Constitution and address instances where persons are classified and the law differentiates between such legally classified groups such as in the case with children. The Constitutional Court found that this guarantee 'lies at the very heart of the Constitution. It permeates and defines the very ethos upon which the Constitution is premised.'[31] When interpreting equality, the context is very important: equality as a component of justice means that one has to treat equals equally and those who are unequal, differently – provided that the basis of differentiating between the two categories of persons is relevant to the purpose served by the distinction. Children with disabilities are therefore not to be treated the same as children without disabilities. However, differentiating between those with and those without disabilities must fully accommodate the needs of each category. In the education context this means that one has to provide education to children with disabilities that conforms to the demands of and the special needs of these children. Substantive equality in this instance can only be effective if the state takes on the positive duty to provide. When dealing with vulnerable and marginalised children, section 9 of the Constitution includes equal access to educational institutions.[32] Section 9(2) furthermore sanctions affirmative action in education that would give preference to previously disadvantaged persons or groups of persons, such as the disabled child. Section 9(3) of the Constitution prohibits unfair discrimination, directly or indirectly, by the state based on, *inter alia*, age and disability.[33] Section 9(4) prohibits unfair discrimination on the same grounds by any person other than the state[34] and section 9(5) creates a rebuttable presumption that discrimination based on either age or disability (among other things) is unfair.

The right to equality goes far beyond equal treatment before the law and non-discrimination. It includes equal access, equal resources and equal opportunities.[35] Equal access to education is being denied when the language of learning and teaching is inappropriate, when the curriculum is inflexible, when the built environments are unsafe, the support services insufficient and legislation inadequate or non-existing.[36] And without access there can be no participation. Furthermore, the *Western Cape Forum* case demonstrated that resources were not being spent equally and the differentiation had no rational connection to a legitimate government purpose.[37] Equal opportunity is understood as a consequence of removing the legal and institutional barriers that stand in the way of people.[38]

Dignity

Human dignity has been described as 'the touchstone of the new political order [in South Africa] and … fundamental to the new Constitution'.[39] Dignity is both a fundamental principle or value underlying human rights and a right in itself.[40]

Human dignity is also a means of understanding what it is to be a bearer of rights.[41] This is the right that bestows inherent worth on children despite being different from adults and one another. It is to be respected as an individual and is an unalienable right and an indispensable part of human rights values.[42] The principle of dignity requires that all people, thus including children with disabilities, are empowered to enjoy the benefits of society on an equal basis and therefore it goes hand in hand with the right to equality.[43]

Education

The right to education is said (Kilkelly 2002, p. 123; Combrinck 2008, p. 299; Akinbola 2010, p. 459) to be both the most important right of children with disabilities and the right most frequently denied. It is an important fundamental human right[44] because it unlocks the exercise and enjoyment of other fundamental rights.[45] It could thus be described as an 'empowerment right' that fulfils the needs of all human beings.[46] This constitutional right creates a positive right that basic education must be provided for every person,[47] including severely and profoundly disabled children. The right to basic education is immediately realisable and justiciable.[48] In South Africa education is a functional area of concurrent national and provincial competence but for the purpose of this chapter only national legislation will be examined.

When the right of children with disabilities to education is at stake, section 29 of the South African Constitution has to be examined. In the disability context, section 29(1) obliges the government to provide basic education (including adult basic education) to everyone, ie. people with and people without disabilities alike. The unqualified and absolute[49] nature of the right requires that the state implements measures and makes budgetary allocations to give effect to the right as a matter of priority.[50] Section 29(2) requires education to be provided in a language that ensures effective and equitable access to that education, which may include sign language[51] and braille. In terms of section 29(3) individuals or organisations, like the applicant in the *Western Cape Forum* case, may establish independent educational institutions. Section 29(4) stipulates that the state may provide subsidies in these instances.[52]

Children's rights

The South African Constitution is renowned for its specific provision for children in section 28 with the rights provided to children over and above the fundamental rights guaranteed to all persons. In the context of education for children with disabilities, the child's right to basic nutrition, shelter, basic health care services and social services (section 28(1)(c))[53] has to be considered because the presence of such a child in a family contributes to poverty and many times to extreme poverty as the mother has to devote all her time to care for the child.[54] In the context of education for children with severe and profound disabilities, the child's right to be protected from maltreatment, neglect, abuse or degradation has to be considered.[55] The Bill of Rights further dictates in section 28(2) that a child's best interests are of paramount importance in every matter affecting that child.[56] The Constitutional Court[57] has bolstered the paramountcy of the best interests of the child by finding that it creates a right that is independent of those specified in section 28(1) of the Constitution.[58]

The Children's Act 38 of 2005

It is an explicit objective of this Act 'to recognise the special needs that children with disabilities may have' and to enhance their constitutional rights (section 2 (*h*)).[59] The rights of children with disabilities are therefore addressed upfront in chapter 2 under the General Principles of the Act and an approach upholding the basic principle of non-discrimination is articulated in section 6(2)(*d*). The Act states unequivocally that a child must be protected from unfair discrimination on the ground of his or her disability or the disability of a family member of the child. Section 6(2)(*f*) mandates that a child's disability must be recognised and an enabling environment must be created to respond to the child's special needs. Any disability that a child may have is specifically stated as one of the factors that must be considered when applying the best interests standard (section 7(1)(*i*)).

Section 11 is *in toto* dedicated to the rights of children with disabilities and children with chronic illness. Section 11(1)(*a*) obliges that due consideration must be given to provide children with disabilities with parental care, family care or special care when that is appropriate.[60] Section 11(1)(*b*) also obliges the participation of children with disabilities in social, cultural, religious and *educational* activities, recognising the special needs that such a child may have. This is an extremely bold step in the light of the failing funding story in the *Western Cape Forum* case. Very importantly section 11(1)(*c*) also obliges providing the child with conditions that ensure dignity, promote self-reliance and facilitate participation in the community. Lastly, section 11(1)(*d*) obliges providing the child and the child's care-giver with the necessary support services.

The South African Schools Act 84 of 1996

In special needs education the segregation of the past extended to incorporate segregation on the basis of disability, and the Schools Act was therefore destined to address the inequalities. The Preamble of the Schools Act boldly reiterates the fundamental values of equality and non-discrimination.[61] Section 5(1) then provides that public schools must admit children and meet their educational needs without unfairly discriminating against them in any way. However, when it comes to attendance at school for learners with 'special education needs' it is watered down because the Minister of Basic Education has to determine the ages of compulsory attendance by notice in the *Government Gazette* (section 3(2)) and after more than 20 years this has not yet been done with a huge effect on the government's accountability, or the lack thereof, in this regard. The funding model of public schools must be equitable and also redress past inequalities in education provision (section 34(1)). The funding of independent schools is done on the basis of a subsidy that may be granted (section

48). Sadly, in the case of learners with special educational needs, the funding model is after 20 years still in flux.[62]

The Member of the Executive Council (MEC) must ensure that there are enough school places for children, including children with disabilities, to attend school in his or her province (section 3(3)).[63] If the MEC cannot comply due to a lack of capacity, he or she must take remedial action as soon as possible and report annually to the Minister on the progress. There is no indication that this was done in the *Western Cape Forum* case and media reports very recently confirmed the struggle that parents have to find a school for children with disabilities (Venter 2018). Section 12(4) of the Schools Act states that the MEC of a province must where reasonably practicable, provide education for learners with 'special education needs at ordinary public schools[64] and provide relevant educational support services for such learners'.[65] The Schools Act also obliges the MEC responsible for education in a province to take all reasonable measures to ensure that physical facilities at public schools are accessible to persons with disabilities.[66] These provisions are in line with the policy that children with special needs should attend mainstream schools as far as possible. This policy has however not been effected into law which leaves aggrieved parties to appeal firstly to the Head of the Education Department and if not successful then to the MEC of Education in the province. If the matter is still not resolved the courts can be approached.

The Schools Act has special provisions concerning the membership of school governing bodies of public schools for learners with special education needs including *inter alia* people with disabilities, representatives of organisations of people with disabilities and experts in the fields of special needs education (section 24). When learners with special needs are accommodated in ordinary public schools the governing body must establish a committee on special education needs (section 30(2)).

In spite of clear legislation and an inclusive policy towards children with special needs there was on the Department of Basic Education's own version,[67] an estimated 597,953 children with disabilities who were out of school in 2012 and it is therefore crucial to find out what happened since the *Western Cape Forum* case.

The aftermath of the failing funding story

The Department of Basic Education has responded to the court's order in the *Western Cape Forum* case with a report to record progress that has been made at national and provincial level on the implementation of the Policy on Inclusive Education that was published in 2015.[68] According to this report (2015, pp. 7 and 70) there seems to be some discord between the provinces in the implementation of the inclusive education model, but in general it may be stated that four provinces succeeded in improving the results of learners with disabilities in ordinary schools. In 2012 119,861 learners with disabilities were accommodated in ordinary schools and 111,598 were in special schools (2015, Tables 13–15 pp. 18–9). However, 3,500 new special schools will have to be built if all learners with disabilities were to be accommodated in special schools (2015, p. 71).[69] Because this is not feasible, full-service schools should be resourced to create a viable alternative. Some ordinary schools were already converted into full-service schools (2015, pp. 21, 27 and 67 *et seq.*). Transportation of learners with special needs remains a huge challenge and could potentially improve access to full service schools and alleviate the pressure on special schools (2015, p. 72). Challenges abound and this report also revealed abuse of children in special school hostels and called for the reporting of such cases to the Human Rights Commission (2015, pp. 24, 51 and 70).[70]

The Department of Basic Education has also very specifically responded on the education of children with severe or profound intellectual disabilities and invited public comment on a 'Draft Policy for the Provision of Quality Education and Support for Children with Severe to Profound Intellectual Disability' in October 2016.[71] Unfortunately, this policy document like many others in that department, is 'not yet … finalised or operationalised'.[72] It is interesting to note that this 2016 Draft Policy (p. 19) refers to the CRC but only Article 23 thereof that children with disabilities should enjoy a full and decent life and be included in the community. Under the heading 'Realising the right to education for children with severe to profound intellectual disability' we are informed of a baseline audit that will be conducted to *inter alia* establish the number of children with severe or profound intellectual disabilities who are at home without services (p. 26); a learning programme that is in the process (p. 27); a transport system that should be available to them (p. 28); and the 'cadre of well-trained specialised teachers and auxiliary support staff' that needs to be developed (p. 30). Under the heading 'Responsibilities of government departments' a 5-year implementation plan is mentioned (pp. 38–39) and nothing about the Minister and the age of compulsory schooling. I did not find any indication that inclusive education will be the law and not merely policy.

The way forward

In spite of a model Constitution emphasising the position of children as rights bearers and clear international standards charting the way forward, Human Rights Watch published the most damning Report in 2015, and the title says it all: '"Complicit in Exclusion" South Africa's Failure to Guarantee an Inclusive Education for Children with Disabilities'.[73] The six key findings were: discrimination accessing education, discrimination due to a lack of reasonable accommodation in school, discriminatory fees and expenses, violence, abuse and neglect in schools, lack of quality education and lack of preparation for life after basic education. The overriding theme seems to be discrimination in the education of children with disabilities.

Even in post-apartheid South Africa discrimination in the education system as it relates to children with disabilities is persistent and challenging children's rights. In customary international law, non-discrimination is the norm but in South Africa Article 2 has not come into full fruition. It is now time that #DiscriminationMustFall and with it exclusion and marginalisation on the ground of disability.

Notes

* This material is based on work supported financially by the National Research Foundation (NRF). Any opinions, findings and conclusions or recommendations expressed in this material are those of the author and therefore the NRF does not accept any liability with regards thereto.

1 Malherbe (2009 p. 405). Also see CESCR General Comment No. 13 paras 6 and 21–24 (CESCR 1999).

2 For more information see Du Plessis and De Groof (2018 p. 15).

3 Sec. 3(1).

4 Most recent South African budget details available at http://www.treasury.gov.za/documents/national%20budget/2018/sars/Budget%202018%20Highlights.pdf [Accessed on 20 July 2018].

5 For detail, see McLaren (2017 pp. 37–73).

6 Statistics available at www.education.gov.za.

7 2011 (5) SA 87 (WCC).

8 Department of Basic Education (2001). White Paper 6 established full-service schools as flagship inclusive schools to admit all learners irrespective of their disability with appropriate support.

9 See the persuasive critique by Ngwena and Pretorius (2012 p. 109) levelled against the SIAS strategy indicating how it fed into 'the apartheidisation of the education system through a phenomenon we can call *disablism*'.

10 '1. States Parties shall respect and ensure the rights set forth in the present Convention to each child within their jurisdiction without discrimination of any kind, irrespective of the child's or his or her parent's or legal guardian's race, colour, sex, language, religion, political or other opinion, national, ethnic or social origin, property, disability, birth or other status.

2. States Parties shall take all appropriate measures to ensure that the child is protected against all forms of discrimination or punishment on the basis of the status, activities, expressed opinions, or beliefs of the child's parents, legal guardians, or family members.'

11 CRC (2006). Until the adoption of the Convention on the Rights of Persons with Disabilities (CRPD), the CRC was the only international human rights treaty that acknowledged 'disability' as a status.

12 Eg. sec. 28 of the Constitution, the Children's Act 38 of 2005 and the Child Justice Act 75 of 2008.

13 *S v M (Centre for Child Law as amicus curiae)* 2008 3 SA 232 (CC) paras. 16–17.

14 'Discrimination' is not defined in the CRC, but see the definition of 'discrimination on the basis of disability' in the CRPD below.

15 Also see Art. 4 of the CRC and CESCR General Comment No. 13 paras. 31 and 34 (CESCR 1999).

16 The court's response was granting a structural interdict enabling the respondents to remedy the wrong, with directions to report back to the court and the applicant on their progress (para. 52), which the respondents did.

17 (CRC 2006) para. 11.

18 See (CRC 2006) para. 14(a) (ibid).

19 Note the correlation between this paragraph and (CRC 2006) para. 31. See also paras. 11 and 21 (ibid).

20 Also General Comment No. 14 paras. 14 and 15 on the obligation of State Parties regarding implementation and the right of the child to have his or her best interests taken as a primary [sic] consideration (CRC 2013).

21 Also see CRC (2001).

22 Available at http://www.acerwc.org/download/south_africa_initial_report_under_the_acrwc. The Committee's Concluding Recommendations is available at http://www.acerwc.org/download/concluding_observations_south_africa/?wpdmdl=8754.

23 See Mezmur (2008) p. 1 *et seq.*
24 The article unfortunately refers to 'handicapped' children.
25 United Nations (2007 p. 5).
26 On Art. 24 see Akinbola (2010 pp. 469–470).
27 Inclusive education is the norm: see CRC (2016) para. 68.
28 *De Vos NO v Minister of Justice and Constitutional Development* 2015 (2) SACR 217 (CC).
29 South Africa adheres to a dualistic approach in this regard.
30 Courts are obliged to consider international law when interpreting the Bill of Rights (sec. 39(1)(*b*) of the Constitution) and must consider international law when interpreting legislation (sec. 233).
31 *Fraser v Children's Court, Pretoria North* 1997 2 BCLR 153 (CC) para. 20.
32 See sec. 29(1) and (2) of the Promotion of Equality and Prevention of Unfair Discrimination Act 4 of 2000, read with item 2 of the Schedule, that unfair exclusion of learners from educational institutions, including learners with special needs, is an unfair practice.
33 Reiterated in sec. 5(1) of the South African Schools Act 84 of 1996. See also *Matukane v Laerskool Potgietersrus* 1996 3 SA 223 (T) 233–234.
34 In this instance the proscription must be further sanctioned through national legislation aimed at either preventing or prohibiting the discrimination.
35 UNESCO/UNICEF (2007 p. 31); Woodhouse (2008 p. 39).
36 See Pendlebury (2009 pp. 24–27).
37 See *Harksen v Lane NO* 1998 (1) SA 300 (CC).
38 Rioux and Riddle (2011 p. 44).
39 *S v Makwanyane* 1995 6 BCLR 778 (CC) para. 329, referring to the 1993 (interim) Constitution.
40 See sec. 1 of the Constitution read with sec. 10 and *Dawood v Minister of Home Affairs; Shalabit v Minister of Home Affairs; Thomas v Minister of Home Affairs* 2000 8 BCLR 837 para. 35.
41 Basser (2011 p. 36).
42 Basser (2011 p. 17).
43 Basser (2011 p. 34). Also see (CESCR 1999) para. 4.
44 Included in the constitutions of at least 59 countries and even when not constitutionally entrenched, still recognised as a legal right of fundamental importance: *Brown v Board of Education of Topeka* 347 US 438 (1954); Veriava and Coomans (2005 p. 57).
45 Such as political, economic, social and cultural rights, see CESCR (1999) para. 1.
46 *Minister of Home Affairs v Watchenuka* 2004 4 SA 326 (SCA) para. 36; Woolman and Fleisch (2009 pp. 117–118).
47 *Ex Parte Gauteng Provincial Legislature: In re Dispute Concerning the Constitutionality of Certain Provisions of the Gauteng School Education Bill of 1995* 1996 3 SA 165 (CC) para. 9 referring to sec. 32(a) of the 1993 Constitution; *Western Cape Forum for Intellectual Disability v Government of the Republic of South Africa* p. 90.
48 Section 29(1)(a) of the Constitution; *Governing Body of the Juma Musjid Primary School v Essay* 2011 7 BCLR 651 (CC) para. 37.
49 But still subject to the general limitations: sec. 36.
50 In particular with reference to primary education: compare sec. 29(1)(a) to sec. 29 (1)(b).
51 Section 6(4) of the Schools Act. A recognised sign language has the status of an official language for the purposes of learning at public schools. See also sec. 6 of the Constitution.
52 See sections 45 and 48 of the Schools Act.
53 For a full exposition see Friedman et al. (2006 pp. 47–9 to 47–18).
54 The family will have access to a care dependency grant (in terms of the Social Assistance Act 13 of 2003) of R1,700 per month (from 1 October 2018) which is often the only income of the family: Department of Basic Education (2011) para. 17. See also Resolution 66/124 of the General Assembly which noted that persons with disabilities face a

greater risk of living in absolute poverty and that 80 per cent of these persons live in developing countries.

55 Section 28(1)(*d*). For a full exposition see Friedman et al. (2006 pp. 47–18 to 47–28).

56 The application of sec. 28(2) in the education context has extensively been dealt with: eg. in *Governing Body of the Juma Musjid Primary School v Essay*; Mawdsley et al. (2010); Reyneke (2013).

57 *Minister of Welfare and Population Development v Fitzpatrick* 2000 3 SA 422 (CC) para. 17.

58 Other constitutional rights that might be relevant are the right to freedom and security of the person (sec. 12), the right to privacy (sec. 14), the right to freedom of association (sec. 18), language and culture (sections 30 and 31) and just administrative action (sec. 33).

59 In line with Rule 15(3)(b) of the Standard Rules on the Equalisation of Opportunities for Persons with Disabilities (1993), which provides for a duty on the state to create a legal basis aimed at achieving the objectives of full participation and equality.

60 Yet, in the *Centre for Child Law v MEC Health and Social Development, Gauteng* North Gauteng High Court unreported case no 37850/2010, the Centre of Child Law applied for a curator *ad litem* to be appointed for a 15-year-old boy with psychiatric problems for whom no suitable accommodation could be found after Weskoppies Hospital refused to admit him into their care as a mental health care user. Again, on 2 August 2018 the Centre and the Departments of Social Development, Education and Health reached a settlement that was made an order of court regarding a 10-year-old girl in similar circumstances: http://www.centreforchildlaw.co.za/ [Accessed on 25 August 2018].

61 See Krüger and Mcconnachie (2017 pp. 538–543) on the impact of the equality principle on education in general. See also sec. 1 of the Promotion of Equality and Prevention of Unfair Discrimination Act 4 of 2000.

62 See Martin (2014 pp. 139–40) on the insufficiency of funding allocated to inclusive education.

63 If this is not the case, appropriate steps should be taken: sec. 3(4). The wishes of the parents are specifically mentioned in relation to the placement of the learner with special needs: sec. 5(6).

64 See also sec. 12(3)(*a*)(ii). The Schools Act recognises two types of schools, namely public (sections 12–33) and independent (sections 45–51) schools. Three types of public schools may be provided: ordinary public schools, schools for learners with special education needs and gender specific schools, sec. 12(3) and sec. 12(6).

65 See also sections 22–25 of the Admission Policy for Ordinary Public Schools published in GN 2432 *GG* 19377 of 19 October 1998 (in terms of sec. 3(4)(i) of the National Educational Policy Act 27 of 1996) which makes provision for learners with special needs to be accommodated in ordinary schools where 'reasonably practical'. Note that in terms of sec. 23 the principal must refer the application to the HoD if the necessary support cannot be provided in an ordinary school.

66 Section 12(5) of the Schools Act. See also sec. 4(*b*) of the National Education Policy Act 27 of 1996. Section 4(*d*) then builds on sec. 4(*b*) by guaranteeing the physically disabled child an education to maximise his or her potential. However, Majangaza reported on 40 physically disabled children at one particular school without any support: 2018.

67 Department of Basic Education (2015) Table 18 p. 21. In the 5- to 15-year-old group 25.9 per cent of children with disabilities were not attending an education institution, *op. cit.* p. 7.

68 Department of Basic Education (2015).

69 There were 5,552 learners on waiting lists hoping to be admitted to special schools in 2014 although the Department admits that it defies the Schools Act to put names on waiting lists: 2015 p. 22.

70 Other challenges are *inter alia* improving curriculum delivery in special schools (p. 34), teachers without the required training in special schools (pp. 37 and 43), introduction of a skills and vocational exit level qualification (p. 39), introduction of South African Sign Language (pp. 62–67) and the non-allocation and under-spending in some provinces (pp. 70–71). On this last point see Majangaza 2018.

71 Available at http://www.education.gov.za/Resources/Legislation/CallforComments/DraftPolicyfortheProvisionofQualityEducationandSupporttoChildrenwithDisability.aspx.

72 Martin (2014 p. 142), referring to the Department of Basic Education's 2012 report.

73 In spite also of the fact that the government announced that it achieved the United Nations Millennium Development Goal on education thus asserting that all children are in school.

References

Abramson, B. 2008. Article 2: The right of non-discrimination. In: A. Alen, J. Vande Lanotte, E. Verhellen, F. Ang, E. Berghmans and M. Verheyde (eds) *A Commentary on the United Nations Convention on the Rights of the Child*. Leiden: Martinus Nijhoff.

African Charter on the Rights and Welfare of the Child, 1990.

African Committee of Experts on the Rights and Welfare of the Child. *Concluding Recommendations on the Republic of South Africa Initial Report on the Status of Implementation of the African Charter on the Rights and Welfare of the Child*. Available at: http://www.acerwc.org/download/concluding_observations_south_africa/?wpdmdl=8754 [Accessed on 26 July 2018].

Akinbola, B. R. 2010. The right to inclusive education in Nigeria: Meeting the needs and challenges of children with disabilities. *African Human Rights Law Journal*, 10, 457–477.

Basser, L. A. 2011. Human dignity. In: H. M. Rioux, L. A. Basser, and M. Jones (eds) *Critical Perspectives on Human Rights and Disability Law*, (pp. 17–36). Leiden; Boston: Martinus Nijhoff.

Bekink, B. and Bekink, M. 2005. Children with disabilities and the right to education: A call for action. *Stellenbosch Law Review*, 1, 125–145.

Bekker, G. 2000. The right to education in the South African Constitution: An introduction. In: L. V. Mashava (ed.) *A Compilation of Essential Documents on the Right to Education Economic and Social Rights Series vol 2* (pp. 1–17). Pretoria: Centre for Human Rights.

Besson, S. 2005. The principle of non-discrimination in the Convention on the Rights of the Child. *International Journal of Children's Rights*, 13, 433–461.

Boezaart, T. 2012. A constitutional perspective on the rights of children with disabilities in an educational context. *Southern African Public Law*, 27(2), 454–471.

Brown v Board of Education of Topeka 347 US 438 (1954). US Supreme Court.

Centre for Child Law v MEC Health and Social Development, Gauteng. North Gauteng High Court unreported case no 37850/2010.

Child Justice Act 75 of 2008.

Children's Act 38 of 2005.

Chürr, C. 2015. Realisation of a child's right to a basic education in the South African school system: Some lessons from Germany. *Potchefstroom Electronic Law Journal*, 18, 2404–2455.

Combrinck, H. 2008. The hidden ones: Children with disabilities in Africa and the right to education. In J. Sloth-Nielsen (ed.). *Children's Rights in Africa: A Legal Perspective* (pp. 299–322). Aldershot: Ashgate.

Committee on Economic, Social and Cultural Rights (CESCR). 1999. General Comment No. 13: The Right to Education (Art. 13 of the Covenant) (1999) E/C.12/1999/10. Available at: http://www.refworld.org/docid/4538838c22.html.

Committee on the Rights of the Child (CRC). 2001. General Comment No. 1 (2001) Article 29 (1), The aims of education. CRC/GC/2001/1. Available at: http://www.refworld.org/docid/4538834d2.html.

Committee on the Rights of the Child (CRC). 2006. General Comment No. 9 (2006) The rights of children with disabilities. CRC/C/GC/9.

Committee on the Rights of the Child (CRC). 2013. General Comment No. 14 (2013) on the right of the child to have his or her best interests taken as a primary consideration (art. 3, para. 1). CRC/C/GC/14.

Committee on the Rights of the Child (CRC). 2016. General Comment No. 20 (2016) on the implementation of the rights of the child during adolescence. CRC/C/GC/20.

Constitution of the Republic of South Africa Act 200 of 1993.

Constitution of the Republic of South Africa, 1996.

Constitutional Court of South Africa. *Dawood v Minister of Home Affairs; Shalabit v Minister of Home Affairs; Thomas v Minister of Home Affairs* [2000]. ZACC 8, 2000 8 BCLR 837.

Constitutional Court of South Africa. *De Vos NO v Minister of Justice and Constitutional Development*, 2015 (2) SACR 217 (CC); 2015 ZACC 21.

Constitutional Court of South Africa. *Ex Parte Gauteng Provincial Legislature: In re Dispute Concerning the Constitutionality of Certain Provisions of the Gauteng School Education Bill of 1995*, 1996 3 SA 165 (CC).

Constitutional Court of South Africa. *Fraser v Children's Court, Pretoria North*, 1997 2 BCLR 153 (CC).

Constitutional Court of South Africa. *Governing Body of the Juma Musjid Primary School v Essay*, 2011 7 BCLR 651 (CC).

Constitutional Court of South Africa. *Harksen v Lane NO*, 1998 (1) SA 300 (CC).

Constitutional Court of South Africa. *Minister of Welfare and Population Development v Fitzpatrick*, 2000 3 SA 422 (CC).

Constitutional Court of South Africa. *S v M (Centre for Child Law as amicus curiae)* 2008 3 SA 232 (CC).

Constitutional Court of South Africa. *S v Makwanyane* 1995 6 BCLR 778 (CC).

Convention on the Rights of Persons with Disabilities (2008).

Convention on the Rights of the Child (1989).

Department of Basic Education. 2001. White Paper 6 Special Needs Education Building an Inclusive Education and Training System (July 2001).

Department of Basic Education. 2011. Draft Framework for a Policy on the Education of Learners with Severe to Profound Intellectual Disability (August 2011).

Department of Basic Education. 2012. Report on Actions taken by the Department of Basic Education to Develop a Framework for the Provision of Services to Children with Severe and Profound Intellectual Disability.

Department of Basic Education. 2015. Report on the Implementation of Education White Paper 6 on Inclusive Education: An overview for the period 2013–2015 (May 2015).

Department of Basic Education. 2016. Education Statistics in South Africa 2014.

Department of Basic Education. 2016a. Draft Policy for the Provision of Quality Education and Support for Children with Severe to Profound Intellectual Disability (October 2016).

Du Plessis, G. and De Groof, J. 2018. Constitutional changes and values of the Schools Act. In: E. De Waal. (ed.) *Pathways to Successful Schooling: South African Schools Act 84 of 1996 – 20 Years On* (pp. 9–24). Claremont: Juta.

Du Plessis, M. 2013. The social model of disability, rights discourse and the impact of South Africa's Education White paper 6 on access to the basic education system for persons with severe or profound intellectual impairment. *Law, Democracy & Development*, 17, 202–225. Available at: http://dx.doi.org/10.4314/Idd.v17i1.10.

Francke, R. L. 2017. High hopes for the first Down Syndrome child in public school. *Daily Voice*, 23 January 2017. Available at: http://www.iol.co.za/news/south-africa/western-cape/high-hopes-for-the-first-down-syndrome-child-in-public-school-7483606 [Accessed on 28 January 2017].

Fredman, S. 2005. Providing equality: Substantive equality and the positive duty to provide. *South African Journal on Human Rights*, 21, 163–190.

Friedman, A., Pantazis, A. and Skelton, A. 2006. Children's rights. In S. Woolman and M. Bishop (eds). *Constitutional Law of South Africa, vol 3.* 2nd edition, (pp. 47–1 to 47–47). Cape Town: Juta.

Hanzungule, Z. 2016. A Case for the Socio-economic Rights of Children with Disabilities in South Africa. Unpublished LLM dissertation, University of Pretoria.

Hodgkin, R., and Newell, P. 2007. *Implementation Handbook for the Convention on the Rights of the Child.* Geneva: UNICEF.

Human Rights Watch. 2015. 'Complicit in Exclusion' South Africa's Failure to Guarantee an Inclusive Education for Children with Disabilities, August 2015.

Human Rights Watch. 2016. South Africa: Crisis for Children with Disabilities. Available at https://www.hrw.org/news/2016/03/14/south-africa-crisis-children-disabilities [Accessed on 24 May 2018].

Hyman, A. 2016. 831 Arrests mar 2016 Fees Must Fall protests. *TimesLive*, 28 October 2016. Available at http://www.timeslive.co.za/local/2016/10/28/831-arrests-mar-2016-Fees-Must-Fall-protests [Accessed on 3 March 2017].

Jones, M. 2011. Inclusion, social inclusion and participation. In M. Rioux, L. A. Basser and M. Jones (eds). *Critical Perspectives on Human Rights and Disability Law*, (pp. 57–82). Leiden, Boston: Martinus Nijhoff.

Kilkelly, U. 2002. Disability and children: The Convention on the Rights of the Child (CRC). In: G. Quinn and G. T. Degener. (eds). *Human Rights and Disability: The Current Use and Future Potential of United Nations Human Rights Instruments in the Context of Disability*, (pp. 119–140). Geneva: United Nations.

Kruger, P. 2015. Critical appraisal of Western Cape Forum for Intellectual Disability v. Government of the Republic of South Africa 2011 5 SA 87 (WCC). *Potchefstroom Electronic Law Journal*, 18, 756–773.

Krüger, R., and Mcconnachie, C. 2017. The impact of the Constitution on learners' rights. In: Boezaart, T. (ed.). *Child Law in South Africa*, 2nd edition, (pp. 534–574). Claremont: Juta.

Lake, L. and Pendlebury, S. 2009. Children's right to basic education. In: S. Pendlebury, L. Lake and C. Smith (eds). *South African Child Gauge 2008/2009.* Cape Town: Children's Institute, University of Cape Town.

Lord, J. E. and Brown, R. 2011. The role of reasonable accommodation in securing substantive equality for persons with disabilities: The UN Convention on the Rights of Persons with Disabilities. In: M. Rioux, L. A. Basser and M. Jones (eds). *Critical Perspectives on Human Rights and Disability Law*, (pp. 273–307). Leiden, Boston: Martinus Nijhoff.

Mabizela, S. 2015. In South Africa, university is open to rich and poor – but what about the missing middle? *The Conversation*, 28 January 2015. Available at: http://www.theconversation.com/in-South-Africa-university-is-open-to-rich-and-poor-but-what-about-the-missing-middle-36801 [Accessed on 24 May 2018].

Majangaza, S. 2018. R530-million of unspent EC budget meant for poor schools given to other provinces. *Dispatch Live*, 13 March 2018. Available at: http://www.dispatchlive.co.za/news/2016/03/09/r530-million-of-unspent-ec-budget-meant-for-poor-schools-given-to-other-provinces/ [Accessed on 13 March 2018].

Malherbe, R. 2009. Education rights. In: Boezaart, T. (ed). *Child Law in South Africa* (pp. 399–419). Claremont: Juta.

Martin, P. 2014. Children's rights to basic education: A review of South Africa's laws and policies. In: S. Pendlebury, L. Lake and C. Smith (eds). *South African Child Gauge 2008/2009* (pp. 99–152). Cape Town: Children's Institute, University of Cape Town.

Mawdsley, R. D., Beckmann, J. L., De Waal, E. and Russo, C. J. 2010. The best interest of the child: A United States and South African perspective. *Journal of Juridical Science*, 1–23.

McLaren, D. 2017. Funding basic education. In: F. Varieva, A. Thom and T. F. Hodgson. (eds). *Basic Education Rights Handbook – Education Rights in South Africa*, (pp. 37–73). Johannesburg: SECTION27.

Mezmur, B. D. 2008. The African Children's Charter versus the UN Convention on the Rights of the Child: A zero-sum game? *Southern African Public Law*, 23, 1–29.

Murungi, L. N. 2015. Inclusive basic education in South Africa: Issues in its conceptualisation and implementation. *Potchefstroom Electronic Law Journal*, 18(3), 3159–3195. Available at: http://dx.doi.org/10.4314/pelj.v18i1.07.

National Educational Policy Act 27 of 1996.

Ngwena, C. and Pretorius, L. 2012. Substantive equality for disabled learners in state provision of basic education: A commentary on Western Cape Forum for Intellectual Disability v Government of the Republic of South Africa. *South African Journal on Human Rights*, 28, 81–115.

Pendlebury, S. 2009. Meaningful access to basic education. In: S. Pendlebury, L. Lake and C. Smith (eds). *South African Child Gauge 2008/2009*, (pp. 24–27). Cape Town: Children's Institute, University of Cape Town.

Promotion of Equality and Prevention of Unfair Discrimination Act 4 of 2000.

Reyneke, M. 2013. *The Best Interests of the Child in School Discipline in South Africa.* Unpublished LLD thesis, Tilburg University

Rioux, M. H. and Riddle, C. A. 2011. Values in disability policy and law: Equality. In: M. Rioux, L. A. Basser and M. Jones (eds). *Critical Perspectives on Human Rights and Disability Law*, (pp. 37–55). Leiden, Boston: Martinus Nijhoff.

South Africa's Initial Country Report on the African Charter on the Rights and Welfare of the Child, 2013. Available at: http://www.acerwc.org/download/south_africa_initial_report_under_the_acrwc [Accessed on 26 July 2018].

South African Schools Act 84 of 1996.

Supreme Court of Appeal of South Africa. *Minister of Home Affairs v Watchenuka*, 2004 4 SA 326 (SCA).

Standard Rules on the Equalisation of Opportunities for Persons with Disabilities. 1993.

Transvaal Provincial Division of the High Court of South Africa. *Matukane v Laerskool Potgietersrus*, 1996 3 SA 223 (T).

UNESCO/UNICEF. 2007. *A Human Rights-based Approach to Education for All: A Framework for the Realization of Children's Right to Education and Rights within Education.* New York, Paris: UNESCO.

United Nations. 2007. *From Exclusion to Equality: Realizing the Rights of Persons with Disabilities.* Geneva: United Nations.

United Nations General Assembly. 2012. *High-level meeting of the general Assembly on the realization of the Millennium Development Goals and other internationally agreed development goals for persons with disabilities.* Resolution 66/124.

Van Bueren, G. 1995. *The International Law on the Rights of the Child.* Dordrecht: Springer.

Venter, Z. 2018. Court orders Pretoria school to admit disabled boy. *Pretoria News*, 9 April 2018. Available at: https://www.iol.co.za/news/south-africa/gauteng/court-orders-pretoria-school-to-admit-disabled-boy-14326323 [Accessed on 11 April 2018].

Veriava, F. and Coomans, F. 2005. The right to education. In D. Brand and C. Heyns (eds). *Socio-Economic Rights in South Africa: International and Constitutional Law*, (pp. 57–83). Pretoria: Pretoria University Law Press.

Western Cape High Court of South Africa, Cape Town. *Western Cape Forum for Intellectual Disability v Government of the Republic of South Africa,* 2011 (5) SA 87 (WCC).

Woodhouse, B. B. 2008. *Hidden in Plain Sight: The Tragedy of Children's Rights from Ben Franklin to Lionel Tate.* Princeton, Oxford: Princeton University Press.

Woolman, S. and Bishop, M. 2009. Education. In: S. Woolman, M. Bishop and J. Brickhill. (eds). *Constitutional Law of South Africa*, 2nd edition, (pp. 57-i to 57–95). Cape Town: Juta.

Woolman, S., and Fleisch, B. 2009. *The Constitution in the Classroom: Law and Education in South Africa 1994–2008.* Pretoria: Pretoria University Law Press.

11 Starting from system building

Child rights protection and the non-discrimination principle in China

Liu Huawen[*]

Introduction

The People's Republic of China (PRC), has almost tripled its population since it gained independence in 1949. By the end of 2017, the total population of mainland China was 1,390.08 million, which includes 31 provinces, autonomous regions and municipalities and the Chinese People's Liberation Army in service, excluding Hong Kong Special Administrative Region, Macao Special Administrative Region and Taiwan Province and overseas Chinese. Art. 2 of the Law of the PRC on the Protection of Minors indicates that a child is a citizen under the age of 18, which is consistent with the definition of the CRC. According to data of the sixth lustrum in China, in 2010, there were 299,668,269 children under the age of 18 years in China, accounting for 22.48 percent of the total population, which included 160,619,971 boys (53.60 percent), and 139,048,298 girls (46.40 percent).[1]

China is a unitary country, and the Communist Party of China (CPC) is the leading party. The CPC and the Chinese government play a key role in the national economic and social development. "Big government–small society" is the main social governance structure in China. In this model, CPC and the governments at different levels are the leading entities for the protection of children's rights, mainly by the formulation and implementation of the national and local laws and policies. During recent years, other actors – communities, schools, non-governmental organizations and so on – have been encouraged to join the efforts for the realization of the rights of the child. One way to promote this is to establish Children's Centers at community or village level around the whole country, in order to involve social workers and other entities to provide services or help to the children.

China approved the United Nations (UN) Convention on the Rights of the Child (CRC) on 29 December 1991 and China became the 110th State Party of the CRC. On 2 April, 1992, CRC came into force for China. China has also ratified the Optional Protocol to the CRC on the Sale of Children, Child Prostitution and Child Pornography (CRC-OPSC) and the Optional Protocol to the CRC on the Involvement of Children in Armed Conflict (CRC-OPAC).

As a State Party to the Convention, China actively fulfills its obligations, and views the protection of children's rights as a top priority in the development of

China's human rights. The protection of children's rights in China has progressed quickly, especially in the awareness of a new perspective on childhood and children's rights and the construction of a system including both laws and policies. However, China is still in a period of economic and social transition, and the urban–rural gap, regional differences and various social issues are still quite obvious. The social conditions including the sound social structure, especially the fact that social work institutions and personnel are not put in place, means that this insufficiency produces obstacles for the implementation of the child rights protection system.

Non-discrimination is the basic principle both for general international human rights law and the CRC in particular. Chinese laws recognize the principle of equality for children. But they seldom use the term "non-discrimination" expressly. This term does not appear in the basic law for the rights of the child – Chinese Law on Protection of the Minors. It may be viewed as not so much useful, considering the lack of justiciability of the principle of equality. The legal principle, like equality itself, is not a sufficient basis to file a case in the judicial court, and it does not result in manifestly better treatment of individuals directly. In fact, in China, judicial cases based upon or in the name of discrimination or equality are very difficult to find. However, in contrast to the judicial approach, it is more commonly administrative efforts that make the equality principle work in daily life in China.

Therefore, to implement the Art. 2 of the CRC on the non-discrimination principle, China needs to integrate the very term of non-discrimination directly into its laws, policies and practices. What is more, it should work effectively in the everyday life of children, guaranteed by legislative, judicial, administrative or other measures.

The principles of child's rights in China

The principle of non-discrimination

This principle is not laid down in Chinese laws with this exact wording. Generally speaking, it is named the principle of equality. Equality before the law is one of the legal principles in the Constitution of China. Art. 3 (3) of the Law of the PRC on the Protection of Minors provides: "Minors shall, regardless of their sex, ethnic status, race, family property background and religious belief, enjoy their rights equally in accordance with law." So, unfortunately, the most relevant national law on the rights of the child in China does not mention the non-discrimination principle directly. This is not conducive to the promotion of the awareness of the non-discrimination principle, let alone access to the judicial remedies for illegal discriminatory treatment. This general legislative gap in the Chinese legal system has drawn a lot of attention and scholars have attempted to advocate a unified anti-discrimination law in China (Li 2018, pp. 214–278).

It is worth noting that the most important policy document – China's Program of Child Development in China (2011–2020) does mention "Creating a fair social environment to ensure that children are not discriminated against on account of household registration, geographic location, gender, ethnicity, beliefs, educational status, physical condition and family property. All children enjoy equal rights and opportunities". It is helpful for the promotion of anti-discrimination advocating in the child rights field.

For the protection of the equal rights of all children, and based upon the principle of non-discrimination stipulated clearly in the CRC, we should emphasize that there is a need to take measures to protect and realize equal opportunities for children living in difficulties, such as children in poverty, girls, physically or mentally disabled children, migrant children, left-behind children, ethnic minorities, children affected by AIDS and so on. There are many children in difficulties, and they are the most dependent groups who need the whole country to take special measures to aid them (Liu 2012).

In fact, the implementation of the principle of non-discrimination is a complicated process. It needs to be fully promoted with political, legal, economic, social and cultural measures. There are many laws providing provisions to protect children living in difficulties at the national level, including the Constitution, the Law on Protection of the Minors, Maternal and Infant Health Care Law, etc. What is more, there are even more policy documents concerned as well. Plan for Disabled Persons' Cause of China and the 13th Five-year Plan for Contain and Prevent AIDS of China lay down the measures to protect the rights of physically or mentally challenged children and children affected by AIDS. Regulation on Prevention and Cure of AIDS came into force on March 1, 2006, which provides practical institutional guarantees to protect children affected by HIV/AIDS from discrimination. It stipulates that people affected by HIV/AIDS and their families have the rights and interests of medical care and education, and every unit or individual shall not discriminate against their rights.

Special care for girls is one of the main concerns. In its Concluding Observations adopted in October 2013, the UN CRC Committee urges China to adopt a comprehensive approach to take effective and systematic action to combat social, cultural and economic discrimination against girls and women, including social and institutional norms and practices that are inconsistent with the provisions of the Convention and that perpetuate discrimination against girls (Committee on the Rights of the Child 2013). The Committee further recommends that the State Party takes immediate legal, policy and awareness-raising measures to prevent sex-selective abortions, female infanticide and abandonment of girls, including by addressing factors that reinforce cultural norms and practices that discriminate against girls.[2] China's laws and policies explicitly prohibit gender discrimination. Among others, the government continually carries out specific projects to prohibit the gender identification of the fetus without medical needs and to stop artificial abortion because of sex preference.

According to statistics, in China the new-born male population was 71.37 million in 2017, and the female population was 67.87 million. The sex ratio of the total population decreased to 104.81 (100 for females), and the sex ratio of the birth population gradually is tending to be balanced. So, it seems that the legal ban and policy prohibition is effective, and the public is generally against the sex preference.

Punishment of the illegal conduct concerned in some areas is controversial and considered unconstitutional. In 2012, the People's High Court of the Zhejiang province adopted a judicial interpretation document criminalizing some conducts concerning the gender identification of the fetus. Prof. Li Buyun, a leading human rights law scholar at the Institute of Law, Chinese Academy of Social Sciences, wrote to the top legislative body in China and the Legislative Affairs Commission of the Standing Committee, National People's Congress to urge the Zhejiang judicial authorities to correct the judicial interpretation *ultra vires* in August 2018 (Zhu 2018, p. 9). Instances of communication such as these are rare – it may mean that the constitutional examination and supervision of the legislative and judicial work in China is to be strengthened and it is conducive to review of the existing laws and policies and the application of legal principles such as the non-discrimination principle.

The principle of best interests of the child

The non-discrimination principle is subsidiary. It works together with other principles of child protection and the essential rights provisions of the laws. The principle of best interests of the child is the most significant one guiding the system and practice of child rights. For non-discrimination, we emphasize that for any child, his or her best interests should be borne in mind.

In China, "All for children" is a popular slogan. When formulating its Plan for National Economic and Social Development, National Human Rights Action Plan, China's Program of Child Development and other relevant national policy documents, the Central Government clearly stipulated the principle of child priority or maximization of the interests of children and required the provinces, autonomous regions and municipalities to implement the principles according to their actual conditions.

When formulating or revising Criminal Law, Criminal Procedure Law and Law on the Protection of Minors, China stipulated in the light of the principle of the best interests of children in order to provide a special and prioritized protection for children. For example, Art. 3 (1) of the Law on the Protection of Minors provides: "Minors shall have the right to life, the right to development, the right

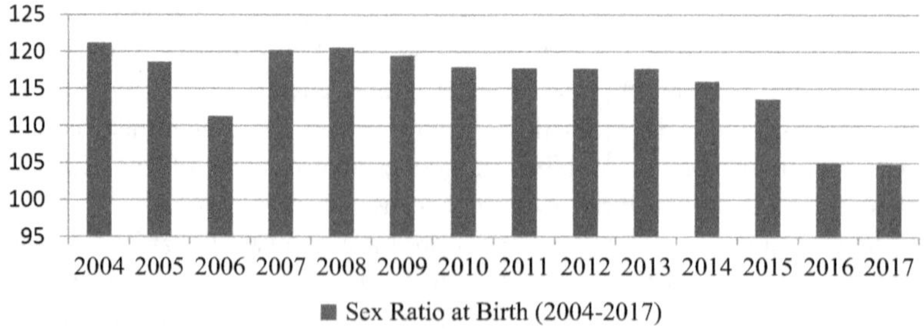

Figure 11.1 Sex ratio at birth (2004–2017)
Source: National Health and Family Planning Commission of the People's Republic of China, 2016. *Statistical Yearbook for Health and Family Planning in China*. Beijing: Peking Union Medical College Press.

to protection and the right to participation, and the government should give them a special and prioritized protection based upon the characteristics of their physical and mental development, and protect their right from infringement".

The realization of the principle of best interests of the child is not only enlightening for the policy makers and legislators, but also quite relevant to the judicial judgment. In judicial practice, the understanding and application of this principle has also produced an actual change. The following two real cases reflect the change in judicial practice that emphasizes the principle.

The right to names is an important right for children and there is a typical case – *Yao Kunyun v. Yao Pengcheng.* [3] In May 2001, the plaintiff, Yao Pengcheng sued the defendant Yao Kunyun (his ex-wife) to demand the resumption of his son's surname. At that time, his son was a student in a primary school and had been using new names for the past 6 years. The plaintiff claimed that without his agreement the defendant changed the surname of the child and therefore infringed on his right. He filed the case to the People's Court in Wuhua District of Kunming City, Yunnan Province. Based on Art. 18 of Marriage Law and Art. 107 (1) of Civil Procedure Law, the Court sentenced that Yao Kunyun should change the child's surname back to the father's surname or mother's surname within 5 days from the date the judgment took effect. Later, the defendant appealed to Kunming Intermediate People's Court but failed to change the original judgment.

In this case, the court did not listen to the voice of the child, and the surname of the child was considered relevant to the right of the father rather than that of the child. The legislation that the Court applied did not provide sufficient support for the protection of the child's rights.

However, with the promotion of the consciousness of children's rights, the above-mentioned legal reasoning has changed. For example, in 2007, the People's Court in Changping District of Beijing decided that whether a child should change his surname should weigh the child's interests and his opinion, and his parents' opinion may not be decisive (Liu 2009).

In this case, Mr. Wang married in March 1993, and his son was born in January 1994. After the divorce, Mr. Wang's ex-wife changed the surname of the child, and he submitted the case to court. Mr. Wang claimed that the name of the child resulted from the common agreement between his wife and him during their marriage. His ex-wife changed the name of the child without consultation with him. Therefore, he asked the court to change the child's name to the original one. Mr. Wang's ex-wife defended that, according to the relevant provisions of the Marriage Law, a child can follow the father's or the mother's family name. Changing name was the child's personal right, not a right of the parents, so the child has the right to decide his or her own name. Moreover, the child had been using this name for more than a year, his school roll and files used this name, and his teachers and classmates were also very familiar with this name. If the name was changed, it would have a negative influence on the child's development.

The Court held that the right of name was the identity right for every citizen. Citizens have the right to use names, change names and protect their names from infringement. Mr. Wang's child has the right to change his name, and Mr. Wang did not provide evidence to prove his child disagrees with the change. Therefore, the judgment rejected Mr. Wang's claim. It reflects the impact of the principle of best interests of the child.

We can see that the basic human rights principles could change the thinking, the model or the result of the judicial work. Although it is difficult to find any typical non-discrimination judicial case in China now, we may see the potential impact of the non-discrimination principle in future.

The principle of ensuring maximum survival and development

The survival and development of children is the principle that is key to protecting children's rights in China. According to the relevant laws and policies in China, governments at different levels adopt measures to promote children's safety, health, welfare and education. With the rapid development of the economy, the protection of children's survival and development has been effectively strengthened. In this regard, the non-discrimination principle demands special attention to vulnerable groups of children.

Children as victims of domestic violence should be protected urgently. They often suffer from unprivileged environments and other negative factors. On December 27, 2015, the Standing Committee of the NPC passed the Anti-Domestic Violence Law of the PRC, which is a historical breakthrough in China. After that, the implementation of the Law has become a key point to the prevention of and fight against family violence and ensuring children's rights. Based upon the Anti-Domestic Violence Law, some local courts issued the habeas corpus (personal protection order) to protect children from domestic violence, signaling the operation of the Law in real life.

Accidental injury in daily life, including food safety, environmental safety and traffic safety, are among the social concerns for children's safety. Discriminatory factors are again involved when we see that unprivileged regions or groups of children are more exposed to unfavorable conditions. On July 31, 2018, the People's Court of Jinyun County, Zhejiang province decided the first public interest case concerning food security for children in that province; a restaurant in a small town, selling food to the nearby middle school students, regularly violated the security standards and was fined and instructed to provide a fund for the compensation of the victims.[4] In 2003, the National Working Committee on Children and Women under the State Council and Ministry of Health began to establish hospital and school injuries monitoring systems in the country, and gradually implemented intervention projects and safety educational activities.

It has been reported by the Chinese official news agency that China's infant and child mortality rates dropped significantly in recent years. About 8.1 per 1,000 infants (those under 12 months old) died in 2015, down from 13.1 in 2010, according to a report released by the National Bureau of Statistics. The child (those under 5 years) mortality rate stood at 10.7 per 1,000 in 2015, down from 16.4 in 2010. However, in both categories there is a marked difference between urban and rural areas, with rural areas having more than double the mortality rates of urban areas. Meanwhile, infant and child mortality showed a significant gap between the developed eastern regions and the less developed western regions, the research said.[5]

The principle of children's participation

Children's right to participation has a policy and legal basis in China. In 2006, Arts. 3 and 14 of the Law on the Protection of Minors stipulated the "right to participate" as a basic right of children in law for the first time. After that, such provisions were also included in the revised regulations for the protection of children in Hunan, Guangdong, Jiangsu and other provinces at local levels. In 2010, China's Program of Child Development (2011–2020) clearly mentioned the principle of children's participation and required children's participation in family life and cultural and social life. Its aim is to create a social environment conducive to children's participation, opening the channels for the expression of children's opinions, and absorbing children's opinions according to their evolving capacity. This is progress compared with China's Program of Child Development in the 1990s and China's Program of Child Development (2001–2010).

On January 18, 2018, the China National Center for Children and Social Sciences Academic Press jointly published the *Annual Report on Children's Participation in China* (2017), which is the first bluebook on children's participation in China. In this book, studies show that there exist variances in their participation between children from urban and rural areas, children from white-collar families and those from blue-collar families, and children whose parents have different levels of education in aspects such as family, school, after school, online and public affairs (Zhou and Zou 2017). However, how to read the differences? Do they reflect the real behavior or desire of the children? Or are they the result of the discriminatory treatment of the parents based upon their social status? The studies attempt to show the reality. But we need to explain and try to face the challenges of the limited resources the disadvantaged groups of children have.

In the judicial proceedings, Art. 270 of the Criminal Procedure Law stipulates that through the appropriate adult presence system, children should be helped to participate in criminal procedure. In public affairs management, opportunities for children's participation in China are also expanding. In 2010, the Office of National Working Committee on Children and Women under State Council drafted The Goal and Strategy of the Child-friendly Cities in China, which encourages local governments to improve the awareness of responsibility to manage children's affairs, and formulate public policies to promote the development of children. In this document, whether the children participate in family, school, community, social life, and take part in decision-making relating to children's affairs in the management of public affairs is the criterion for evaluation of the child-friendly city. Definitely, the quantity and quality of participation of the children depends upon the implementation of the principle of non-discrimination.

The new concept of children and the mainstreaming of children's rights in China

The new concept of children

To promote and protect children's rights, it is necessary to understand the new concept of children and their rights. In other words, to understand children and their rights from a new perspective according to the UN CRC. The new concept of children is a basic knowledge of children, childhood and the children's rights. It reflects the ideological foundation of the CRC, and also provides significant guidance for Chinese legislation and policy making and law and policy implementation. It also helps in the understanding of the non-discrimination principle.

It includes three basic opinions or perspectives. First, the child should be viewed as a human being. No matter how small and weak she or he is, a child has the same status as any human being, just like adults, and these rights include the right to life, the right to food and so on. The child is the rights holder, not an adjunct or subordinate to the adult, family and other institutions. The child cannot be just considered as objective of protection. Second, a child should be viewed as a child. She or he shall enjoy some unique legal protection designed just for them. Childhood is a specific stage of life and has its own independent value. Children cannot always be regarded as incomplete, and their childhood cannot only be considered as the preparation for adulthood. Actually, for many rights like the right to food, the child can enjoy them directly and fully. Third, the child should be treated according to her or his evolving capacity. Children are a big group below the age of 18, and their childhood can be divided into different stages during which their needs and capacities are different. Children at different stages must be provided with appropriate treatment (Bu 2000).

The new concept or outline of children provides a leading guidance for China to formulate relevant child policies and laws and to protect the right of children in practice. During the past decade, children's independent personality has received more and more recognition and attention, though still there is a long way to go to raise the awareness of this new concept.

Mainstreaming of children's rights in China

The Chinese government has formulated relevant policies and laws to protect children's rights. They are conducive to the mainstreaming of children's rights in China. Meanwhile, based upon them, civil society can also advocate children's rights, supervise and evaluate the government's work, and promote the development of children's rights mainstreaming.

Art. 7 (2) of the Law on the Protection of Minors declares that the State Council and local people's governments at various levels shall provide leadership over the effective protection of children; and they shall include this work in their national or local economic and social development plans and annual plans and include the budgets needed in their governmental budgets.

In 2016, the National Human Rights Action Plan (2016–2020) emphasizes "the principle of 'putting children first' shall be upheld, the responsibility of the governments and the whole of society for the protection of children's rights shall be highlighted, and the goals set in the National Program for Children's Development in China (2011–2020) shall be fully realized". The action plan elaborates the measures the governments at different levels should take for children's rights.

The mainstreaming of children's rights is significant for the realization of children's rights. However, the mainstreaming of children's rights cannot be simply understood as a slogan. Legislation and policy making is just the first step. It means the law and policy's implementation as well. Both standards or rules and actions are needed. This is the full meaning of mainstreaming of human rights. During the mainstreaming process, the non-discrimination principle is the very basic principle for the child rights approach. Otherwise, it is not a real human rights approach. In China, the laws and policy documents advocate the equality right of the child and emphasize the aid or special protection for vulnerable groups such as children. They encourage governments, schools, families and other actors to take joint efforts to promote the development of children. However, the non-discrimination principle is not directly mentioned.

Challenge and proposal to the protection of children's rights in China

Advocate the new understanding of child's rights and non-discrimination principle

More people are accepting the new understanding of childhood and children's rights, but it still needs to be rooted in society. The advocacy of the new understanding not only requires the State to strengthen top-level design, but also requires the wide participation of the public. Due to the influence of traditional culture there is still a view of patriarchal and unequal status of girls in many families. The meanings of the new outline of children's rights have not yet become the common sense of child protection in China, and the awareness of equal protection for children in difficulties needs to constantly improve in fields such as education, health and social services.

"Human rights education" is an important part of the Chinese National Human Rights Action Plans. There is not any obstacle to teach and elaborate the principle of non-discrimination in China. Theoretically, it is a widespread legal concept. Though, formally, it is not used as a Chinese legal principle, it is helpful to understand the legal purposes and existing principles and rules in the law. The author wants to predict that the Chinese laws and policies and their practices will accept the non-discrimination principle expressively in future.

Improve the system and strengthen the State legislation and law enforcement

At the legislative level, the law itself may not be clear enough for operation. For example, 36 times "ipso jure", seven times "competent departments", 12 times "related departments", and three times "related regulations" show in the Law of the PRC on the Protection of Minors. These ambiguous legal provisions have increased the difficulty of implementing the law, and are not conducive to the better protection of children.

As far as the non-discrimination principle is concerned, there is a lack of standards to prevent and correct the discriminatory treatment of the child. In this regard, China should in a timely manner review existing laws from the perspective of human rights, focusing on the promotion of children's rights, gender equality and so on.

Simply making laws is not enough – China should also pay attention to the implementation of existing laws, and make children's rights in the law really work in real life, especially to ensure every child is protected fully and equally. For example, though the laws have prohibited the violation of disabled children for a long time, it is only recently that we have seen the first criminal case on the forced begging of disabled children sentenced in the year 2007 by the People's Court of Futian District, Shenzhen, Guangdong province, in which three persons were fined and imprisoned for between 14 months and 2 years (Liu et al. 2007). Considering the abuse of disabled children in this case, including serious illegal detention, corporal punishment and other illegal acts over a long time, the penalties cannot be viewed as sufficient.

Expand financial input, make full use of all kinds of resources and realize the balanced protection of children's rights in various regions

As the largest developing country in the world, local development inside China is quite uneven. There are obvious differences between the eastern and western regions, urban and rural areas in the fields of education, health, and social welfare. Therefore, the Chinese Government should actively play a strong role to keep a balanced economic and social development of the country. It can promote the human rights cause around the country. For instance, through poverty alleviation policies and projects and other efforts, improve the conditions of under developed areas for guaranteeing of the rights of the child.

The gap in education among the regions is an important one. In order to enhance the construction of schools in poverty-stricken areas, China has provided a series of special funds to waive the tuition and miscellaneous fees for students in compulsory education around the country including in rural areas, especially the poverty-stricken areas, carry out the three-year action plan for preschool education and ordinary high school transformation programs, and upgrade the quality of vocational education. In addition to national finance, UNICEF, Save the Children, Plan International and other international organizations also provide funds for the protection of children in China. During the past years, domestic foundations have also actively helped poor areas to improve the school conditions and provide support for the development of basic education, vocational education, and for the basic essential services for 2- and 3-year-old babies of the indigent families, left-behind children in rural areas, and other children with special needs.

However, in any case, we should not regard funding as the only way to resolve the problem, or simply consider the protection of children's rights as a financial matter. Other than the input of money, we still need a strong political will and widespread awareness on the protection of children's rights. Mainstreaming of children's rights into the political, legal, and social work, and trying to create new child friendly environments is a complicated process. However, financial and resources allocation is a crucial step and needs to be done in accordance with the principle of best interests of children and the principle of non-discrimination.

Care for left-behind children in rural areas, perfecting information collection and working mechanism

"Left-behind children" are the special groups of children in rural areas that are a result of the unbalanced development of China's economy. Many peasants leave their children behind at home and go to work in the cities far away. In February 2016, the State Council issued the Opinions on Strengthening the Care and Protection of Left-behind Children in Rural Areas. It defines the left-behind children as children less than 16 years of age whose parents live away as migrant workers or one parent is migrant worker outside while the other has no guardianship capability. Based upon a survey jointly carried out in 2016 by the Ministry of Civil Affairs, the Ministry of Education and the Ministry of Public Security, it is said that there are about 9 million left-behind children in China (Ma 2016). The household registration system in China, introduced in the 1950s, ties people's access to public services to their residential status – basically, urban or rural. Because the reform of the household system to remove the distinction between urban and rural residents has not been completed, it is not easy for the children of migrant workers to go and live together with their parent(s) in the city. In other words, the rural residents cannot move to urban areas easily and be treated equally. The left-behind children often live with their grandparents or other close relatives, and the quality of the guardianship is often questionable.

In recent years, Central Government has supported the implementation of the Pilot Project for Community Care Services for Left-behind Children in Rural Areas, which has benefited a large number of left-behind children. From the end of March 2016 to the end of July 2016, the Ministry of Civil Affairs, Ministry of Education, and Ministry of Public Security jointly carried out a nationwide survey of rural left-behind children. This action provides a basic data support to fully reflect the situation of rural left-behind children. It will help to further refine and perfect the policies and measures to strengthen care protection, strengthen the care service deployment and resource integration, and establish a detailed database of rural left-behind children.

In the long run, the key to the problem of left-behind children is to reduce the number and prevent them from being left-behind. Reunion and living with their parents are the rights of children and that is the most favorable way to bring up the child. On the one hand, peasants should be encouraged to work or start their own businesses in their hometowns. On the other hand, through the reform of households, social security and educational systems, the government can create conditions for migrant workers to live more easily with their youngest children in their working city, and receive the social services of education, medical treatment and so on. In the long run, the phenomenon of left-behind children will still exist, and government and society should take effective measures to care for and protect the right of left-behind children. Obviously, the non-discrimination principle can help prevent the discriminatory treatment of both the migrant workers and their children. It is an important rule for the solution of the problem in the long run.

Face the changes in the number of newborns and meet the needs of child-related social services

On October 29, 2015, China issued the "two-child policy" applicable around the country, which means that within the framework of the national policy of family planning, China abolished the "one-child policy" that had been implemented for 35 years. The implementation of the new policy will be conducive to optimizing the population structure, increasing the supply of labor force, reducing the pressure of an aging population, promoting the balanced development of the population and the sustainable development of the economy.

State policy is an important, but not decisive, factor affecting fertility rate. Due to concerns for the high cost of education, medical care and development of the child, many families are unwilling to have a second child. It is worth noting that the Compulsory Education Law of the PRC stipulates that school-age children over the age of 6 should receive compulsory education and China has not incorporated pre-school education into the national compulsory education system. This means that families now bear the burden of pre-school education of the children. For the best interests of children, the State may include pre-school education in the scope of compulsory education. Meanwhile, there is no unified national welfare system for the children yet. Medical care for the child may also mean a financial burden for the families in China.

According to the Department of Population and Employment Statistics (part of the National Bureau of Statistics), the number of births in 2017 was 17.23 million, which is a decrease of 630,000 compared with 2016, and the birth rate was 12.43 percent, which is also lower than the previous year (Zhang 2018). This shows that the expected peak of pregnancy is not very obvious, which means that China will also enter the list of low-fertility countries.

Even the growth of the birth rate is slower than expected. There are more newborn babies in China. The sudden change of policy and the consequent rise of the new-born population produces pressure on China's maternal and child health care, compulsory education and so on. The number of high-risk pregnant women and the cases of birth defects in new-born babies will increase. The infrastructure of health is insufficient and the resources for childcare are lacking. The contradiction between supply and demand for preschool education is more obvious. Beijing and other cities have a huge "deficit" of kindergartens.

Due to the pressure of the development of the aging society and the reluctance of families to have more than one child, the author can predict that soon China will lift the ban of baby birth completely and give up its family planning policy at last. This may make the limitation of the social services and resources even more serious.

When resources are in short supply, equal and fair access to them is challenging. For the rights of children and their parents, governments are attempting to improve services and solve problems, and in this process, the principle of non-discrimination can play an important role and help to make public health services accessible for all children and their parents. Additionally, a special arrangement for vulnerable groups should be considered. This is a new challenge for China to protect the rights of the child, especially from a non-discrimination perspective.

Conclusion

With economic and social development, China is more actively taking efforts to promote human rights, including the rights of the child. The Implementation of the UN CRC is enlightening in China for the promotion of both awareness of and practices for the rights of the child.

In the Report to the 19th National Congress of the CPC, Xi Jinping, the General Secretary of the CPC and the President of the PRC, pointed out that Chinese socialism has entered a new era, and the principal contradiction or challenge faced by Chinese society has evolved into the contradiction between unbalanced and inadequate development and the people's ever-growing needs for a better life. This is the background of the child rights promotion and protection in China.

As a developing country, China has achieved a lot in awareness raising on the rights of the child, and witnessed big progress in legislation and policy making. But challenges still exist for directly incorporating the non-discrimination principle of CRC into Chinese law and Chinese judicial practices. Population policy change, educational and medical care reforms, rural left-behind children, girl's rights and security issues are the main concerns now relating to the rights of the child in China.

For the protection of children's rights, China should continue to deepen the understanding and strengthen the implementation of the purposes and principles of CRC, keep raising the awareness of the new rights-oriented concept of childhood and the principles of CRC including the best interests of children and non-discrimination, improving child protection mechanisms involving both governments and other actors in society, and creating child-friendly environments with joint efforts.

Children's rights, and human rights in China, have been under scrutiny and are still on the way to being improved. The laws and policies on child welfare are fragmented and still on the way to being more unified and completed. Legislation and policy making are the starting points for further action. The new direction is clear and encouraging, but there are still challenges and obstacles to overcome, promisingly and uneasily.

Notes

* Professor of International Human Rights Law, Assistant Director of Institute of International Law, Chinese Academy of Social Sciences (CASS); Executive Director, Center for Human Rights Studies, CASS.

1 Tabulation on the 2010 population Census of the People's Republic of China, available from: http://www.stats.gov.cn/tjsj/pcsj/rkpc/6rp/indexch.htm [Accessed 16 August 2018].

2 Concluding observations on the combined third and fourth periodic reports of China, adopted by the Committee at its sixty-fourth session (16 September–4 October 2013), CRC/C/CHN/CO/3–4, 29 Ocober, 2013, para. 29.

3 Decision No. 1514 of Civil Final (2001). Kunming: Kunming Intermediate People's Court of Yunnan Province, China.

4 Yao, G., Li, W., Decision of the first public interests case on the food security of the minors made in Zhejiang province declared. *China Women's Daily*, 15 August, B1.

5 China's child mortality rates drop, regional differences remain. Xinhua News Agency. 4 November,2016, available from: http://www.chinadaily.com.cn/china/2016-11/04/content_27272588.htm [Accessed 22 August 2018].

References

Bu, W. 2000. Defending the childhood. *Reading*, 252(3), 45–50.

Committee on the Rights of the Child (CRC). 2013. Concluding observations on the combined third and fourth periodic reports of China, adopted by the Committee at its sixty-fourth session (16 September–4 October 2013). CRC/C/CHN/CO/3–4.

Department of Population and Employment Statistics of the National Bureau of Statistics. 2017. *Statistics Yearbook of Population and Employment in China (2017)*. Beijing: China Statistics Press.

Li, Z. 2018. *Anti-discrimination: Ideas, Systems and Practice*. Beijing: Peking University.

Liu, C., Xiao, F. and Xie, T. 2007. Three suspects sentenced penalties for enforcing minors to beg. *Guangzhou Daily*, 22 August, A5.

Liu, H. (chief ed.). 2009. *Rights of the Child and Legal Protection*. Shanghai: People's Press.

Liu, J. 2012. Strategic thinking of China's child welfare times. *Academia*, 134(2), 51–58.

Liu, J. 2010. *State Responsibility and Child Welfare*. Beijing: China Social Press.

Ma, C. 2016. Parents leave behind 9 million children in China. *China Daily*. Available at: http://www.chinadaily.com.cn/china/2016-11/10/content_27334436.htm [Accessed 16 August 2018].

National Health and Family Planning Commission of the People's Republic of China. 2016. *Statistical Yearbook for Health and Family Planning in China*. Beijing: Peking Union Medical College Press.

Wang, X. 2005. *On Children's Rights: A Preliminary Comparative Study in the Context of China*. Beijing: Social Sciences Academic Press.

Yuan, L. (chief ed.). 2017. *Annual Report on Children's Participation in China (2017)*. Beijing: Social Sciences Academic Press.

Zhang, Y. 2018. Birth of the baby is both family and national issue. *People's Daily Overseas Edition*, 7 August, 7.

Zhou, J. and Zou, X. 2017. Children's participation among different groups: A comparative study in terms of family background. In: Yuan, L. (chief ed.) *Annual Report on Children's Participation in China*, (pp. 75–115). Beijing: Social Sciences Academic Press.

Zhu, N. 2018. Legislative Affairs Commission of the Standing Committee, National People's Congress urges the relevant authorities to correct the judicial interpretation ultra vires by local court according to its Record Review power. *Legal Daily*, 14 August, 9.

12 The importance of Article 2 of the Convention on the Rights of the Child for refugee children

Sonia Human

Introduction

To qualify for refugee status, a refugee child, like any other applicant, will have to prove that she is outside her country of origin; that she is unable or unwilling to seek or to take advantage of the protection of that country, or to return there; that the inability or unwillingness is attributable to a well-founded fear of being persecuted; and the fear of persecution is based on race, religion, nationality, membership of a particular social group or political opinion. The definition reflects a bias in favour of an adult male paradigm that directly impacts on asylum procedures and adjudication of asylum applications, in particular in the understanding of "persecution" and "a well-founded fear" (Bhabha 2004, p. 228). The absence of age and even gender as grounds for persecution in the refugee definition militates against a concept of "refugee identity" for a child and in principle, constitutes discrimination (Bhabha 2003, pp. 266–269). A full understanding of the unique needs and entitlements is therefore critical to challenge the discriminatory nature of the adult paradigm of the refugee definition. In view of unprecedented refugee flows, states increasingly introduce legislative and interstate arrangements aimed at restricting access to asylum and the provision of legal rights to refugees (Gorlick 2000, p. 2). Increasingly restrictive interpretations of the refugee definition and consequently limiting access to refugee status determination procedures, directly impacts on refugee children and adds to their vulnerability. It is submitted that Article 2 of the Convention on the Rights of the Child (hereafter CRC), has the potential to challenge certain preconceptions, such as the adult male paradigm of the refugee definition, that have had the effect of denying protection to refugee children under the Refugee Convention (Edwards 2003, p. 47). As a threshold right, Article 2 requires a detailed interrogation of child-specific discrimination in the context of refugee law, thereby advancing the understanding and development of age-sensitive interpretations of refugee law.

The Refugee Convention (UNHCR 1951), supplemented by the 1967 Protocol (UNHCR 1967) is the key treaty in the international refugee regime. Since the inception of the Refugee Convention, the field of international human rights law has changed and developed in an exponential fashion (Hathaway 2005,

p. 119). The scope of refugee protection is therefore no longer limited to the norms of refugee law, but extends "to all the necessary measures to ensure that refugees are effectively protected, including through national legislation, and in compliance with their obligations under international human rights and humanitarian law instruments bearing directly on refugees" (UNHCR 1997a, No. 81). International human rights law therefore makes a significant contribution in strengthening refugees' protection (Gorlick 2000, p. 1; McAdam 2007, pp. 10–12). One is even tempted to question the continued relevance of the Refugee Convention in view of the extensive body of international human rights law (McAdam 2007, p. 12). There is, however, no doubt that the Refugee Convention remains unique as the specificity of refugees' entitlements:

> is to ensure that those whose basic rights are not protected (for a Convention reason) in their own country are, if able to reach an asylum state, entitled to invoke rights of substitute protection in any state party to the Refugee Convention.
>
> (Hathaway 2005, pp. 5, 119–126, 153; McAdam 2007, p. 5)

In this sense, refugee law has been described as a "remedial or palliative branch of human rights law" (Hathaway 2005, p. 5).

As the title indicates, the Refugee Convention only addresses the status of refugees, and aspects such as admission of refugees, access to asylum procedures and finding of durable solutions are not dealt with (Goodwin-Gill 1995, p. 406). States retain exclusive authority to regulate entry into their territory and to decide on the extent and nature of human rights protection of those within its territory and subject to its jurisdiction (Goodwin-Gill 1995, p. 406). As far as refugee children are concerned, other than recommended measures aimed at family unity and providing for access at least at the level of primary education there are no provisions specifically aimed at them (Goodwin-Gill 1995, p. 407).

In order to discuss the importance of Article 2 for refugee children, context will be provided by giving a brief overview of the Refugee Convention as a human rights treaty as supplemented by the normative framework provided by the CRC. This will provide the basis for the discussion of the principle of non-discrimination in refugee law. In what follows, the exclusive focus will be on Article 2 and its role in refugee law.

The Refugee Convention as a human rights treaty

The Refugee Convention is infused with a human rights dimension. This is evident from the Preamble, which reads as follows:

> Considering that the Charter of the United Nations and the Universal Declaration of Human Rights have affirmed the principle that human beings shall enjoy fundamental rights and freedoms without discrimination.

> Considering that the United Nations has, on various occasions, manifested its profound concern for refugees and endeavoured to assure refugees the widest possible exercise of fundamental rights and freedoms.

The direct line of descent with the human rights focus of the UN Charter and the Universal Declaration of Human Rights is unambiguous (Gorlick 2000, p. 5; McAdam 2007, pp. 29–31).[1] Since the adoption of the Refugee Convention, the number of international and regional human rights treaties have proliferated, whereby states have formally accepted legal obligations for human rights ranging from civil and political rights to economic, social and cultural rights (Gorlick 2000, pp. 11–12).[2] As a living document, the content of the Refugee Convention must therefore be analysed in the broader context of international human rights law as well as humanitarian law (Edwards 2003, p. 47).[3] This holistic approach is very important, as these bodies of law complement the safeguards for refugees as set out in the Refugee Convention. In addition, as explained by Edwards, these bodies of law reinforce the non-discriminatory basis of international law in general, which impacts on international refugee law in particular (Edwards 2003, p. 47).[4]

The one international human rights treaty that contributes significantly to the human rights dimension of the Refugee Convention is the United Nations Convention on the Rights of the Child (hereafter the CRC) (Goodwin-Gill 1995, pp. 406–407). More than any other treaty, in the context of this discussion, the value of the CRC is that it brings the much needed child-specific focus to refugee issues. The CRC broadens the concept of protection in as far as refugee children are concerned, to not only include rights and processes, but also to extend protection to all the developmental needs of a refugee child (Goodwin-Gill 1995, p. 410). The fundamental importance of the CRC has been recognised by the United Nations High Commissioner for Refugees (hereafter UNHCR), and it is used as the normative framework for all matters concerning refugee children (Goodwin-Gill and McAdam 2007, p. 477; UNHCR 1979, par. 14).

The Refugee Convention, read with the CRC, therefore sets the most comprehensive standards encompassing every aspect of a refugee child's life. Bierwith refers to this as a "complementary relationship [affording] optimal protection for the refugee child; the 1951 Convention seeks to protect the rights of the child as a refugee, whilst the CRC serves to guard the child's rights as a child" (Bierwith 2005, p. 101).

The CRC is also the first international treaty that contains a provision in Article 22 focussing on refugee children, and states are required to ensure that a child who is seeking refugee status or who is considered to be a refugee, receive appropriate protection and humanitarian assistance in the enjoyment of the rights set out in the Convention, as well as other international human rights or humanitarian instruments to which the States are party. The content of Article 22 once again underscores the interchange between refugee law, international human rights law and humanitarian law (Goodwin-Gill 1995, pp. 413–414).[5] It brings a holistic approach to the protection and development of the refugee child and provides a legal and normative framework that provides a standard for any intervention (Goodwin-Gill 1995, pp. 410, 415).

In what follows, a brief discussion of the meaning of non-discrimination in the context of international refugee law will be give, before Article 2 of the CRC will be elaborated upon with regard to specific issues in refugee law.

Non-discrimination and international refugee law

The principles of non-discrimination and equality are regarded as the "most frequently declared norms of international human rights law" (Bayefsky 1990, p. 1) and enshrine the notion that dignity and equality is to be accorded to all human beings (Breen 2003, p. 751; Pobjoy 2010, pp. 184, 201). Hathaway is of the opinion that of all the various protections guaranteed by international human rights law, the duty of non-discrimination has the potential to be of the greatest value to refugees (Hathaway 2005, p. 123). The centrality of non-discrimination is reflected in the Charter of the United Nations, promoting "the equal rights of men and women" in the Preamble. Furthermore, the Charter calls upon the United Nations to "achieve international co-operation in promoting and encouraging respect for human rights and for fundamental freedoms for all without distinction as to race, sex, language or religion". These goals were given legally binding force in the International Covenant on Civil and Political Rights (hereafter ICCPR) and the International Covenant on Economic, Social and Cultural Rights (hereafter ICESCR).[6]

It is however Article 26 of the ICCPR (1976) that is seen as the core guarantee of non-discrimination in international human rights law (Hathaway 2005, p. 125; Pobjoy 2010, p. 203), and it reads as follows:

> All persons are equal before the law and are entitled without any discrimination to the equal protection of the law. In this respect, the law shall prohibit any discrimination and guarantee to all persons equal and effective protection against discrimination on any ground such as race, colour, sex, language, religion, political or other opinion, national or social origin, property, birth or other status.

It is important to note that the scope of Article 26 is not limited to the rights provided in the ICCPR, but that it provides an independent and autonomous guarantee of non-discrimination (Pobjoy 2010, p. 204; Hathaway 2005, p. 125; OHCHR, 1989). All refugees are therefore entitled to rely on Article 26 and, as a minimum, it requires of any decision maker to critically examine the rationale for differential treatment between refugees and citizens (Hathaway 2005, pp. 123–147). It must, however, be noted that, in reflecting on his discussion of the jurisprudence of the Human Rights Committee in Article 26, Hathaway reaches the conclusion that despite its wide ambit, non-discrimination law has not yet developed to the point that refugees can safely assume that they will benefit from all the rights afforded to citizens (Hathaway 2005, pp. 124–147, 238).

In contrast to the scope of Article 26 of the ICCPR (1976), the scope of Article 3 of the Refugee Convention is far more limited. In terms of Article 3, the provisions of the Convention must be applied to refugees without discrimination as to race, religion or country of origin. Article 3 is clearly aimed at prevention of discrimination between and among subsets of refugees, but only based on the three listed grounds (Hathaway 2005, p. 251).[7]

As a living document, the Refugee Convention cannot be applied in a manner that is isolated from the human rights paradigm, especially the universality of the right not to be discriminated against (Hathaway 2005, p. 67).[8] Article 3 of the Refugee Convention must therefore be read with the non-discriminatory provisions of the ICCPR (1976) and the ICESCR (1976) to appreciate the extensive guarantee of non-discrimination not only between and among refugee sub-populations, but also between refugees and citizens (Hathaway 2005, p. 259).[9] Article 3 of the Refugee Convention must obviously also be read with the one child-specific non-discrimination provision, namely Article 2 of the CRC. The value of Article 2 can be found in the fact that it has the potential to make a significant contribution to the understanding of a refugee child's "refugee identity", and to thereby draw attention to the numerous levels of discrimination faced by these children.[10]

CRC Article 2 and refugee children

Refugee children, as their adult counterparts, flee their country of origin as a result of human rights violations. These human rights violations are linked to discrimination based on race, religion, nationality, membership of a particular social group, political opinion or age (Goodwin-Gill & McAdam 2007, p. 70).[11]Hathaway (2005, p. 352) elaborates further on the theme of discrimination in the following day:

> [R]efugee status is a recognition of the special imperative to respond to the needs of persons in flight from risk prompted by discrimination – the prohibition of which is the most central human rights commitment of the international community. Simply put, refugees are persons who are seriously at risk because of who they are or what they believe.

Unfortunately, human rights violations do not end once a refugee child crosses on international border (Fritsch et al. 2010, pp. 627–633).[12] The one reality that adds to their vulnerability is a double jeopardy of discrimination faced by them once they become non-citizens. Here they face discrimination in the sense that they are viewed as refugees, subsumed within the male adult paradigm of migration laws, policies and procedures with little concern for their vulnerabilities as children (Bhabha 2001, pp. 293–295). On the other hand, they also face discrimination in terms of care and protection as they tend to be identified as children in need of care and protection but often their distinctive needs as refugees are not fully acknowledged and understood (Bhabha 2003, pp. 266–267). This form of discrimination is not necessarily intentional, but nevertheless amounts to discrimination if there is no objective justification for treating different situations in a similar fashion (Besson 2005, p. 451).[13] In order to determine if situations are similar and should therefore be treated in a similar way, the criterion of comparison is a comparison between children. In the context of the discussion, the relevant comparison is one between the specific refugee child and a child citizen. Access to legal representation or guardianship where appropriate, the failure to initiate family tracing, the lack of proficient translation services and the consideration of asylum as a remedy, are only some of the consequences of this form of discrimination (Bhabha 2004, p. 243). The failure to fully interrogate Article 2 of the CRC as a point of departure is also evident when durable solutions for a particular refugee child are considered. In refugee law discourse, durable solutions are typically understood to entail voluntary repatriation, local integration or third country settlement (Goodwin-Gill 1995, p. 407). Goodwin-Gill captures the inappropriateness of this understanding where refugee children are involved as follows, "Solutions for children, however have another dimension; they cannot be mortgaged to some future time and place, but to be durable must contribute now to the full development of the child" (Goodwin-Gill 1995, p. 407).

Therefore, in contract to achieving post-flight goals which often have to be postponed for reasons such as lack of political will or a lack of available resources, Article 2 is the triggering provision that requires a decision-maker to identify a child-specific durable solution that entails a total approach to the protection and development of such a child. It is not necessary to look further than the CRC to find content to such durable solutions (Goodwin-Gill 1995, p. 412). Psychosocial well-being; health and nutrition; personal liberty and security; access to education; and the right to a name and nationality are obvious examples (UNHCR 1997b; Detrick 1999, pp. 367–367; Van Bueren 1995, pp. 366–372).

It is argued that Article 2 is a core-minimum right and in all probability the most important legal guarantee that a refugee child can rely on the moment she comes under the *de facto* or *de jure* jurisdiction of a State party to the Refugee Convention (Hathaway 2005, pp. 123, 278). As a threshold right and a legal guarantee it "unlocks" six claims to protection, which should immediately and unconditionally be recognised (Hathaway 2005, p. 279). First, the refugee child is entitled to enter and remain in the country of destination until they are found not to be a Convention refugee. Second, refugee children may not be arbitrarily detained, especially not with adult refugees if they are unaccompanied or separated. Third, pending the outcome of an asylum adjudication, their right to life, survival and development should be implemented (CESCR 2009, par. 30).[14] Fourth, respect for the human dignity of every refugee child requires respect for the preservation of family unity, as well as the preservation of language, culture and religion. Fifth, priority must be given to birth registration and identity documents and preventing statelessness. Sixth, remedies should be made available to a refugee child, should any of the above rights of protection be infringed.[15]

Sadly, the six claims to protection are ignored and violated on a daily basis. It therefore came as no surprise that the United Nations Committee on the Rights of the Child (hereafter Children's Rights Committee) dedicated the Day of General Discussion in 2012 to "The rights of all children in the context of international migration". Underlying the decision to focus on this theme was the concern that children in the context of international migration face multiple forms of discrimination in transit and in destination countries (CRC 2012a, p. 36).

In the Background Paper to the 2012 General Day of Discussion, the human rights challenges affecting children in the context of international migration are discussed in quite some detail. The majority of these violations can directly be linked to violations of the six claims to protection as set out above (CRC 2012b, pp. 18–32).[16] It is submitted that the basis for the human rights violations can be found on a domestic level, where State parties to the CRC fail to engage with the content of Article 2.

In the Report of the Day of General Discussion, a number of recommendations are made (CRC 2012a, pp. 15–22). In making the recommendations, the Committee on the Rights of the Child emphasised that a child is first and foremost a child, whatever the condition she may find herself in (CRC 2012a, p. 15). The Committee also reiterated that:

> States and relevant actors [need] to undertake holistic and comprehensive approaches for identifying and addressing the rights of children affected by migration based on all provisions and principles of the Convention, avoiding categorisation or distinctions of different types of children, situations or rights. In reiterating that all children involved in or directly affected by international migration are entitled to the enjoyment of their rights, regardless of age, sex, ethnic or national origin and economic or documentation status, whether accompanied or unaccompanied, documented or undocumented.

Support is given to the point made above, namely that CRC Article 2 is probably the most important legal guarantee a refugee child can claim.[17]

On a domestic level, Article 2 must therefore be seen as a threshold provision which must be upheld and which requires age-sensitive interpretations of refugee law, further complemented by the CRC and relevant provisions of international human rights law and humanitarian law (Edwards 2003, p. 47). Article 2 contains two sets of duties, complementing each other (Besson 2005, p. 454). First, a duty of respect implies that a state may not in any way discriminate against any child, in other words also a refugee child, in the enjoyment of all the rights in the CRC. In the second place, duties of result requires of states to take all the necessary measures to ensure that every child under its jurisdiction is protected against all forms of discrimination, based on the status or attributes of the child's parents, legal guardians or family members (Besson 2005, p. 454). The measures are not limited to legislation, but also require changes in administration and resource allocation (Besson 2005, p. 454). It even includes educational measures to create awareness of the plight of refugee children and to counter racist and xenophobic behaviour towards them.

The most basic aspect of the refugee experience has been described as "the need to escape, to be accepted, and to be sheltered" (Hathaway 2005, p. 94). The importance of Article 2 as a threshold right, is that it has the potential to address these risks in a child-specific manner. Article 2 contributes to an understanding of child-specific forms of persecution and introduces the differential treatment required of refugee child's claim to asylum. Article 2 requires that the need to be accepted is judged in a manner that interrogates the adult male-centred nature of asylum procedures. Article 2 is key in addressing the refugee child's need to shelter as it unlocks all the rights in the CRC in order to contribute to the survival, protection and development of the child.

Over and above the fact that Article 2 must be seen as a threshold right, there are a number of further reasons why Article 2 is of such importance for refugee children. First, it requires for any decision made regarding a refugee child, that any unequal treatment compared to a child in the country of destination, must be "property justified according to consistently applied, persuasive, and acceptable criteria" (Hathaway 2005, p. 124). Second, Article 2 makes it clear that children have a right not be discriminated against in the enjoyment of all the rights set out in the CRC. The extent of the rights in the CRC basically covers every aspect of a refugee child's life. For example, a refugee child may not be discriminated against in the exercise of her right to life, survival and development in terms of Article 6. Article 6 probably contains the most basic and essential rights any child is entitled to, even more so a refugee child (Van Bueren 2000, pp. 208–209).

Third, Article 2 is a directly justiciable provision and can be relied upon as an immediately realisable right (Besson 2005, p. 447).[18] Fourth, Article 2 applies to all children under a State's jurisdiction. Refugee children may consequently not be discriminated against in the enjoyment of their rights as set out in the Convention because they are non-citizens (Besson 2005, pp. 449–450). In the fifth place, States must explicitly report on the measures taken in complying with their obligations in terms of Article 2 (Besson 2005, p. 455). The detailed extent to which a State must report on non-discriminatory measures is indicative of the importance of the principle of non-discrimination (Besson 2005, pp. 455–456; Detrick 1999, p. 365).[19]

The discussion will not be complete without a brief reference to the absence of gender in the refugee definition.[20] The failure to engage with these vulnerabilities has an impact on the institutional ideology of those who are responsible for the practical administration of asylum, as they tend to operate with a "traditional male-centered notion of persecution", which excludes refugee women and refugee children as they are viewed as passive bystanders and unlikely victims of persecution (Bhabha 2004, p. 228). The absence of age in the refugee definition also works towards asylum procedures which "take no account of gender or age-based specificities, thus procedural biases further disadvantage child applicants" (Bhabha 2004, p. 229). The discriminatory nature of such institutional ideologies and procedural biases are obvious. The value of Article 2 is, therefore, that it requires that institutional ideologies and administrative processes to be aligned with child-specific interpretations of a well-founded fear of persecution. Any differential treatment of refugee children which is not in accordance with the law, which does not pursue a legitimate aim and remain proportionate to the aim pursued, will amount to discrimination against refugee children vis-à-vis refugee adults.

As far as the concept of "persecution" is concerned, the interchange between international human rights law and refugee law has greatly contributed to an understanding of persecution "as the sustained or systemic failure of state protection in relation to one of the core entitlements which has been recognised by the international community" (Hathaway 1991, p. 112 cited by Carmody 2010, p. 28). In view of the universal ratification of the CRC, one can support an argument that this signifies near universal consensus of the core entitlements due to children (Carmody 2010, p. 28). Further support for this viewpoint can be found in the 1997 Guidelines (UNHCR 1997b, par. 8.7) where the following is stated:

> [U]nder the Convention on the Rights of the Child, children are recognized specific human rights, and that the manner in which those rights may be violated as well as the nature of such violations may be different from those that may occur in the case of adults. Certain policies and practices constituting gross violations of specific rights of the child may, under certain circumstances, lead to situations that fall within the scope of the Refugee Convention.

In general, the 1994 Guidelines on Protection and Care (UNHCR 1994), the Handbook on Procedures and Criteria for Determining Refugee Status (UNHCR 1979) and the 1997 Guidelines, provide justification for differential treatment as far as the onus of proof is on a refugee child to prove a well-founded fear of persecution. The 1997 Guidelines (UNHCR 1997b, par. 8.6) for example, emphasise the need to give "particular regard to a child's stage of development, possible limited knowledge of conditions in the country of origin and their significance to the legal concept of refugee status, as well as her special vulnerability". Article 2 of the CRC is once again key in ensuring an age-sensitive approach to the substantive claim of the refugee child (Edwards 2003, p. 57). Article 2 provides a basis to focus on the individuality of a refugee child's claim, and to uphold the right not to be discriminated against in the enjoyment of all the rights in the CRC. Unfortunately, it appears that it is on a domestic level that there is a failure to use Article 2 as a basis to focus on the individuality of a refugee child's claim (Bierwith 2005, pp. 103–105).

Too often, the consequences are detention, deportation, lack of attention to refugee-specific claims in the care and protection system and other discrimination vis-à-vis citizen children (Goodwin-Gill 1995, p. 412; Bhabha 2004, p. 243).

Conclusion

All refugee children are the beneficiaries of a broad range of human rights as set out in international instruments such as the UDHR, the ICCP and the ICESCR. The principle of non-discrimination runs like a golden thread through these instruments and provides the legal and moral imperative to treat all human beings, even refugee children as of equal worth (Bhabha 2003, p. 258). Unfortunately, as non-citizens, refugee children are discriminated against as a refugee and as a child who happens to be a refugee. They often experience the harshest realities after flight (Goodwin-Gill 1995, p. 412). Very often the reason for flight was based on discrimination that is age related. Human rights violations such as forcible or underage recruitment into the armed forces, underage marriage, female genital mutilation, forced prostitution and trafficking are well-known forms of child-specific persecution (Edwards 2003, p. 57).

The value of Article 2 is that is establishes the imperative obligation of state parties to the CRC to vigorously engage with child-specific forms of discrimination in the refugee context. The guarantee of non-discrimination extends beyond children who have been afforded refugee status to children who are seeking asylum (Van Bueren 1995, p. 362). Refugee children are therefore entitled to all the rights guaranteed to citizen children as set out in the CRC. As a minimum, Article 2 requires that any unequal treatment be "properly justified according to consistently applied, persuasive and acceptable criteria" (McCrudden in Hathaway 2005, p. 124).

Understood in this way, the contribution hopefully opens up dialogue for an understanding of the importance of Article 2 in establishing a refugee identity for every refugee child and thereby providing a sound legal basis to challenge the adult male paradigm in refugee law.

Notes

1 McAdam, 2007 points out that early UN General Assembly resolutions support the underlying human rights basis of the Refugee Convention, with an emphasis on assisting the most needy, affirming basic principles relating to solutions and recommending increased protection activities. The result is a treaty that has even been called a "Convention on the Human Rights for Refugees".

2 There are numerous examples such as the International Covenant on Civil and Political Rights, the International Covenant on Economic, Social and Cultural Rights, the Convention on the Elimination of Racial Discrimination and the Convention Against Torture, to name a few. On a regional level, the European Convention for the Protection of Human Rights and Fundamental Freedoms and the African Charter on Human and Peoples' Rights are two examples.

3 UNHCR emphasised the interrelationship between the Refugee Convention and international human rights law as the follows: "The human rights base of the Convention roots it quite directly in the broader framework of human rights instruments of which it is an integral part, albeit with a very particular focus. The various human rights treaty monitoring bodies and the jurisprudence developed by regional bodies such as the European Court of Human Rights and the Inter-American Court of Human Rights are an important complement in this regard, not least since they recognize that refugees and asylum-seekers benefit both from specific Convention-based protection and from the range of human rights protections as they apply to all people regardless of status." UNHCR 2001, par. 4.

4 Bayefsky describes the principles of equality and non-discrimination as "the most frequently declared norms of international human rights law". Also see Pobjoy 2010, p. 184 and pp. 202–203 for the centrality of the concept of non-discrimination in international human rights law.

5 In the context of humanitarian law, the special protection needs of children were provided for in the context of the 1949 Geneva Conventions. The 1977 Additional Protocols expressly confirm that children are entitled to special protection and that they should be provided with the care and aid they require. It is notable that the Geneva Conventions and the Protocols link the protection of the child with the maintenance of family life. This link is a recurring theme in international law and is of great significance as far as unaccompanied and separated refugee children are concerned.

6 See Art 2 and Art 26 in the ICCPR (1976) and Art 2 in the ICESCR (1976). Although the UDHR has no legally binding force in the strict sense of the word, it contains

provisions such as Articles 1, 2 and 7 that clearly shows a commitment to eradicate discrimination.

7 For a detailed discussion see Hathway 2005, pp. 236–260.

8 See *Sepet and Bulbul v Secretary of State for the Home Department*, [2003] UKHL 15 (UKHL, Mar. 20, 2003) at par. 11 where Lord Bingham approved of the following observation in *R v Secretary of State for the Home Department, ex parte Adan and Aitseguer*, [1999] 3 WLR 1274 (UKCA July 23, 1999): "[I]t is clear that the signatory states intended that the convention should afford continuing protection for refugees in the changing circumstances of the present and future world. In our view, the Convention has to be regarded as a living instrument".

9 As Art 2 in both the ICCPR (1976) and the ICESCR (1976) only prohibits discrimination in relation to a right established in the respective Covenants, the importance of Art 26 of the ICCPR is once again highlighted as an independent and free-standing right.

10 Besson 2005, pp. 452, 456–457 highlights the fact that refugee children are not only protected against discrimination in terms of Art 2 of the CRC but that they also enjoy "positive" measures of discrimination in terms of Art 22 of the CRC. Detrick 1999, p. 368 also emphasises that none of the major international or regional human rights conventions contains a provision similar to Art 22, providing special protection to refugee and asylum-seeking children.

11 The further ground which can be added is gender, as refugee children face the double impact of discrimination based on age and gender. See Edwards 2003, pp. 46–59 in this regard. Attention must also be drawn to the overlap between the grounds of discrimination mentioned above and the non-discrimination provisions in the main international human rights treaties such as the ICCPR, the ICESCR and the CRC.

12 Fritsch et al (2010) provides an overview of the harsh realities faced by unaccompanied refugee minors.

13 Besson explains on 451 as follows: "[D]iscrimination in the context of children's rights implies a difference of treatment in similar situations or a similar treatment of different situations, whether this discrimination is intentional or not".

14 Par. 30 reads as follows: "The ground of nationality should no bar access to Covenant rights, e.g. all children within a state, including those with an undocumented status, have a right to receive education and access to adequate food and affordable health care. The Covenant rights apply to everyone including non-nationals, such as refugees, asylum-seekers, regardless of legal status and documentation".

15 The importance of Articles 3 and 12 of the CRC must be highlighted in this regard.

16 Examples include criminalization of migration; absence of consideration of the best interest of a child in migration situations; restrictions on the right to family life and family reunification procedures; migration related detention; denial of access to economic, social and cultural rights and basic services; and lack of birth registration and statelessness.

17 In this regard, also see Joint General comment No.3 (CMW 2017a) and No.22 (CMW 2017c) as well as the Joint General comment No.4 (CMW 2017b) and No.23 (CMW 2017d).

18 This is in contrast to Art 26 of the ICCPR that is, according to Hathaway 2005, p.129, in fact an *entitlement* "without any discrimination to the equal protection of the law" [own emphasis added]. Credit is given to Pobjoy 2010, p. 187 for referring to Art 26 as a provision that has the potential to "drill down" and remedy the discriminatory allocation of rights. It is argued that Art 2 of the CRC, more than Art 26 of the ICCPR has the potential to "drill down" and remedy discriminatory measures.

19 The Committee on the Rights of the Child specifically requests States parties to indicate in their reports: "The domestic legislation and procedures in place, including to determine refugee status and ensure and protect the rights of asylum-seeking and refugee children, as well as any safeguards established and remedies made available to the child". States parties

are also required to report on the number of asylum-seeking and refugee children, with specific reference to age, gender, country of origin, nationality and if they are accompanied or unaccompanied (Par. 120). Sates parties must also provide information on how the best interest of the child are given primary consideration in "[I]mmigration, asylum-seeking and refugee procedures" (Par. 35). As Article 12 of the CRC provides a right to be heard in asylum-seeking procedures, States parties must also provide information on measures taken to ensure that the right is implemented (Par. 43).

20 Although significant progress has been made in recent times in relation to the recognition of gender-related claims to refugee status, the particular vulnerabilities of refugee girls must be highlighted (Edwards 2003, pp. 51–57). Like refugee women, they face rape, sexual abuse, trafficking and especially child marriage.

References

Bayefsky, A. F. 1990. The principle of equality or non-discrimination in international law. *Human Rights Law Journal*, 11, 1–2.

Besson, S. 2005. The principle of non-discrimination in the Convention on the Rights of the Child. *The International Journal of Children's Rights*, 13, 433–461.

Bhabha, J. 2001. Minors or aliens? Inconsistent state intervention and separated child asylum seekers. *European Journal of Migrations and Law*, 3, 293–295.

Bhabha, J. 2003. More than their share of sorrows: International migration law and the rights of children. *Saint Louis University Public Law Review*, 22, 253–274.

Bhabha, J. 2004. Demography and rights: Women, children and access to asylum. *International Journal of Refugee Law*, 16, 227–243.

Bierwith, C. 2005. The protection of refugee and asylum seeking children, the Convention on the Rights of the Child and the work of the Committee on the Rights of the Child. *Refugee Survey Quarterly*, 24(2), 98–114.

Breen, C. 2003. Refugee law in Ireland: Disregarding the rights of the child citizen, discriminating against the rights of the child. *International Journal of Refugee Law*, 15(4), 750–785.

Carmody, L. C. 2010. To what extent has the Convention on the Rights of the Child acted as a lens for the refocus of refugee protection mechanisms, to affect improved protection measures and adherence to human rights standards for child refugees? Unpublished LLM Minor Dissertation.

CESCR. 2009. General comment No. 20: Non-discrimination in economic, social and cultural rights (art. 2, par. 2, of the International Covenant on Economic, Social and Cultural Rights). 2 July 2009. UN Committee on Economic, Social and Cultural Rights.

CMW. 2017a. Joint general comment No. 3 of the Committee on the Protection of the Rights of All Migrant Workers and Members of Their Families and No. 22 (2017) of the Committee on the Rights of the Child on the general principles regarding the human rights of children in the context of international migration. 16 November 2017. UN Committee on the Protection of the Rights of All Migrant Workers and Members of Their Families.

CMW. 2017b. Joint general comment No. 4 (2017) of the Committee on the Protection of the Rights of All Migrant Workers and Members of Their Families. 16 November 2017. UN Committee on the Protection of the Rights of All Migrant Workers and Members of Their Families.

CMW. 2017c. Joint general comment No.22 (2017) of the Committee on the Rights of the Child on the general principles regarding the human rights of children in the context of international migration. 16 November 2017. UN Committee on the Protection of the Rights of All Migrant Workers and Members of Their Families.

CMW. 2017d. Joint general comment No.23 (2017) of the Committee on the Rights of the Child on State obligations regarding the human rights of children in the context of international migration in countries of origin, transit, destination and return. 16 November 2017. UN Committee on the Protection of the Rights of All Migrant Workers and Members of Their Families.

CRC. 1996. General Guidelines for periodic reports: 20/11/96 CRC/C/58 Committee on the Rights of the Child. General Guidelines regarding the form and contents of periodic reports to be submitted by States parties under art. 44, para. 1 (b), of the Convention. Adopted by the Committee at its 343rd meeting (thirteenth session) on 11 October 1996. Committee on the Rights of the Child.

CRC. 2012a. Day of General Discussion on the Rights of All Children in the Context of International Migration. Committee on the Rights of the Child.

CRC. 2012b. Day of General Discussion. The Rights of All Children in the Context of International Migration: Background paper. Committee on the Rights of the Child.

Detrick, S. 1999. *A Commentary on the Convention on the Rights of the Child*. The Hague: Martinus Nijhoff Publishers.

Edwards, A. 2003. Age and gender dimensions in international refugee law. In: E. Feller, V. Türk and F. Nicholson, (eds). *Refugee Protection in International Law: UNHCR's Global Consultations on International Protection*, (pp. 46–80). Cambridge: Cambridge University Press.

Fritsch, C., Johnson, E. and Juska, A. 2010. The plight of Zimbabwean unaccompanied refugee minors in South Africa: A call for comprehensive legislative action. *Denver Journal of International Law and Policy*, 38(4), 623–658.

Goodwin-Gill, G. S. 1995. Unaccompanied refugee minors. The role and place of international law in the pursuit of durable solutions. *The International Journal of Children's Rights*, 3, 405–416.

Goodwin-Gill, G. S. and McAdam, J. 2007. *The Refugee in International Law*. 3rd edition. Oxford: Oxford University Press.

Gorlick, B. 2000. Human rights and refugees: enhancing protection through international human rights law. *Nordic Journal of International Law*, 69(2), 117–177.

Hathaway, J. 2005. *The Rights of Refugees Under International Law*. Cambridge: Cambridge University Press.

ICCPR. 1976. International Convention on Civil and Political Rights. General Assembly resolution 2200A (XXI) of 16 December 1966, entry into force 23 March 1976, in accordance with Article 49. United Nations High Commissioner for Human Rights.

ICESCR. 1976. International Covenant on Economic Social and Cultural Rights. General Assembly resolution 2200A (XXI) of 16 December 1966, entry into force 3 January 1976, in accordance with Article 27. United Nations High Commissioner for Human Rights.

McAdam, J., 2007. *Complementary Protection in International Refugee Law*. Oxford: Oxford University Press.

OHCHR. 1989. General Comment No.18: Non-discrimination. HRI/GEN/1, U., 1989. Human Rights Committee.

Pobjoy, J. 2010. Treating like alike: The principle of non-discrimination as a tool to mandate the equal treatment of refugees and beneficiaries of complementary protection. *Melbourne University Law Review*, 34, 181–229.

UNHCR. 1951. Convention relating to the Status of Refugees. United Nations High Commissioner for Refugees.

UNHCR. 1967. Protocol Relating to the Status of Refugees. United Nations High Commissioner for Refugees.

UNHCR. 1979. Handbook on Procedures and Criteria for Determining Refugee Status under the 1951 Convention and the 1967 Protocol relating to the Status of Refugees U. N. Doc. HCR/IP/4/Eng/REV.1 (1992)

UNHCR. 1994. Refugee Children: Guidelines on Protection and Care. UN High Commissioner for Refugees. Available at: http://www.unhcr.org/cgi-bin/texis/vtx/protect.

UNHCR. 1997a. Executive Committee Conclusion No. 81 (1997). United Nations High Commissioner for Refugees.

UNHCR. 1997b. Guidelines on Policies and Procedures in dealing with Unaccompanied Children Seeking Asylum. (February 1997). United Nations High Commissioner for Human Rights.

UNHCR. 2001. Note on International Protection. UNDoc A/AC. 96/951 (13 September 2001). United Nations High Commissioner for Refugees.

Van Bueren, G. 1995. *The International Law on the Rights of the Child*. Dordrecht: Martinus Nijhoff Publishers.

Van Bueren, G. 2000. The United Nations Convention on the Rights of the Child: An evolutionary revolution. I: C. J. Dave (ed.). Introduction to Child Law in South Africa. Lansdown: Juta & Co, Ltd.

13 Birth and status

The ongoing discrimination against children in Scots law based on parentage

Gillian Black

Introduction

In Scotland,* the Government's strategic mission is to make Scotland "the best place in the world to grow up" (The Scottish Government 2017). Compliance with the UNCRC protections is a fundamental strand of this. Although the Convention has not been implemented in Scots law, and therefore cannot be directly invoked before the Scottish courts,[1] there is nevertheless an explicit commitment on the part of the Scottish Government to recognise Convention rights. Section 1 of the Children and Young People (Scotland) Act 2014, for example, states: "The Scottish Ministers must… keep under consideration whether there are any steps which they could take which would or might secure better or further effect in Scotland of the UNCRC requirements", while section 2 obliges specified public authorities to "publish… a report of what steps… taken in… [a three year] period to secure better or further effect within its areas of responsibility of the UNCRC requirements". Despite this clear commitment to respecting UNCRC rights, the Concluding Observations provided by the Committee on the Rights of the Child to the United Kingdom in July 2016 highlighted a number of areas where Scots law could be improved.[2] While these are spread across a wide range of issues and Convention articles, it is fair to say that they are usually high-profile and well-articulated concerns (often linked to issues of juvenile justice or poverty), which are on the Scottish Government's radar, even if the problems persist.[3]

Yet away from the spotlight, a small and undeniably niche area of discrimination persists: discrimination on grounds of birth and/or status in the succession to titles, coats of arms, honours or dignities. Children who are born to unmarried parents in Scotland, or who are not the full genetic children of their parents, are not entitled to inherit titles or peerages (such as Baronet or Lord), or coats of arms, or dignities. This differential treatment amounts to discrimination against children on grounds of their illegitimate status and birth, in terms of Article 2 UNCRC.[4] In particular, Article 2(2) provides: "States Parties shall take all appropriate measures to ensure that the child is protected against all forms of discrimination or punishment on the basis of the status, activities, expressed opinions, or beliefs of the child's parents". To treat children differently as regards succession based on whether their parents are married or unmarried, or genetic or non-genetic, is to discriminate against children based on the status of their parents, and is contrary to the aims and ethos of the UNCRC.

In exploring the nature of this discrimination in Scots law the chapter will first set out the nature of "titles, coats of arms, honours and dignities", before moving on to define illegitimacy and the relationship between illegitimacy and assisted conception. Having identified the nature of titles and the exclusion for illegitimacy, I then assess whether this treatment is indeed discriminatory in terms of Article 2 UNCRC, and conclude with some thoughts on the need for, and shape of, law reform. The first step therefore is to set out briefly the nature of the titles at the heart of this.

Titles, coats of arms, honours and dignities

Scots law recognises a range of titles, honours and dignities. The baronetage and peerage comprises titles – such as Baronet, Earl or Duke – which descend to the holder's heirs.[5] Honours and dignities include the Great Offices of State, such as the Royal Standard Bearer, or the Lord High Constable of Scotland.[6] Coats of arms are heraldic devices, used to identify the individual and may often incorporate a symbolic reference to the individual's surname.[7] They are unique to the bearer, and can be transmitted to the bearer's heir. Under Scots law (discussed in more detail below), succession to these titles, honours and coats of arms requires the heir to be the full genetic child of married parents: anyone who is born out of wedlock, or who is born to married parents but not genetically related to both of them, is excluded from the succession.

Such titles, honours and coats of arms are undoubtedly the exception rather than the norm for children in Scotland. Yet while not many Scots will have a peerage in the family, the numbers are not entirely insignificant. There are over 300 peerages and more than 1200 baronetcies in existence, which can only transmit to a legitimate heir.[8] When these are added to the tens of thousands of coats of arms matriculated in Scotland, there is the potential for a significant minority of children to be affected by this discrimination to the succession perpetuated by Scots law, based on birth and status. This is of even greater concern in the case of those titles which carry the right to sit in the House of Lords, the upper chamber of the UK Parliament at Westminster. To maintain discrimination in the succession to those titles, based on status and genetics at birth, and thereby in who can exercise legislative power, is a serious concern.

Perhaps most compellingly, even where a child is not directly affected, he or she still suffers indirectly by virtue of this ongoing discrimination. The message it sends out is, in itself, damaging: by recognising that state-endorsed discrimination against children, based on the marital status of their parents, or their (lack of) genetic connection to their parents, is still accepted in Scotland today. This creates a two-tier system which differentiates between children according to factors which are beyond their control and which, critically, the law has deemed irrelevant in all other situations. The discrimination here affects children whom the state has recognised as the legal children of their parents for all purposes – except the succession to titles. The cumulative effect is that Scots law, and the state, continues to recognise and uphold differential treatment based on birth status.

Before turning to examine the legal position, two further points should be noted. First, the discrimination in the succession to titles, honours, coats of arms and dignities is legally embedded. The requirement for legitimacy cannot be overcome by a specific testamentary provision by the parents, stating that they wish to transfer the title to a specific named child: only law reform can redress this imbalance. Second, discrimination here usually goes hand-in-hand with sex discrimination. Succession to titles and peerages and coats of arms is typically predicated on primogeniture, or male succession. Daughters are almost always excluded, not by any statutory or common law measure, but by the terms of the original grant or charter in each individual case.[9] The succession to titles, peerages, coats of arms and so forth is therefore often doubly discriminatory by excluding heirs based on status *and* on sex. Because the exclusion of women from the succession is individual to each title or coat of arms, there is no statute to overturn to redress this. However, in the case of the Queen or King, the right of succession has now been amended by the Succession to the Crown Act 2013, so that the next in line to the throne is not determined by the sex of the individual. A similar measure could be implemented to ensure that there is no discrimination on grounds of sex in the succession to titles and so forth.[10] As this discrimination is not state-sponsored in the same way as discrimination on grounds of status, further analysis is beyond the scope of the current chapter. (see Agnew and Black 2018). Nonetheless, it is essential to recognise that sex discrimination also exists in this field.

For ease of reference, "titles, coats of arms, honours, and dignities" will be referred to hereafter, cumulatively, as "titles".

Status and birth: illegitimacy

Article 2 of the UNCRC enjoins States Parties to ensure that children can enjoy the Convention rights without discrimination, including discrimination on grounds of "birth or other status",[11] and moreover that they are protected against all forms of discrimination or punishment based on "status, activities, expressed opinions, or beliefs of the child's parents, legal guardians or family members".[12] Status is thus expressly protected by Article 2. To what extent are children in Scots law discriminated against on grounds of status? The good news is that, on the face of it, and as a general rule, they are not. Following reforms in 2006, the Law Reform (Parent and Child) (Scotland) Act 1986 as amended (the "1986 Act") is explicit in ensuring that all children are equal:

> Section 1. Abolition of status of illegitimacy
>
> 1 (1) *No person whose status is governed by Scots law shall be illegitimate*; and accordingly the fact that a person's parents are not or have not been married to each other shall be left out of account in –
>
> (a) Determining the person's legal status; or
> (b) Establishing the legal relationship between the person and any other person…

1 (6) It shall no longer be competent to bring an action for a declarator of legitimacy, legitimation or illegitimacy.[13]

In fact, this clear and unambiguous wording in the 1986 Act was the result of revisions introduced by the Family Law (Scotland) Act 2006 (the "2006 Act"). The introductory wording setting out the principle that no child shall be illegitimate was part of the 2006 reforms. Prior to that, the original wording of the 1986 Act had simply removed the *effect*, but not the *status*, of illegitimacy. This can be seen in the original title of section 1, "Legal equality of children", and the fact that section 1 simply stated: "The fact that a person's parents are not or have not been married to each other shall be left out of account in establishing any relationship between the person and any other person". This contrasts with the new opening wording that no person in Scots law shall be illegitimate.

Between the 1986 Act and the 2006 amendments, illegitimacy continued to apply in two circumstances: domicile and succession to titles. In the case of domicile, a child born to unmarried parents continued to take his or her mother's domicile.[14] When the Scottish Parliament enacted the 2006 revisions, as well as abolishing the legal status of illegitimacy, it also removed the ongoing discrimination which affected domicile.[15] Despite these important reforms, succession to titles, coats of arms, honours and dignities remains unchanged. As set out in section 9 of the 1986 Act (in both its original and revised forms): "Nothing in this Act shall... (c) apply to any title, coat of arms, honour or dignity transmissible on the death of the holder thereof or affect the succession thereto or the devolution thereof"

This exclusion from the scope of the Act means that birth status remains relevant, and the succession to titles, coats of arms, honours, and dignities is consequently discriminatory.

It is of particular note that this exclusion in section 9 was not revised by the Scottish Parliament in 2006, when the other revisions regarding illegitimacy were enacted. Specific repeal had been advocated as early as 1992 by the Lord Lyon, one of the Great Offices of State in Scotland, responsible for regulating heraldry, including all grants of coats of arms.[16] In a response to a Scottish Law Commission consultation in 1992, the Lord Lyon said that the exclusion for coats of arms was "unreasonable and unnecessary" and that the reference to coats of arms in section 9 should be repealed.[17] The only explanation offered for the Scottish Parliament's failure to address this in 2006 relates to the devolution settlement between the UK and Scottish Governments, whereby matters of heraldry and titles remain areas of law reserved to Westminster.[18] As stated in the explanatory notes to the 2006 Act (which introduced the amendment), the revised section removes "as far as it is possible and competent" the status of illegitimacy.[19] Since matters heraldic are outwith the legislative competence of the Scottish Parliament, this may well be the reason for leaving the section 9 exclusion in place – albeit a pragmatic rather than a principled one. However, it is disappointing that there was apparently no attempt to seek the consent of the Westminster Parliament to such an amendment, as would be constitutionally possible in terms of section 30 of the Scotland Act 1998.

Defining illegitimacy

Children who are illegitimate in the eyes of the law are accorded a different status, and treated differently, in Scotland, in relation to the succession to titles. But what makes a child illegitimate?

The most obvious answer is the non-marriage of the parents. Although it is typically the child who suffers from this status, it is of course something which is entirely beyond their control, as has been judicially recognised by the (now) President of the UK Supreme Court, Lady Hale, a "distinction which is based solely on the accident of birth outside wedlock, for which the [illegitimate child] is not responsible".[20] Excluding the children of unmarried parents from the succession to titles is of particular concern in a jurisdiction where half of all births each year are to unmarried parents.[21] But the legal ramifications of illegitimacy go considerably further. Where a child has been donor conceived, then he or she will also be viewed as illegitimate for these purposes: since the *genetic* parents are not married, it will be irrelevant whether the child's *legal* parents are or are not married.[22]

The relevant legislative regime in the United Kingdom is the Human Fertilisation and Embryology Act 2008 (the "2008 Act"). The 2008 Act sets out, in sections 33–45, who will be the legal parents where a woman or a couple have conceived using donor eggs, donor sperm, or double donation. In all cases, the woman who carries the pregnancy will be the mother (Human Fertilisation and Embryology Act 2008a). Her spouse or partner will be recognised as the legal parent when the appropriate statutory measures in sections 34–45 have been complied with, depending on whether the couple are married and whether the second parent is male or female. Thus, a married couple can conceive using donor gametes, and will be the legal parents. The sperm and/or egg donor will not, solely by virtue of donation, have any legal status at all as regards the child (Human Fertilisation and Embryology Act 2008b). There is a clear break between genetics and parentage under the 2008 Act, to recognise the legal intention of the couple who have sought treatment to conceive the child. The child's birth certificate will record this couple as the legal parents and on the face of the certificate, there will be nothing at all to indicate that the child was conceived through donor gametes. Where the parents are same sex, then biology will reveal what the birth certificate otherwise conceals.

While the 2008 Act confers legal parental status based on consent and intention, there is a critical statutory exception. As with the 1986 Act, the legislation grants one right up front, and then undermines this with a later exception: the legal parents are defined in sections 33–45, but section 48 states:

> In relation to Scotland… [sections 33–47] do not apply to any title, coat of arms, honour or dignity transmissible on the death of its holder or affect the succession to any such title, coats of arms or dignity.
>
> (Human Fertilisation and Embryology Act 2008c)[23]

When a child is recognised by the state, through its statutory regime, as the legal child of married parents, why should that child still be excluded from the succession to titles where the conception relied on donor gametes? The answer to this is at the very heart of what a parent is, in Scots law.

Defining parents

Scots law has no single statutory definition of a "parent". Where definitions do exist, they are typically framed in terms of the holders of parental responsibilities and rights.[24] However, for the purposes of identifying who holds parental responsibilities and rights in relation to a child, the Children (Scotland) Act 1995 provides arguably the "core" definition of parent, as "the genetic father or mother".[25] Thus, in Scots law, parents are not identified through social parenting, intention, responsibility, or any other model of parenting.[26] The touchstone is whether the two parents have contributed the required genetic material. This comes to the fore when one party seeks a declarator of parentage or non-parentage. Scots law recognises established common law presumptions: the mother is certain (*mater semper certa est*) and the father is the man married to the mother at the time of birth or conception (*pater est quem nuptiae demonstrant*). In the case of the father, this is now recognised as a statutory presumption in the 1986 Act. Section 5(1)(a) recognises the traditional presumption, while section 5(1)(b) introduces a new presumption for unmarried parents, such that the father is presumed to be the man named on the birth certificate. These presumptions both turn on the social reality: who is fulfilling the role of the father, through being married to the mother, or named on the birth certificate? Yet this social reality can be challenged – and overturned – through genetics alone. Where a man can produce a DNA test (or other evidence), then the court has no option but to grant the declarator of parentage or non-parentage, in terms of section 7 of the 1986 Act.[27] External factors, such as the social reality or the best interests of the child have no role to play, in contrast to other jurisdictions, such as France, Germany, and the US. These jurisdictions afford greater protection to the social reality by conferring judicial discretion as to whether to admit DNA evidence or recognising statutory limitations on who can bring a challenge[28]: parentage is viewed as more than simply genetics. Critically, the best interests of the child are at the heart of DNA disputes. In the US, the court may deny a motion for genetic testing to determine paternity where this is not in the best interests of the child,[29] while in Germany, the best interests of the (minor) child may outweigh the claims of the person seeking DNA clarification of genetics.[30]

Continuing to recognise a residual role for illegitimacy informs much wider discourses about parents and parentage, and confers validity on the conceptualisation of parentage as genetic. Yet this masks the underlying social reality:

> Kinship is, as many anthropologists have noted, a social and cultural construct. The importance accorded to the biological link varies according to cultures.... Rules that determine parenthood are often presented as universal laws and as such not open to criticism, but this is far from the truth.
>
> (Everett and Yeatman 2010, p. 307.)

In Scots law, the unchallenged emphasis on biology means that genetics still reigns supreme when it comes to establishing parentage and transferring titles. To be an "heir" means to be the genetic as well as the legal child. And this means that children conceived through donor reproduction are viewed as illegitimate, since their *genetic* parents are not married. The fact that their legal parents may be married is rendered irrelevant. The combined effect of this is that "illegitimate" speaks not only to the marital status of the parents, but also their genetic connection to the child.

Article 2: UNCRC and discrimination

It can be questioned whether the requirement for children to be "legitimate" in order to succeed to titles is in fact discriminatory, and whether it harms children. The European Court of Human Rights has recognised judicially that nobiliary titles and peerages are not "possessions", and therefore property rights, such as Article 1 of Protocol 1 ECHR, are *not* engaged.[31] Thus, where the discrimination is only recognised in conjunction with another Convention right (whether in terms of Article 2(1) UNCRC or Article 14 ECHR), it can be difficult to identify which Convention right has been infringed. This limits quite considerably the effect of Article 2(1) UNCRC, which (as with Article 14 ECHR) confines the protection against discrimination to that suffered in the context of other Convention rights. However, as early as *Marckx v Belgium* in 1979, the ECtHR held that discrimination against children born out of marriage will infringe Article 8 ECHR, unless justified as necessary.[32] When we turn to the UNCRC, it seems likely that Article 3 (best interests of the child) will be infringed by this ongoing recognition of illegitimacy, thereby bringing Article 2(1) into play. And even with this limitation as regards Article 2(1), Article 2(2) goes on to proscribe discrimination based on the "status... of the child's parents". Since the legal status of the child's parents – in not being married – is at the very heart of the discrimination against the child for being illegitimate, this would seem to be a clear breach of Article 2 UNCRC in Scots law.

A breach of Article 2, and the discrimination it perpetuates, leads to a number of harms. As mentioned previously, all children suffer when the state continues to uphold a discriminatory regime. Moreover, children are particularly susceptible to discrimination because of their youth, because "they are relatively powerless and depend on others for the realization of their rights".[33] This point was specifically highlighted in a 2005 General Comment from the Committee on the Rights of the Child on implementing child rights in early childhood. While the concerns voiced in that report focused on deprivation, poverty, violence, and exclusion from education, for example, the need to respect – and the consequent risks of respecting – cultural tradition is one which resonates in this area. Recognising and venerating local cultural traditions can be an important part of childhood and the fabric of a given society but, by its very nature, may bring an inherent risk of discrimination. The General Comment therefore encourages States Parties to "respect traditional values, *provided these are not discriminatory*".[34] This could conceivably apply to the tradition of titles and, particularly, coats of arms.

More critically, there will often be property and financial consequences arising from the succession to titles. While the land and moveable property of the parents will be separate from the title, and may be open to free testamentary transmission, it is common for the family to wish to keep the title with the heritable and moveable property. Children who are "illegitimate" as regards succession to titles may consequently be cut out of the succession to the family lands and possessions, in favour of the person who is to inherit the title. Whatever the reason for the exclusion, the approach in Scotland means that some children may effectively be excluded from succession to valuable property by virtue of being legally excluded from succession to titles. The dangers here are recognised (in a wider context) in the joint report produced by the Committee on the Rights of the Child and the Committee on the Elimination of Discrimination against Women. Their 2014 Report calls upon States Parties: "To challenge sociocultural norms and attitudes that underlie harmful practices, including male-dominated power structures, sex- and gender-based discrimination and age hierarchies".[35] Continuing to limit succession to titles to legitimate children fosters discriminatory power structures and property rights.

The cumulative effect of Scots law in this area is that Article 2 UNCRC is breached both as regards status (illegitimacy) and birth (distinguishing between children born of genetic parents and those born through donor gametes). Only children both to married and genetic (or "natural") parents may succeed to titles. In fact, these provisions are doubly discriminatory, since not only are children barred from inheriting from their *legal* parents, but they are also excluded from succeeding to any titles, honours, coats of arms, etc. held by their *genetic* parents. The focus on genetics bars the way to inherit from their legal parents, while the focus on legality bars the succession from their genetic parents. Children born as a result of donor conception are therefore excluded on both sides of the equation.

The overall result is clearly out of step with the social reality, where the majority of Scots children today are born to unmarried parents, and where assisted reproduction is also the lived reality for many families. The final question to be addressed is whether law reform can tackle this.

The need for law reform?

There are three potential options to address this discrimination in Scots law, with the first to be to do nothing. It is unclear how many individuals are affected but, in the absence of evidence of large numbers, this may be perceived as an unimportant area of discrimination. Moreover, it could be argued that this is a traditional and historic area of law and society and the need to respect and uphold a cultural tradition provides a valid reason for maintaining such distinctions.

This is not persuasive. If the state is prepared to recognise two people as the legal parents of a child for all purposes, that child should have the benefit and all the advantages that derive from this legal recognition, including succession to titles. As noted earlier, perpetuating this discrimination sends a signal to *all* children, whether directly affected by it or not, that the state is prepared to make a distinction based on birth and status. And for those children conceived through donor gametes, it sends a message that they are not quite fully legitimate, even if there are no titles or honours to pass down. Even if the numbers affected are small, any discrimination is a cause for concern.

The second option would be to abolish the whole system of titles, honours, coats of arms, and dignities – an approach taken by other countries to varying degrees, such as Germany. If the system is dismantled, then there can be no ongoing discrimination. Yet this seems a disproportionate response. There may be separate reasons for the abolition of titles, but the specific problem under consideration – discrimination against illegitimate children – can be addressed by a much more moderate reform. It is possible to tackle the discrimination without doing away with the system itself.

The third approach therefore is the one I would advocate. By removing the statutory exceptions and exclusions, the state could simply accept that where a child is recognised, in law, as the child of his or her parents, this legal status should apply in all circumstances. Discrimination on grounds of genetics or legitimacy should not be relevant for succession to titles, as they are not relevant for any other legal purpose. This approach is also supported by Article 2 UNCRC. Since the current rules operate to deprive a child of title he or she would otherwise inherit, it is not in the best interests of that child to continue to maintain a discriminatory approach.

Conclusion

Scotland cannot be said to meet its obligations under Article 2 UNCRC while it continues to recognise the status of "illegitimacy" for certain children. As has been shown, this definition applies both as regards the marital status of the parents and their genetic connection to the child. The harm that arises from this discriminatory treatment is two-fold. First, the very practical consequence for such illegitimate children is that they are debarred from succeeding to titles, honours, coats of arms, and dignities. Second, all children in Scotland are impoverished by the very existence of this ongoing two-tier status, whereby the full genetic children of married parents are afforded all legal rights, while illegitimate and/or non-genetic children are excluded from certain rights in succession. Maintaining this exception for titles maintains the status of illegitimacy for all. Relatively straightforward law reform could tackle this discrimination, by ensuring that a child can inherit a title from his/her legal parents, without the need to look behind this to marital status or genetics. Removing the very last legal consequence of illegitimacy would be a small but significant step on the way to making Scotland the best country in the world to grow up in.

Notes

* Constitutional Note: Scotland is part of the United Kingdom, and since 1999 it has had a devolved legislature. In terms of the Scotland Act 1998, some areas of regulation are reserved to the UK Parliament at Westminster, with all other areas being devolved to the Scottish Parliament. While family law and child law are devolved, assisted reproduction is reserved, and legislation regulating human fertilisation and embryology is common to the United Kingdom as a whole. This chapter focuses on Scots law, and covers both reserved and devolved matters. It will accordingly refer to UK legislation to the extent that it applies in Scotland.

1 For a debate on the merits of implementation, see Elaine E. Sutherland, "Supplementary Written Evidence to the Education and Culture Committee of the Scottish Parliament", 28 October 2013; and Kenneth Norrie, "Oral Evidence to the Education and Culture Committee of the Scottish Parliament", 3 September 2013, col.2682.

2 Committee on the Rights of the Child, "Concluding Observations on the fifth periodic report of the United Kingdom of Great Britain and Northern Ireland", CRC/C/GBR/CO/5, 12 July 2016.

3 Examples of reforms to tackle some of these concerns include legislation introduced in March 2018 to raise the age of criminal responsibility from 8 to 12: the Age of Criminal Responsibility (Scotland) Bill. The age of 8 had been highlighted in the Concluding Observations in 2016 as a source of concern. In addition to that specific response, a number of newer policies and consultations are focused on improving support and conditions for Scots children, including the (admittedly controversial) Named Persons Scheme in the Children and Young People (Scotland) Act 2014 (not yet in force) and, at the time of writing, a major new consultation launched on Part 1 of the Children (Scotland) Act 1995, looking at various aspects of parental responsibilities and rights: https://consult.gov.scot/family-law/children-scotland-act/. This most recent consultation closed in September 2018, and is likely to lead to law reform to further enhance children's rights.

4 This differential treatment also appears to place the UK in breach of its obligations under the European Convention on the Status of Legal Children Born out of Wedlock (1975), Article 9 of which states "A child born out of wedlock shall have the same right of succession in the estate of its father and its mother and of a member of its father's or mother's family, as if it had been born in wedlock." Discrimination is also prohibited under the ECHR. However, the focus of this chapter is primarily on UNCRC obligations.

5 The peerage also includes "life peers", where the title is personal to the holder, and does not descend to his or her heirs.

6 The latter is a hereditary title which has been in the Hay family for over 700 years.

7 For example, in Scotland, coats of arms borne by anyone with the surname "Stewart" will often contain the distinctive "chequy azure and argent" device (that is, like a chequerboard, in blue and silver) which identifies the Stewart name and clan.

8 See the figures referenced in Agnew and Black (2018).

9 Title can in some cases transmit to or through the female line. See Sir Crispin Agnew of Lochnaw Bt, "The Baronets of Nova Scotia", (1979) 1 The Double Tressure (Journal of the Heraldry Society of Scotland); *Ruthven of Freeland Petitioner* 1977 SLT (Lyon Ct) 2; Agnew and Black (2018).

10 A number of private bills have been introduced to achieve this but, so far, none has succeeded. For example, the Equality (Titles) Bill 2012–13 introduced by Lord Lucas of Crudwell (2013) and the Succession to Peerages Bill [HL] 2015–16. The current attempt is the Succession to Peerages Bill, introduced in June 2017, and not currently progressing. It may be that such a move would need to be initiated by the Government, to be successful.

11 UNCRC Article 2(1).

12 Art 2(2).

13 Section 1 of the Law Reform (Parent and Child) (Scotland) Act 1986, as amended. Emphasis added.

14 Section 9(1)(a) of the 1986 Act, as originally enacted.

15 Section 9(1)(a) of the 1986 Act has been repealed.

16 For further information, see http://www.lyon-court.com.

17 Scottish Law Commission *Report on Family Law*, 1992, para 17.11.

18 Scotland Act, Schedule 5, para 2(2).

19 Scottish Parliamentary Corporate Body, "Family Law (Scotland) Bill Revised Explanatory Notes" (2005), para 35.

20 *Johnson v Secretary of State for the Home Department* [2016] UKSC 26, at [34] per Lady Hale. This case concerned the adverse impact of illegitimacy in the different context of citizenship and deportation.

21 Although the percentage varies from year to year, the figure has been higher than 50 per cent in every year since 2008. The latest figures, from 2016, show that 50.9 per cent of children in Scotland were born to unmarried parents, slightly down on 51.2 per cent in 2015: National Records of Scotland, *Scotland's Population: The Registrar General's Annual Review of Demographic Trends* (National Records of Scotland, 2016).

22 The same effect arises where the child has been adopted or carried by a surrogate: in each case, the child's legal parents are different from the child's genetic parents, and the link for succession to titles has been broken. However, adoption and surrogacy are excluded from the scope of this current work because, in both cases, the birth parents will be the first legal parents: the law steps in at a later stage to transfer legal parental status to the new (non-genetic) parents, under the relevant legislation (the Adoption and Children (Scotland) Act 2007 and the Human Fertilisation and Embryology Act 2008 section 54, respectively). This is different from donor conception, where the legal parents are, from the outset, identified based on consent to treatment in the clinic with the donor gametes, rather than genetics, and the genetic parents have no legal recognition: the link between genetics and parentage is set aside at the outset.

23 A similar measure applies to titles in England, Wales and Northern Ireland in terms of section 48(7) of the 2008 Act.

24 See the Adoption and Children (Scotland) Act 2007, where sections 29(4) and 31(15) talk about the parent who has parental responsibilities and rights, and compare with section 30(1) and (7), for example, which talks about the "natural" parent. In the Children's Hearings (Scotland) Act 2011, there is no definition of "parent", but the definition of "relevant person" refers to a parent in the context of parental responsibilities and rights.

25 Children (Scotland) Act 1995, section 15(1), with appropriate exceptions for the application of other legislation governing assisted conception, surrogacy, and adoption.

26 For further discussion, see Sutherland 2014; Black 2018.

27 Where there is evidence that the legal parental title derives from consent to treatment under the Human Fertilisation and Embryology Act 2008, then a declarator of

parentage/non-parentage will be tied to compliance with the consent regime in the 2008 Act: *L v B* [2017] SC EDIN 79, following English decisions such as *In the matter of the Human Fertilisation and Embryology Act 2008 (Cases A, B, C, D, E, F, and G)* [2015] EWHC (Fam) 2602.

28 In France, a DNA test can only be legally carried out on the orders of a judge (French Penal Code art. 226–228), while in Germany, only a limited class of persons can challenge the title of a man currently filling the role of father (BGB s.1600(1)). In the US, under the Uniform Parentage Act 2017, the court will consider a range of factors, including best interest, before deciding whether to order DNA testing to establish parentage: §.612(b).

29 USA's Uniform Parentage Act 2017 §.612(b).

30 BGB, §.1598(a)(3).

31 *de la Cierva Osorio de Moscoso v Spain* (Applications no. 4127/98, 41503/98, 41717/98 and 45726/98) Judgment of 28 October 1998, unreported. Moreover, the UNCRC does not explicitly protect any property rights of children: there is no equivalent to Article 1, Protocol 1 of the ECHR.

32 *Marckx v Belgium (Application 6683/74) [1979] ECHR 2.*

33 Committee on the Rights of the Child, "Implementing Child Rights in Early Childhood" (General Comment No. 7, 2005), para 11.

34 Committee on the Rights of the Child, "Implementing Child Rights in Early Childhood" (General Comment No. 7, 2005), para 8, emphasis added.

35 Joint general recommendation No. 31 of the Committee on the Elimination of Discrimination against Women/General comment No. 18 of the Committee on the Rights of the Child on harmful practices, November 2014, para 74.

References

Agnew, C. and Black, G.2018. The significance of status and genetics in succession to titles, honours, dignities and coats of arms: Making the case for reform. *Cambridge Law Journal*, 77(2), 321–348.

Black, G.2018. Identifying the legal parent/child relationship and the biological prerogative: Who then is my parent? *Juridical Review*, 22 (January 9).

Everett, K. and Yeatman, L.2010. Are some parents more natural than others? *Child Family Law Quarterly*, 22(3), 290–309.

Human Fertilisation and Embryology Act. 2008a. *c.2* (section 33). The United Kingdom. Available at: https://www.legislation.gov.uk/ukpga/2008/22/section/33.

Human Fertilisation and Embryology Act. 2008b. *c2* (sections 41, 47). The United Kingdom. Available at: https://www.legislation.gov.uk/ukpga/2008/22/pdfs/ukpga_20080022_en.pdf.

Human Fertilisation and Embryology Act. 2008c. *c.2* (section 48(8)). The United Kingdom. Available at: https://www.legislation.gov.uk/ukpga/2008/22/pdfs/ukpga_20080022_en.pdf.

Sutherland, E. E. 2014. "It is a wise father …". *Journal of the Law Society of Scotland.* Available at: http://www.journalonline.co.uk/Magazine/59-6/1014070.aspx.

National Records of Scotland. 2016. Scotland's population 2016 – The Registrar General's annual review of demographic trends. Available at: https://www.nrscotland.gov.uk/statistics-and-data/statistics/stats-at-a-glance/registrar-generals-annual-review/2016

The Scottish Government. 2017. *Government Outcome: Children, Young People and Families.* Available at: http://www.gov.scot/About/Performance/scotPerforms/outcome/childfamilies.

Index

For Product Safety Concerns and Information please contact our EU representative GPSR@taylorandfrancis.com
Taylor & Francis Verlag GmbH, Kaufingerstraße 24, 80331 München, Germany

www.ingramcontent.com/pod-product-compliance
Lightning Source LLC
LaVergne TN
LVHW011128300926
849160LV00008B/558

* 9 7 8 1 0 3 2 2 4 1 4 5 6 *